THE EXPERT CONSUMER

The Expert Consumer

Associations and Professionals in Consumer Society

Edited by
ALAIN CHATRIOT
Ecole des Hautes Etudes en Sciences Sociales, Paris, France

MARIE-EMMANUELLE CHESSEL
Ecole des Hautes Etudes en Sciences Sociales, Paris, France

MATTHEW HILTON
University of Birmingham, UK

Routledge
Taylor & Francis Group
LONDON AND NEW YORK

First published 2006 by Ashgate Publishing

2 Park Square, Milton Park, Abingdon, Oxfordshire OX14 4RN
711 Third Avenue, New York, NY 10017

Routledge is an imprint of the Taylor & Francis Group, an informa business

First issued in paperback 2017

British Library Cataloguing in Publication Data
The expert consumer : associations and professionals in consumer society.—(The history of retailing and consumption)
1.Consumers—History—Congresses 2.Consumption (Economics)—History—Congresses
I.Chatriot, Alain II.Chessel, Marie-Emmanuelle III.Hilton, Matthew
381.3'09

Library of Congress Cataloging-in-Publication Data
The expert consumer : associations and professionals in consumer society / edited by Alain Chatriot, Marie-Emmanuelle Chessel, and Matthew Hilton.
p. cm.—(The history of retailing and consumption)
Includes index.
ISBN 0-7546-5501-6 (alk. paper)
1. Consumers—Europe—History. 2. Consumers—United States—History. 3. Consumer protection—Europe—History. 4. Consumer protection—United States—History. 5. Consumption (Economics)—Europe—History. 6. Consumption (Economics)—United States—History. I. Chatriot, Alain. II. Chessel, Marie-Emmanuelle. III. Hilton, Matthew. IV. Series.

HC240.9.C6E98 2006
339.4'7—dc22

2005024152

ISBN 13: 978-0-7546-5501-5 (hbk)
ISBN 13: 978-1-138-26307-9 (pbk)

Contents

Acknowledgements

This book is the product of an international colloquium (*Au nom du consommateur*) held at the *Ecole Nationale d'Administration* in Paris in June 2004. The colloquium and this volume would not have been possible without financial assistance from: the *Centre de Recherches Historiques* at the *Ecole des Hautes Etudes en Sciences Sociales*, the *Centre International de Recherche, d'Echange et d'Information sur la Distribution* (CIREID, Lille-Métropole), the *Maison des Sciences de l'Homme*, the organisation *Le Mouvement Social*, the Ministry of Foreign Affairs, France, the British Academy, and especially the Mairie de Paris. We would like to thank all those who participated in this conference, especially the members of the conference's scientific committee, the commentators and those presenters whose papers we were unfortunately not able to include in this volume: Maurice Aymard, Dominique Barjot, Gérard Béaur, Régis Boulat, Sophie Chauveau, Lizabeth Cohen, Christoph Conrad, Geoffrey Crossick, Joy Cushman, Olivier Dard, Jean-Claude Daumas, Pierre-Antoine Dessaux, Tracey Deutsch, Victoria de Grazia, Laura Lee Downs, Patrick Fridenson, Ellen Furlough, Céline Granjou, Stephen L. Harp, Heinz-Gerhard Haupt, Sheryl Kroen, Erik Langlinay, Yves Lequin, Michel Lescure, Michel Margairaz, Véronique Pouillard, Pierre Rosanvallon, Armand-Denis Schor, Alessandro Stanziani, Anne Sudrow and Gunnar Trumbull. For help with the translations of various chapters we are grateful to Susan Emanuel (Chapters 7 and 10), Rosemary Williams (Chapter 2) and Erik Haakenstad (Chapter 4), and for final editorial assistance, Matt Vaughan Wilson.

List of Contributors

Alain Chatriot is Chargé de recherche in History at the CNRS (*Centre National de la Recherche Scientifique*), based at the *Centre de recherches historiques* (*Ecole des Hautes Etudes en Sciences Sociales*, Paris). He is the author of *La démocratie sociale à la française* (Paris, 2002) and is currently working on a study of French agricultural policies in the twentieth century.

Marie-Emmanuelle Chessel is Chargée de recherche in History at the CNRS (*Centre National de la Recherche Scientifique*), based at the *Centre de recherches historiques* (*Ecole des Hautes Etudes en Sciences Sociales*, Paris). She is the author of *La Publicité: naissance d'une profession, 1900-1940* (Paris, 1998) and is currently working on the history of the French Consumers' League.

Joëlle Droux is Master Assistant in the History Department of the University of Geneva. She is the author of a Ph. D. on the history of the nursing profession in Switzerland in the nineteenth and twentieth centuries which is to be published in 2006. She is currently working on the history of the child protection movement in Switzerland in the twentieth century.

Lawrence B. Glickman is Associate Professor of History at the University of South Carolina. He is the author of *A Living Wage: American Workers and the Making of Consumer Society* (Ithaca, 1997) and the editor of *Consumer Society in American History: A Reader* (Ithaca, 1999). He is currently writing, *Use Your Buying Power for Justice: Consumer Activism in America from the Boston Tea Party to the Twenty-First Century.*

Carolyn M. Goldstein is Curator at Lowell National Historical Park in Lowell, Massachusetts. She is the author of *Do It Yourself: Home Improvement in 20th-Century America* (Princeton, 1998). Her book about the home economics movement and American consumers will be published by the University of North Carolina Press.

Matthew Hilton is Reader in Social History at the University of Birmingham. He is the author of *Smoking in British Popular Culture* (Manchester, 2000) and *Consumerism in Twentieth-Century Britain* (Cambridge, 2003). He is currently working on a study of the international consumer movement.

Odile Join-Lambert is a historian at the *Institut de Recherches Economiques et Sociales*. She is the author of *Le receveur des postes, entre l'Etat et l'usager* (Paris, 2001).

Yves Lochard is a researcher in Sociology at the *Institut de Recherches Economiques et Sociales*. He is the author of *Fortune du pauvre* (Paris, 1998) and *L'expert associatif, le savant et le politique* (edited with Maud Simonet-Cusset, Paris, 2003). He has been working on associations and their values.

Robert N. Mayer is Professor of Family and Consumer Studies at the University of Utah. He is associate editor of the *Encyclopedia of the Consumer Movement* (Oxford, 1997), and his articles appear frequently in the *Journal of Consumer Affairs* and the *Journal of Consumer Policy*. His current research focuses on consumer privacy.

Katherine Pence is an Assistant Professor of History at Baruch College at the City University of New York in Manhattan. She has published a number of articles on consumption in post-war East and West Germany. Her monograph *From Rations to Fashions: Gender, Politics and Consumption in the Cold War Germanys* as well as a volume co-edited with Paul Betts (Sussex University) entitled *Socialist Modern: East German Politics, Society and Culture* are forthcoming.

Iselin Theien is a postdoctoral fellow in Contemporary History at the University of Oslo. She completed her doctoral thesis (on Norwegian fascism) at the University of Oxford in 2001, and from 2001-2003 she was a research fellow at the Institute for Social Research in Oslo, researching the history of the Norwegian consumer co-operative movement (forthcoming 2006 as part of a multi-authored book in Norwegian). Her publications include *Affluence and Activism: Organised Consumers in the Post-War Era* (Oslo, 2004), edited with Even Lange.

Julien Vincent is writing his doctoral dissertation on the 'ethics of political economy' and its uses, with special reference to the Christian Social Union (1889-1914). He is attached to Wolfson College, University of Cambridge, and to the *Institut d'Histoire Moderne et Contemporaine* in Paris.

Introduction

Alain Chatriot, Marie-Emmanuelle Chessel and Matthew Hilton

Who speaks for the consumer? In modern western society it seems everything is done in the name of the consumer. In the private marketplace, prices, products and services are changed and updated in the interests of consumers. Yet in the public sector too – be it education, health or welfare – reforms and changes are made for the 'consumers' of state and municipal services. More broadly, voters in elections are appealed to in their roles as consumers, whereas the discourses of choice, rights and freedom are increasingly equated with the desires of individuals to spend their money, no matter what area of life. One could even argue that wars are fought in the name of the consumer, insofar as they secure supplies of essential goods which maintain the standards of living of those who enjoy the benefits of the consumer society. The consumer has assumed a centrality within economic, social and cultural life and it is for the consumer that so much policy is made. Yet consumers themselves rarely speak alone: today's consumers must compete with a variety of other agents and institutions to define and defend their interests. Precisely because the consumer is defined as everybody, then everybody can volunteer themselves as the expert on consumer affairs.

Over the course of the twentieth century, in Europe as in America, the list of 'expert consumers' is endless. As the essays in this volume demonstrate, many discussions about the consumer emanate from within the bureaucracies of private and public organisations. Professional associations and organised business interests often work to ensure that their voices are heard more frequently than those of consumers themselves. During the period of post-Second World War reconstruction, when the consumer and consumption assumed a renewed importance in social and economic planning arrangements, more often the authority on consumption was less the consumer and more the politician, the marketing expert, the social and economic planner, the diplomat and the state. Even in the late-twentieth century, when the consumer movement was perhaps at its most influential, consumer voices competed with other trade union, co-operative, manufacturing, retailing and professional interests in the institutions of state-sponsored consumer protection. In discussions over specific items of consumption – food and health – industry can often be more ready than consumers to speak as the experts, especially over high-publicity food scandals. And when consumers themselves do organise, specific agendas can emerge which give the organised consumer voice a narrower social, economic or cultural interest, be it through religious, philanthropic, citizen or gender-based groups.

Of course, in this regard the consumer is no different from any other identity within modern society, be it worker, citizen, taxpayer or voter, since organisations, interests and agendas emerge which speak for them. But the consumer interest has usually been perceived to be more diverse than that of the worker, and the range of expert consumers has been greater than that found within an admittedly fractious trade union movement. But perhaps too it is this multitude of voices which explains the hegemony of consumer society today. At the heart of the society of consumption stands an entity, an agent, an identity, a being and a citizen about whom all can speak and whom all can attempt to define, translate and shape to serve the interests of so much else. In an age of affluence, we might all be consumers, but just what type of consumer is another question altogether. The very malleability of the consumer identity enables consumer society itself to progress onwards supposedly in the interests of all. But what is clear is that the consumer society does not necessarily become the society of the consumer. In the dynamism of modern capitalism, consumers are as much the objects as the agents of change.

If active, expert, politically-minded consumers therefore do not appear at the centre of the very society built in their name, then so too have they not become the primary focus of historical scholarship. Even in the turn to the study of consumption over the last two decades, consumers have not always been given a voice, and they have become the problem to be investigated rather than the actors to whom the scholar should listen. In a sense, consumers lay hidden by their own shadow, at one and the same time being the centre of the contemporary world, yet being pushed to the sidelines in the analysis of that world. Thus we observe dimly the consumer in history, recognising his or her importance but failing to examine how they have spoken for themselves or how others have spoken for them. Arguably, we note the existence of a consumer consciousness in the food riots and protests of the eighteenth-century 'moral economy', though the articulation of such a consciousness by the historian has been one of ascription rather than transcription.[1] In the transition to mass consumption, only certain facets of consumer behaviour have been explored. It is as though the historian has acted as the department store owner, Octave Mouret, of Zola's *Au bonheur des dames*. Standing upon the balcony of scholarship, the historian casts his eye over the consuming masses in the store below, knowing, dissecting and directing their needs and desires, but always speaking for the consumer, never acknowledging the widest range of interests which motivate the consumer beyond the store and on, even, to the ballot box. Historians have recognised the fundamental changes to social life with the onset of urbanisation and industrialisation – specifically, the separation of the sphere of production from the sphere of consumption – though they have insufficiently explored what this means for the new consumer as a political being. Jean Baudrillard in France and Michael Young in the United Kingdom both argued that in the consumer society, the pervasive nature of the world of goods would lead to a growing consciousness and authoritative voice among consumers, just as the experience of the relations of production in the nineteenth century gave rise to a politicised labour consciousness.[2] Yet, in their analyses of consumer society, historians have not extensively examined this politicisation of the consumer or the movements to promote expert consumer knowledge, and much remains to be understood of the processes that have given rise to the various dominant and subordinate meanings of 'the consumer'.

The aim of this collection is not to 'rescue' the consumer apparently hidden from history. Much is now known of the economic, social and cultural life of the consumer and what has become clear is that such a rescue is, in any case, complicated by the sheer diversity of factors influencing consumer choices and uses. But what remains to be understood is how this entity, so central to the society of mass consumption over the last one hundred years, has been defined and spoken for and then politicised by a range of experts who have sought to ensure their definition of the consumer has either directed policy, become linked with notions of citizenship, been enshrined within the institutions of modern governance or has simply eclipsed other meanings of the consumer that may have pushed capitalist development in other directions. The tone here ought not to be conspiratorial, since the assertion is simply that in speaking for the consumer, manufacturers, retailers, governments, moral pressure movements, political parties and consumers themselves have all played a role in defining the being at the heart of the consumer society and hence the heart of the modern world itself. And at the centre of all these voices of expertise, stands the consumer his or herself. In the chapters which follow, although all explore the various sites of expertise, the expertise expressed by consumers themselves remains a persistent strand of investigation.

The current state of the historiography: a US model?

Despite the problems of the existing scholarship, the history of consumer society is now a truly international affair. Whereas the output of American historians has been the most prolific, the subject has become well-established in the United Kingdom and, over the last decade, in Germany as well.[3] In France, the topic has not received the same degree of prominence, notwithstanding recent important overviews of the eighteenth century, the work of American historians of France, or the studies conducted by French sociologists.[4] The great irony of this absence of a historical interest in consumer society and consumer politics in France is of course the widespread regard given to French critical theory of the post-1968 era. An Anglophone literature has continually referred to the dominance of French theory in the founding texts of consumption studies. A criticism made was that the models which emerged from the milieu of the political and theoretical experimentalism of May 1968 did not necessarily apply to the empirical realities of modern society. Nevertheless, it is remarkable the extent to which Guy Debord's notion of the 'spectacle', Jean Baudrillard's focus on free-floating chains of signification, Michel de Certeau's emphasis on *bricolage* or moments of *poiësis* (active re-creation) and later Bourdieu's insights into the nature of *habitus*, have all continued to shape studies of consumer society, especially those which focus on more cultural phenomena.[5] They found their equivalents in the Birmingham Centre for Contemporary Cultural Studies, with its emphasis on the ability of consumers to negotiate and appropriate the meanings of goods, and French critical theory has been especially incorporated into anglophone scholarship on consumption.[6] Most recently, there has been a turn away from the consequences of the culturalist interpretations of consumption, if not cultural studies as a whole, though this is not to deny the incredible importance such studies have had in improving our understanding of people's interactions with material culture.[7]

In recent years, historians have extended the analysis of consumer society, questioning the logic of the cultural approach. If consumption forms such a central part of modern identity then does it not follow that people's political identities have been moulded by their consuming interests? Furthermore, if consumption is said to be such a crucial aspect of contemporary economic development, then does it not also follow that organised economic interests have politicised the notion of the consumer in order to serve their own purposes? A number of edited collections, focussing on Europe and the United States, have begun tentatively to explore the political aspects of consumption, examining the role of the state, the relationship between consumption and citizenship and the extent to which consumer interests have been defined and shaped by a range of actors.[8] These texts have opened up a new field of interest within studies of consumer society, particularly within the United States. Indeed, the literature is now so well developed there that it naturally gives rise to certain American models for the history of consumer politics, such that transatlantic exchanges are likely to be reversed from the direction begun by French critical theory. At the conference upon which this volume was based a recurring theme among an emerging French, German and wider European scholarship was the dominance of models based upon American, and occasionally British, experiences.[9] It is the challenge for this scholarship to reject, overturn or complicate these models.

It is easy to speculate as to why understandings of consumer expertise has developed most prominently in the United States. Many left-leaning scholars of consumer society have clearly sought to explore the antecedents to the individualist culture arguably promoted most aggressively in the 1980s by President Reagan, but in so doing they have drawn upon a labour movement tradition which has been just as much about fighting to participate in the 'American way of life' as it has been about overturning the structures of society and economy.[10] And whereas European critics may have reacted against the excesses of commercialism at particular moments in time – most notably in 1968 – there has existed in the US an ongoing debate about luxury, tempered always by a protestant self-denying ethic. Undoubtedly, the critiques of consumerism were bolstered by the émigrés of the Frankfurt School mid-century but, as Daniel Horowitz has shown in his two books on the morality of the market, the jeremiad has been a persistent presence in American literary, cultural and intellectual life. Most recently, in *The Anxieties of Affluence*, he has charted the post-Second World War unease with excess, analysing a series of popular and well-known figures: J. K. Galbraith, Vance Packard, Betty Friedan, Paul Goodman, Martin Luther King, Rachel Carson, Michael Harrington, Ralph Nader, Paul Ehrlich, Christopher Lasch and Robert Bellah. The latter three were read, and then met, by President Carter who took on board their complaints in his infamous 'malaise' speech of 1979 in which he suggested the problems of American society lay not in the policies of his government but in a deeper sickness of the people who increasingly turned inwards towards self-gratification.[11] From the 1980s, one could argue that this liberal unease or guilt has been transferred to the discipline of history itself as a series of ground-breaking books have denounced or sought alternatives to the American capitalist dream of consumer abundance.[12]

Perhaps because of this discomfort with materialism shared by many privileged American academics there exists a remarkable degree of agreement in recent works on consumer politics in the United States. Although a model of historical development has been most recently and clearly set out by Lizabeth Cohen in her *The Consumers' Republic*, the literature as a whole marks out several stages in the nature of consumer expertise.[13] Firstly, one can point to the various precursors of a modern consumer protection regime operating through the grassroots mobilisation of workers and consumers from the nineteenth century through to the 1920s. Although T. H. Breen might argue that the boycotts and commercial protests of the American revolution constituted the first organised consumer movement, most have pointed to the boycotts and 'buycotts' of the anti-slavery campaigners.[14] In this volume, Lawrence Glickman (Chapter 1) sets out the forerunners to twentieth-century consumer politics, all of which provided important precedents in the ability of consumers to act as the moral experts on market relations. In his study of the 'free produce' stores of the anti-slavery movement, the 'non-intercourse' associations of the Southern opponents of the free labour North and the campaigns to uphold the sanctity of the Sabbath by evangelical Sabbatarians, he admits the contradictory aims of these divergent groups but nevertheless emphasises their role in enabling consumers to think of themselves as potential active agents in the marketplace. Previous scholarship has noted the origins of such activism later in the nineteenth century, notably in the National Consumers League which aimed to defend the rights of retail and garment workers by mobilising middle-class purchasing power away from the stores which did not stock 'white label' products. In Chapter 3, Marie-Emmanuelle Chessel traces the history of the National Consumers League to demonstrate how, at the start of the twentieth century, it began to embrace other consumer issues as it lobbied for the reform of social welfare legislation, thereby providing a link to more explicitly consumerist organisations of a later period. To this range of 'progressive' consumer politics we might add the fights for a 'living wage' by trade unionists and the embrace of co-operation (though limited in comparison to Europe) by various wings of the labour movement.[15] The point that is always emphasised in this literature is the other-directed nature of activism, as consumers sought not to defend their own individual purchasing decisions, but the rights of other citizens to share a decent standard of living.

The second period to have caught the attention of American historians is that of the interwar years and, specifically, the New Deal era. This is the age which witnessed the birth of the modern, comparative-testing consumer movement, first through Consumers' Research and then through the more enduring Consumers Union following a split in 1936.[16] It also saw the expansion of women's participation in politics and the rise of a number of organisations which used women's expertise as consumers to attempt to reform society. In Chapter 4, Carolyn Goldstein examines the role of women professionals who were brought into the Department of Agriculture's Bureau of Home Economics from 1923 where they worked with producers to improve the quality of commercial goods and sought to educate housewives into making more rational family buying decisions. But these women were only one group of consumer who were being recognised as experts in this period. At the more radical end of the political spectrum, the League of Women Shoppers, set up in New York in 1935, continued the agenda of the National Consumers League in fighting for workers' pay and conditions, but also campaigned more broadly for a more equitable tax system, price control, social security and fair and stable labour-management relations.[17] These two examples of expert consumers emerging 'from below' were matched by a greater attention to the consumer and consumption within political economy. Kathleen Donohue has recently charted the transition from a producerist to a consumerist worldview, setting out the gradual rise to prominence of consumption as the factor believed to be at the heart of economic change in the United States. By 1941, Franklin D. Roosevelt was able to identify 'four essential human freedoms': from fear, of speech, of religion and from want. This recognition of consumption or want as a fundamental economic and social right stands in contrast to the attitude of most within the classical tradition who regarded consumption 'as little more than the destruction of wealth'.[18] She goes on to describe the incorporation of consumerist agendas within the institutions of the New Deal, particularly the Consumers' Advisory Board of the National Recovery Administration and the Office of the Consumers' Counsel within the Agricultural Adjustment Administration. These bodies, along with the Office of Price Administration during the Second World War, have been almost celebrated within recent historical writing, not least because, as Cohen puts it, the New Deal mobilised and institutionalised 'citizen consumers' who fought for their individual rights at the same time as using their economic power for the greater good of the US economic recovery.[19] The broader vision of consumers articulated by these various experts therefore stands in contrast to the apparently more individualistic and materialistic consumer of the late-twentieth century.

The third stage in the politics of consumption has not received quite the same degree of historical attention and has been most clearly set out by Cohen. She argues that in the Consumers' Republic, from the 1950s to the 1970s, material acquisition was celebrated as the very essence of the American way of life: 'an economy, culture, and politics built around the promises of mass consumption, both in terms of material life and the more idealistic goals of greater freedom, democracy and equality'.[20] But because consumption was so central to democracy, it also enabled interesting engagements with consumer society, be it through African Americans' struggles to participate in the good life or through the intellectual critiques outlined by Horowitz. And, furthermore, it proved to be the golden age of consumer protection, as legislators safeguarded the rights of individuals within the marketplace. Most prominently, President John F. Kennedy, in March 1962, set out the four fundamental consumer rights (the right to safety; the right to be informed; the right to choose; the right to be heard) which have subsequently provided the core principles for consumer movements around the world as well as the benchmarks for the assessment of any consumer protection regime.

But despite these highly nuanced accounts of consumer society, many historians have essentially written the obituary for a more engaged notion of consumer activism. Gary Cross has brought the story almost to a close by suggesting that consumerism (that is, the culture of commerce, as opposed to the organised consumer movement and consumer protection) was the 'ism' that won, implying that consumers have been stripped of their wider rights and responsibilities as citizens and have been reduced instead to atomised, individualistic shoppers.[21] Likewise, Horowitz finds little of interest for the post-Jimmy Carter years, suggesting instead that the engagement with the market has been replaced with a post-moralistic celebration of the virtues of commercial society, in which consumer expertise no longer lies with consumers themselves but with the political economists aligned with commercial interests.[22] Cohen herself argues that de-regulation, 'Reaganomics' and the ascendancy of anti-consumer citizen forces has resulted in the creation of the 'Consumerized Republic', a society in which our roles as consumers, citizens, taxpayers and voters have been combined, promoting a view of life where all market transactions and government policies are judged according to narrow criteria of individual satisfaction. It is a pessimistic end to a fascinating subject and one which needs to be explored and examined further, else scholars outside of America may come to reflect the unease that many left-leaning scholars of a particular generation still have with the goods that they themselves enjoy.

Nevertheless, the overwhelming strength of the American scholarship is its locating of the consumer at the heart of the twentieth century. Indeed, the work of these historians, combining social, cultural, economic, political and intellectual history, suggests together that history itself can be re-written in the name of the consumer. It is this that is perhaps the greatest lesson for an expanding body of work in Europe, notwithstanding the evident problems with some of the finer details of the model of change in the nature of the expert consumer. For instance, there is perhaps too rigid a division between the pre- and post-Second World War periods, too neatly assuming the existence of an enriched consumer politics in the former and its gradual demise in the latter. This has resulted in too ready a championing of the incorporation of the consumer in the New Deal programmes when not all experts were listened to with equal measure. Similarly, while it is still necessary to uncover all the forms of consumer mobilisation for the earlier period, we have to begin to assess the relative importance of each of these groups of consumers, both in terms of their size, impact on specific policies and contribution to the general discourse of the politics of consumption. For the later period, the general narrative of decline has meant the achievements of consumer movements have not been observed while the era of globalisation and the emergence of a new expert consumer with an eye on the world trade system has been almost entirely overlooked. There are clearly areas where the American context requires further exploration and one should be careful in assuming that a quantitatively more developed literature provides a model for the testing and assessment of consumer politics in other states and regimes. In the contributions to this collection there exist a series of papers which point to both the specificities of different national contexts within Europe, as well as raising further questions about consumer society that point the way forward for future research on both sides of the Atlantic.

The expert consumer in Europe, America and beyond

Nevertheless, the US scholarship certainly provides a base from which a model or periodisation of the history of the expert consumer can be developed. Indeed, in one of the most recent contributions to the study of twentieth-century consumption, Victoria's de Grazia's authoritative *Irresistible Empire*, the author outlines how the US 'Market Empire' conquered 'old Europe'.[23] In some senses de Grazia reasserts an older Americanisation thesis, in her emphasis on the almost inevitable success of US measures of the good life, yet she argues convincingly for the hegemony of the US model of consumer capitalism in contrast to a more fragmented European economy whose only real anti-capitalist alternatives – fascism and communism – would ultimately fail.[24] De Grazia overplays the differences between old Europe and new America, implying that Europe on its own would not have been able to develop a mass consumption society, but she rightly points to the crucial transatlantic exchanges and dialogues between individuals, institutions, politicians and academics. These exchanges suggest that, rather than assuming the imposition of an American model, the responses to a transatlantic capitalism might have much in common and that it would be useful to identify the commonalities in the development of consumer expertise from the late-nineteenth century. Consumers, and those other groups concerned with their welfare and needs, identified similar problems of the market regardless of the nation-state they found themselves in and a two-way traffic in consumerist ideas took place across the Atlantic. Thus, while the Marshall Plan may have brought all the power of the US state to bear on post-Second World War European productivity missions, elsewhere US expert consumers borrowed from European experiences, be it in the boycotts of the anti-slavery movement, the late-nineteenth century anti-sweating campaigns, or the forms of consumer protection legislated across Europe in the 1960s and 1970s.

Consequently, in this volume we have located the contributions within three broad thematic areas which roughly correspond with three general periods. These borrow heavily from the greater knowledge set out by historians of the US, but are suggestive of an international development of consumer expertise. Firstly, we can identify a period of early consumer activism from the nineteenth century through to the First World War, though in many instances it continued into the interwar period as well. At this time, early efforts to mobilise consumers as experts were centred on items of necessity and were consequently focussed on the problems faced by ordinary workers: consumers were to be united with producers in the cause of labour conditions. Secondly, the period covering the interwar decades, followed by the Second World War itself, might be seen as the moment of expert consumer professionalisation, when governments first called upon organisations to represent the mass of consumers in official institutions. Frequently, these representatives were selected from the various types of consumer activist, which were taken to be co-terminus with women's organisations, though representatives were more often chosen from amongst the world of commerce and the professions, especially those connected to the new consumer disciplines of marketing, advertising, home economics, retailing and academic economists concerned with the consumption function. Thirdly, a final section focuses on the post-Second World War period, a time when economic reconstruction created a new generation of affluent consumers across the industrialised world and a related movement for greater protection in the marketplace. Ever-increasing consumption became tied up with a Cold War rhetoric, though the tremendous sweep of consumer protection measures which were implemented were as much concerned with restraining the free market as further liberating it.

The principal organisations connected to the first period are undoubtedly the consumers' co-operatives, a movement which marks a clear distinction between Europe and the US due to the sheer scale of the enterprises involved. Their history has been traced elsewhere and it is clear that their leaders were often assumed to be the main expert consumers in their respective countries.[25] Although the level of involvement in representative situations varied from country to country, the power of co-operatives at the vanguard of an emerging consumer consciousness continued well into the twentieth century. In Britain, France and Belgium, co-operative thought dominated consumerist ideas and, particularly in the Scandinavian countries, their representative role continued well beyond the Second World War (see Chapter 8 by Theien) whereas, elsewhere, new organisations of housewives and affluent consumers began to eclipse the co-operatives as expert consumers. What is significant about the co-operative movement, however, and which links it to other forms of consumer organising covered in this volume, is its concern with the relations of production and the condition of workers. Although the dividend on purchases formally established co-operation as a consumer movement, its ultimate aim was the improvement of standards of living for its worker-consumer members, the struggle over costs removing a distinction between price and pay.

Other attempts to improve workers' lives did not necessarily constitute such a grassroots movement, but important links were established with trade unions and socialist and social democratic political parties. Many of the precedents for consumer concern with the productive origins of commodities began in the early nineteenth century (Glickman, Chapter 1) but, towards the end of the nineteenth century, the labour movement itself saw the importance of working with consumers to improve working conditions. The anti-sweating movement provided the inspiration for Clementina Black, Honorary Secretary of the Women's Trade Union Association, to call for a specific 'consumers' league' in Britain in 1887. Her own organisation failed to endure however, yet the idea subsequently took hold in the US before being picked up by a variety of civic-minded groups in Europe, many of whom were inspired by religious principle. Indeed, this suggests that consumer expertise lay not only in a knowledge of abstract economic processes and theories, but in the consciences of consumers who argued persuasively that morality was not a topic to be divorced from the market. In her study of the French *Ligue Sociale d'Acheteurs*, Marie-Emmanuelle Chessel in Chapter 3 compares this organisation's work with the American National Consumers League with which it was linked, and draws out the strong element of social Catholicism running through its operations. Consumers' leagues represented one of the first attempts to create an international consumer movement (along with the co-operatives) and similar organisations were found across western Europe, all of which focussed their activities on developing 'white lists' of reputable traders who recognised certain standards in their employment conditions. The consumer concern with the worker was not just restricted to the consumers' leagues, however. Julien Vincent in Chapter 2 explores the religious motivations behind much ethical consumerism. His case study of the Christian Social Union in Britain sets out the precise theological underpinnings of this late nineteenth-century social reform wing of the Anglican Church and further challenges historians to explore the role of religion in consumption. Indeed, there is a book waiting to be written on the history of religion and consumption, perhaps beginning as early as the ritualistic removal and washing of clothes as pre-requisites to spiritual cleanliness found in Leviticus and moving forward to the fair-trade movement of the present day and the role played by bodies such as the Mothers' Union, Jubilee 2000, Christian Aid and CAFOD (Catholic Agency for Overseas Development), many of which recently came together in the Make Poverty History campaign.

In many ways, this concern with basic needs and the questions of poverty reached a highpoint at the end of the First World War, when shortages and rationing schemes caused consumers to protest on the street. Civil disobedience, consumer agitation and even riots were witnessed across Europe and beyond to the extent that questions over bread were an important factor in the revolutionary atmosphere at the end of the war, not least in Russia.[26] But the threat of consumer mobilisation also provoked a recognition that the consumer could be an expert with a role to play in the workings of state and society. In Britain, the Ministry of Food established a Consumers' Council to advise on the everyday concerns and problems faced by working-class shoppers. In Germany, Belinda Davis has gone so far as to suggest that the sympathetic recognition of the legitimacy of food protests mobilised the state into introducing rationing schemes, though ultimately these were insufficient to quell mounting protests.[27]

Of lasting significance were the precedents such consumer concerns set for interwar governments. The 1920s and 1930s saw the beginnings of the second period to be examined in this volume, that of the growing professionalisation of expert consumerism, when consumer groups were increasingly invited to speak to public bodies at a time when various forms of knowledge were increasingly bound up within professional associations.[28] But while consumers attached to the labour movement may have positioned themselves as the experts on getting and spending, so too did other professionals emerge as expert consumers, especially in advertising and marketing.[29] As mentioned above, Carolyn Goldstein's essay (Chapter 4) discusses the incorporation of professional female home economists into the American federal government, but in Europe as a whole, a range of actors were invited to present their expertise in the centralised planning environments of the 1920s and 1930s. Here, the notion of expertise is useful because it invokes the tremendous diversity of groups which have been invited by states to articulate a consumer or a citizen interest. Social scientists, in studies of the complexity of judicial proceedings and issues of the environment, have pointed to the problems of legitimacy for groups who have offered themselves as impartial and detached experts.[30] Especially in pluralist political systems, expertise is often tied to economic interests and is articulated through the lobbying activities of pressure groups or the advocacy of hired professionals. This is seen no more clearly than in the reports of state-sponsored commissions which profess to offer a neutral assessment of the public interest, but which, in practice, offer a notion of expertise dependent on the negotiation and compromises between competing interests.[31]

In this contested political arena, in which various groups posit themselves as the expert consumer (for instance in the field of HIV/AIDS patient groups)[32], consumers themselves can be crowded out by other interests and voices. In the US, the New Deal went some way into incorporating various consumer professionals into the state apparatus, though often consumers themselves were overwhelmed by the range of agricultural and industrial interests which also offered to speak in the name of the consumer. In Europe, in the interwar period, although co-operators remained powerful advocates of the consumer cause, no such corporatist involvement of consumers took place. New organisations of consumers did emerge however and as governments increasingly intervened into all areas of life during the Second World War, new groups of women's organisations and consumer professionals frequently found themselves advising state departments. Ina Zweiniger-Bargielowska has shown in her analysis of British austerity measures how housewives' organisations assumed a greater importance over the discussion of the rights to basic consumer items.[33] Indeed, all over Europe, it would be women's organisations in the late 1940s and 1950s which first pushed for a greater attention to consumer matters in the gradual move towards the implementation of consumer protection regimes in the 1960s. But nutritionists, economists, business confederations, trade unions and marketing experts all entered the debates over consumption. In Chapter 5, Joëlle Droux's case study of rationing in Switzerland between 1939 and 1945 argues that the wartime situation was used by a variety of groups to speak for the consumer.[34] Just as Lewis Mumford and John K. Galbraith hoped to use the American Office of Price Administration to promote 'chastened consumption' so too did nutritionists, moralists, journalists and women's groups attempt to use rationing to promote a simpler diet, supposedly more in keeping with traditional Swiss values. However, this created a distance between the aims of administrators and the needs and desires of many consumers, a gap which companies were only too keen to fill as they developed marketing strategies which emphasised the nutritional and traditional qualities of their standardised goods.

Just as the First World War set important precedents in paying attention to expert consumers, so too did the Second World War further extend these developments. As countries moved to reconstruct their economies, consumers became an importance focus for governments seeking to legitimate their measures. Although different forms of consumer citizenship would emerge, and not all countries would place consumption at the heart of a national ideology to quite the same extent as in the US, attention was nevertheless given to consumption across a variety of regimes. This is no better highlighted than in Katherine Pence's analysis of consumer citizenship in both East and West Germany in Chapter 6. She emphasises the differences between directly competing socialist and social-market systems which, all the same, emphasised the role of the consumer in reconstruction. Both countries saw and encouraged the mobilisation of women as consumers, though the patriotic consumption they were called upon to engage in was to serve very different ideological ends.

Certain institutional developments, however, suggest that the differences between states ought not to be overemphasised, particularly in western Europe. In the third period to be covered here – that of the affluent consumer society in the second half of the twentieth century – consumption was clearly linked to notions of democracy and the enjoyment of the good life. This was an idea especially promoted by the expert consumers mobilised by the Marshall Plan. According to de Grazia and other historians, Cohen's 'consumers' republic' was exported to Europe through the administrators and marketing professionals of the Marshall Plan who spread the message that individual prosperity and satisfaction were intricately bound up with the success of democracy.[35] How propaganda met with different institutional, political and cultural traditions is another matter, however, and what is apparent is the range of different consumer protection regimes which emerged in Europe as well as the very different forms of consumer expertise. As has been argued for an earlier debate about Americanisation, US models had to confront the prevalence of more state-oriented forms of economic and social participation in Europe.[36] Certainly, the evidence of expert consumerism across

Europe in the 1950s and 1960s either makes the American model irrelevant to Europe or else renders it an ideal type, against which national consumer protection systems developed.

But what also marks the third period is the mobilisation of consumer expertise by consumers themselves. Gunnar Trumbull, in his work on France and Germany, has argued that consumer protection outcomes depend very much on the interactions between the organised interests of producers and consumers.[37] Whichever group manages to persuade the state that it speaks with the most expertise and authority is able to mould the consumer protection regime more in line with their own interests. Furthermore, in Scandinavia, a social democratic system of consumer protection has been produced which has been as much an inspiration to consumer activists around the world as the highly active American consumer advocates such as Ralph Nader. As Iselin Theien demonstrates in Chapter 8, in Norway and Sweden, strong state-sponsored consumer institutions have existed with a high degree of input from the co-operative movement. As such, few private comparative-testing consumer organisations have developed in these countries, as compared to western Europe, especially Britain, France, Belgium and the Netherlands. They have, instead, pioneered state consumer activities such as the appointment of consumer councils and, in particular, consumer ministries and ombudsmen. In France, too, a strong central state has existed, which has led to pioneering developments in state-sponsored consumer protection measures. Yet, as Alain Chatriot argues in Chapter 7, the state was also responsive to organised consumers as a valuable part of civil society. The consumer protection measures which emerged in the 1970s (and which culminated in the formulation of a consumption code) were as much a response to a fragmented, but nevertheless vociferous, consumer movement as they were to the internal dynamics of an increasingly interventionist state.

In comparing these different national consumption regimes, it further brings into question the notion of an American model of consumer expertise. If the 'corporatist' consumer representative systems of the Scandinavian countries, as well as Germany and the Netherlands, contrasts with the stronger consumer movements of France and the UK, both, in turn, are at odds with the more pluralist system of consumer advocacy in the United States. In Chapter 9, Robert Mayer overviews four principal organisations connected with the modern consumer movement in the US and concludes that 'expertise' is not so much attributed to those groups who can mobilise the most numbers or who have the ear of government through the political traditions of a country, but through the ability of each consumer group to raise funds from the private sector. Expertise, already linked to advocacy within a pluralist conflict of interest, is also linked with the entrepreneurial skill each consumer group has in mobilising its resources, rather than to the state-directed incorporation of an expert consumer into a particular institution.

Such a system necessarily heightens the competition between different consumer groups and expert consumers, a situation which is replicated in less pluralistic political systems. Because of the diverse groups which have made up the consumer movement in France – from housewives' groups to trade unions to rural associations – at times different actors have sought to put themselves forward as the true expert on consumer affairs. In their study of a local Parisian residents' association at the end of the 1960s, Odile Join-Lambert and Yves Lochard note in Chapter 10 how the group deliberately chose to cast its expertise differently from that of the 'consumer' of commodities and the 'user' of public services. Instead, they developed a more generalist interpretation of using collective services tied to a wider vision of the development of a *quartier* or an *arrondissement.* The notion of expertise was thus cast more broadly than that found in the professionalised institutions of the mainstream consumer movement and it attempted to invoke a more grass-roots citizen consciousness which engaged with the diverse aspects of consumer and civil society.

This proliferation of consumer expertise in the latter half of the twentieth century is the subject of Matthew Hilton's concluding chapter on consumer movements around the world. He traces the origins and spread of consumer organising in the United States and Europe during the period of economic reconstruction. But just as consumer society itself has expanded so too has the number of people who have wished to have a say in the organisation of the society being built in their name. Just as an economic system became increasingly globalised and marketing professionals took their expertise about consumer behaviour around the world, so too did the consumer movement become a global phenomenon. Consumer organisations have pushed for better value for money, but also for a range of protection mechanisms to make the market a fairer and more equitable place. Furthermore, the consumer movement has spread well beyond the borders of the industrialised world and has taken on board the agendas of poor, developing-world consumers, concerned less with value for money and more with access to basic needs.

This last chapter serves to remind us that just as the expert consumer seemed to reach its apotheosis in the late-twentieth century, it also gave rise to new consumer voices and new consumer problems in a range of different economic, social and political contexts. What becomes clear, then, at the beginning of the twenty-first century, is that no one group has successfully managed to make itself the 'expert consumer' and that the fight to speak authoritatively about the marketplace will remain as contested as it has ever been. Over the course of the long twentieth century, expert consumerism has seemingly become more professionalised and organised, yet the very diversity of the market place – and, hence, the consumer interest – has meant expert consumers continue to proliferate. Indeed, in the period of the last one or two decades, not covered by this volume, a whole range of new consumer activists have emerged which seek to offer new forms of expertise which steer consumer society in new directions. Ethical shoppers, green consumers, fair traders, faith-based groups, advocates of voluntary simplicity and anti-capitalist protestors have continued to offer forms of expert knowledge which promote the agendas of specific groups of consumers and which have the potential to adapt the market to the interests of various actors. In many senses, the expert consumer remains both the label various groups attach to themselves as well as the goal of those who aim to speak above and beyond all other experts in the marketplace.

Notes

1 E. P. Thompson, 'The Moral Economy of the English Crowd in the Eighteenth Century', *Past and Present*, 50 (1971): 76-136.

2 Michael Young, *The Chipped White Cups of Dover: A Discussion of the Possibility of a New Progressive Party* (London, 1960); Jean Baudrillard, 'Consumer Society', in Mark Poster (ed.), *Jean Baudrillard: Selected Writings* (Oxford, 1988), p. 55.

3 For some overviews and useful bibliographies of US scholarship see Lawrence B. Glickman (ed.), *Consumer Society in American History: A Reader* (Ithaca, 1999). For Britain see the discussion in Matthew Hilton, *Consumerism in Twentieth-Century Britain: The Search for a Historical Movement* (Cambridge, 2003). For Germany, see A. Colfino and R. Koshar, 'Regimes of Consumer Culture: New Narratives in Twentieth-Century German History', *German History*, 19:2 (2001): 135-61; Hartmut Kaeble, Jurgen Kocka and Hannes Siegrist (eds), *Europäische Konsumgeschichte: Zur Gesellschafts- und Kulturgeschichte des Konsums (18 bis 20 Jahrhundert)* (Frankfurt am Main, 1997); Hartmut Berghoff (ed.), *Konsumpolitik: Die Regulierung des privaten Verbrauchs im 20 Jahrhundert* (Göttingen, 2003); Michael Prinz (ed.), *Der lange Weg in den Überfluss: Anfänge und Entwicklung der Konsumgesellschaft seit der Vormoderne* (Paderborn, 2003); plus the special issue on 'Au bonheur des Allemands: consommateurs et consommation au XXe siècle', *Le mouvement Social*, 206 (2004).

4 Daniel Roche, *Histoire des choses banales: naissance de la consommation dans les sociétés traditionnelles, XVIIe – XIXe siècles* (Paris, 1997); M. Wieviorka, *L'Etat, le patronat et les consommateurs: étude des mouvements de consommateurs* (Paris, 1977); M. Ruffat, *Le contre-pouvoir consommateur aux Etats-Unis: du mouvement social au groupe d'intérêt* (Paris, 1987); L. Pinto, *La constitution du 'consommateur' comme catégorie de l'espace public* (Paris, 1989); Ellen Furlough, *Consumer Cooperation in Modern France: The Politics of Consumption* (Ithaca, 1991); Rosalind Williams, *Dreamworlds: Mass Consumption in Late Nineteenth Century France* (Berkeley, 1982); M. B. Miller, *The Bon Marché: Bourgeois Culture and the Department Store, 1869-1920* (Princeton, 1981); Lisa Tiersten, *Marianne in the Market: Envisioning Consumer Society in Fin-de-Siècle France* (Berkeley, 2001).

5 Guy Debord, *Society of the Spectacle* (Detroit, 1983); Jean Baudrillard, *Consumer Society: Myths and Structures* (London, 1998); Michel de Certeau, *The Practice of Everyday Life* (London, 1984); Pierre Bourdieu, *Distinction: A Social Critique of the Judgement of Taste* (London, 1984).

6 For overviews of the main theories of consumer society, and of the influence of French critical theory (among others), see: Celia Lury, *Consumer Culture* (Oxford, 1996); Peter Corrigan, *The Sociology of Consumption: An Introduction* (London, 1997); Don Slater, *Consumer Culture and Modernity* (Oxford, 1997); Steven Miles, *Consumerism as a Way of Life* (London, 1998); Hugh Mackay (ed.), *Consumption and Everyday Life* (London, 1997); R. Bocock, *Consumption* (London, 1993); Mike Featherstone, *Consumer Culture and Postmodernism* (London, 1991); Daniel Miller (ed.), *Acknowledging Consumption:*

A Review of New Studies (London, 1995); Isabelle Szmigin, *Understanding the Consumer* (London, 2003); N. Herpin, *Sociologie de la consommation* (Paris, 2001).

7 For some criticisms see Thomas Frank, *One Market Under God: Extreme Capitalism, Market Populism, and the End of Economic Democracy* (London, 2001); Joseph Heath and Andrew Potter, *Nation of Rebels: Why Counterculture Became Consumer Culture* (New York, 2004).

8 Victoria de Grazia and Ellen Furlough (eds), *The Sex of Things: Gender and Consumption in Historical Perspective* (Berkeley, 1996); Susan Strasser, Charles McGovern and Matthias Judt (eds), *Getting and Spending: European and American Consumer Societies in the Twentieth Century* (Cambridge, 1998); Martin Daunton and Matthew Hilton (eds), *The Politics of Consumption: Material Culture and Citizenship in Europe and America* (Oxford, 2001); Neva R. Goodwin, Frank Ackerman and David Kiron (eds), *The Consumer Society* (Washington, DC, 1997); Juliet B. Schor and Douglas B. Holt (eds), *The Consumer Society Reader* (New York, 2000); Glickman, *Consumer Society.*

9 All 24 of the papers presented at this conference have appeared in Alain Chatriot, Marie-Emmanuelle Chessel and Matthew Hilton (eds), *Au Nom du Consommateur: Consommation et Politique en Europe et aux États-Unis au XXe Siècle* (Paris, 2004).

10 For instance, see Lawrence B. Glickman, *A Living Wage: American Workers and the Making of Consumer Society* (Ithaca, 1997); Lawrence B. Glickman, 'Workers of the World, Consume: Ira Steward and the Origins of the Labour Consumerism', *International Labour and Working Class History*, 52 (1997): 72-86.

11 Daniel Horowitz, *The Morality of Spending: Attitudes Towards the Consumer Society in America, 1875-1940* (Baltimore, 1985); Daniel Horowitz, *The Anxieties of Affluence: Critiques of American Consumer Culture, 1939-1979* (Amherst, 2004).

12 R. W. Fox and T. J. Jackson Lears (eds), *The Culture of Consumption: Critical Essays in American History, 1880-1980* (New York, 1983); Warren I. Susman, *Culture as History: The Transformation of American Society in the Twentieth Century* (New York, 1984); T. J. Jackson Lears, *No Place of Grace: Antimodernism and the Transformation of American Culture, 1880-1920* (New York, 1981).

13 Lizabeth Cohen, *A Consumers' Republic: The Politics of Mass Consumption in Postwar America* (New York, 2003).

14 T. H. Breen, *The Marketplace of Revolution: How Consumer Politics Shaped American Independence* (Oxford, 2004).

15 Glickman, *Living Wage*; Dana Frank, *Purchasing Power: Consumer Organising, Gender, and the Seattle Labour Movement, 1919-1929* (Cambridge, 1994).

16 Charles McGovern, 'Consumption and Citizenship in the United States, 1900-1940', in Strasser *et al.*, *Getting and Spending*, pp. 37-58; Lawrence B. Glickman, 'The Strike in the Temple of Consumption: Consumer Activism and Twentieth-Century American Political Culture', *Journal of American History*, 88:1 (2001): 99-128; Robert N. Mayer, *The Consumer Movement: Guardians of the Marketplace* (Boston, 1989); Norman Isaac Silber, *Test and Protest: The Influence of Consumers Union* (New York, 1983); Michael Pertschuk, *Revolt Against Regulation: The Rise and Pause of the Consumer Movement* (Berkely, CA, 1982); Mark V. Nadel, *The Politics of Consumer Protection* (New York, 1971).

17 Tracey Deutsch, 'Des consommatrices américaines très engagées, du New Deal à la guerre froide', in Chatriot, Chessel and Hilton, *Au Nom du Consommateur*, pp. 361-75.

18 Kathleen G. Donohue, *Freedom from Want: American Liberalism and the Idea of the Consumer* (Baltimore, 2003), p. 2.

19 Cohen, *Consumers' Republic*; Meg Jacobs, '"How About Some Meat?" The Office of Price Administration, Consumption Politics, and State-Building from the Bottom Up, 1941-1946', *Journal of American History*, 84:3 (1997): 910-41; Meg Jacobs, '"Democracy's Third Estate: New Deal Politics and the Construction of a "Consuming Public"', *International Labour and Working-Class History*, 55 (1999): 27-51; Meg Jacobs, *Pocketbook Politics: Economic Citizenship in Twentieth-Century America* (Princeton, NJ, 2005).

20 Cohen, *Consumers' Republic*, p. 7.

21 G. Cross, *An All-Consuming Century: Why Commercialism Won in Modern America* (New York, 2000).

22 The main culprit for Horowitz being James B. Twitchell, *Adcult USA: The Triumph of Advertising in American Culture* (New York, 1996) and *Lead Us Into Temptation: The Triumph of American Materialism* (New York, 1999).

23 Victoria de Grazia, *Irresistible Empire: America's Advance Through Twentieth-Century Europe* (Cambridge, MA, 2005).

24 For an introduction to the Americanisation debate see Richard Pells, *Not Like Us: How Europeans Loved, Hated, and Transformed American Culture Since World War II* (New York, 1997).

25 Ellen Furlough and Carl Strikwerda (eds), *Consumers Against Capitalism? Consumer Cooperation in Europe, North America and Japan, 1840-1990* (Oxford, 1999).

26 Dana Frank, 'Housewives, Socialists and the Politics of Food: The 1917 New York Cost-of-Living Protests', *Feminist Studies*, 11 (1985): 255-85; J. Smart, 'Feminists, Food and the Fair Price: The Cost of Living Demonstrations in Melbourne, August-September 1917', *Labour History*, 50 (1986): 113-31; T. Kaplan, 'Female Consciousness and Collective Action: The Case of Barcelona, 1910-1918', *Signs*, 7 (1982): 545-66; L. T. Lih, *Bread and Authority in Russia, 1914-1921* (Los Angeles, 1990); Eric Hobsbawm, *Age of Extremes: The Short Twentieth-Century, 1914-1991* (London, 1994), pp. 60-61; Erik Langlinay, 'Consommation et ravitaillement en France Durant la Première Guerre mondiale', in Chatriot, Chessel and Hilton, *Au Nom du Consommateur*, pp. 29-44.

27 Belinda J. Davis, *Home Fires Burning: Food, Politics and Everyday Life in World War I Berlin* (Chapel Hill, 2000).

28 M. Burrage and R. Thorstendhal (eds), *Professions in Theory and History* (London, 1990); Alain Desrosières and Laurent Thévenot, *Les catégories socio-professionnelles* (Paris, 2000); Roland Marchand, *Advertising the American Dream: Making Way for Modernity, 1920* -1940 (Berkeley, 1985).

29 Marie-Emmanuelle Chessel, *La publicité: naissance d'une profession (1900-1940)* (Paris, 1998); Romain Laufer and Catherine Paradeise, *Le prince bureaucrate: Machiavel au pays du marketing* (Paris, 1982); Frank Cochoy, *Une histoire du marketing: discipliner l'économie de marché* (Paris, 1999); Gilles Marion, *L'idéologie marketing* (Paris, 2004); Christoph Conrad, 'Observer les consommateurs: études de marché et histoire de la consommation en Allemagne, des années 1930 aux années 1960', *Le Mouvement Social*, 206 (2004): 17-39.

30 Laurence Dumoulin, Stéphane La Branche, Cécile Robert and Philippe Warin (eds), *Le recours aux experts: raisons et usages politique* (Grenoble, 2005); Danièle Bourcier and Monique de Bonis, *Les paradoxes de l'expertise: savoir ou juger?* (Le Plessis Robinson,

1999); Jacques Theys, 'L'expert contre le citoyen? Le cas de l'environnement', in Christian Join-Lambert (ed.), *L'Etat moderne et l'administration: nouveaux contextes, nouvelles éthiques, nouveaux experts* (Paris, 1994), pp. 151-65.

31 Alain Chatriot, *La démocratie sociale à la française: l'expérience du Conseil national économique 1924-1940* (Paris, 2002).

32 Sébastien Dalgalarrondo, *Sida: la course aux molécules* (Paris, 2004), pp. 79-125; Chris Bonell and Matthew Hilton, 'Consumerism in Health Care: The Case of a Voluntary Sector HIV Prevention Organization', *Voluntas*, 13:1 (2002): 27-46; Sophie Chauveau, 'Malades ou Consommateurs? La consommation de médicaments en France dans le second XXe siècle', in Chatriot, Chessel and Hilton, *Au Nom du Consommateur*, pp. 182-198.

33 I. Zweiniger-Bargielowska, *Austerity in Britain: Rationing, Controls and Consumption 1939-1955* (Oxford, 2000).

34 See also Jakob Tanner, 'The Rationing System, Food Policy, and Nutritional Science during the Second World War: A Comparative View of Switzerland', in Carola Lentz (ed.), *Changing Food Habits: Case Studies from Africa, South America and Europe* (Australia, 1999), pp. 211-42.

35 de Grazia, *Irresistible Empire*; Sheryl Kroen, 'A Political History of the Consumer', *Historical Journal* 47:2 (2004): 709-36; Sheryl Kroen, 'Negotiations with the American Way: The Consumer and the Social Contract in Post-War Europe', in John Brewer and Frank Trentmann (eds), *Consuming Cultures. Global Perspectives* (forthcoming).

36 V. de Grazia, 'Changing Consumption Regimes in Europe, 1930-1970: Comparative Perspectives on the Distribution Problem', in Strasser *et al.*, *Getting and Spending*, pp. 59-83.

37 G. Trumbull, *The Contested Consumer: The Politics of Product Market Regulation in France and Germany* (forthcoming).

Part 1
Early Consumer Activism

Chapter 1

'Through the Medium of Their Pockets': Sabbatarianism, Free Produce, Non Intercourse and the Significance of 'Early Modern' Consumer Activism

Lawrence B. Glickman

Despite a growing interest in the history of consumer society and its relationship to politics, historians have tended to treat the topic of consumer activism in a piecemeal way and in isolation, focusing on one particular episode or another. Those scholars who have proposed a more systematic understanding of consumer activism have inaccurately characterized it as an episodic twentieth-century development. After an obligatory mention of the boycotts of the Revolutionary era, historians of modern consumer activism in the United States have, for the most part, leapfrogged the nineteenth century entirely to examine what they take to be the birth of modern consumer activism in the Progressive era. For their part, scholars of Revolutionary boycotters have made little attempt to trace the impact of these actions on subsequent generations. American consumer activism is, in either version, discontinuous. From either the eighteenth- or twentieth-century perspective, then, the storyline is similar. Consumer activism, though born in the 1770s, was dormant for more than a century before emerging in the twentieth century, and even then it was a periodic phenomena characteristic only of certain decades: the 1900s, 1930s, 1960s and 1990s.[1]

Sharing many of these assumptions, when I began researching the history of American consumer activism I understood it to be fundamentally a twentieth-century phenomenon. Having previously studied the American labour movement in the late nineteenth century, I knew that many of the ideas embraced by twentieth-century consumer organizations had roots in that period. For example, the union label movement began in the 1870s, the so-called 'labour boycott' – the shunning of non-union or anti-union employers and businesses – was popularized in the 1880s, the decade when the word 'boycott' itself was coined and, in general, labour reformers and many trade unionists embraced in the late-nineteenth century what I have called a 'consumerist turn' in labour ideology, a turn whose chief postulate was that consumption provided an essential and powerful mode of solidarity in an increasingly market-linked economy.[2] All of these ideas and practices seemed so novel and so modern – and so many of their articulators confidently proclaimed them to be so – that I did not recognize that these postbellum workers were themselves (generally unwitting) inheritors rather than inventors of most of these ideas and practices. Consequently, in the process of researching what I took to be the history of consumer activism, I understood the late nineteenth-century labour movement to be the beginning or prehistory of a tradition that only matured organizationally in the twentieth century with the emergence of such groups as the National Consumers League in the Progressive Era, Consumers' Research, Consumers Union, and the League of Women Shoppers, in the 1930s, and the Consumers' Education and Protection Association as well as the organizations associated with Ralph Nader in the 1960s.

The broad scope and significance of consumer activism, however, only became apparent as I explored the minutes, newspapers and pamphlets of organizations, such as 'free produce' societies, 'non intercourse' associations, Sabbatarian groups – all of which made their appearance in the late 1820s and persisted throughout the antebellum period. Free produce advocates called upon abolitionists to eschew goods made by slave labour and, alternatively, to purchase only free labour produce. White Southern advocates of non intercourse used precisely the same methods – the boycott and buycott – and very similar rhetoric for the exact opposite cause: the maintenance of a slave labour economy and the weakening of the free labour North. Sabbatarians, inspired by the evangelical fervour of the second Great Awakening, called on Christians, North and South, to uphold the sanctity of the Sabbath by boycotting businesses that violated the Fourth Commandment. I stumbled upon these groups, starting with free produce, when I came across brief but suggestive references to their consumer politics, almost always in works that were in the field of antebellum American history rather than consumer history. These movements are not unknown to specialists in antebellum American history but their use of consumer tactics, while detected by several historians, has not been the source of sustained commentary. It is a paradox that scholars of the antebellum period, who have done so much to highlight the political significance of the 'market revolution,' have had very little to say about the relation of the developments that fall under this rubric to the other economic revolution which began roughly at the same time, the 'consumer revolution.' The result is that free produce, non intercourse, and Sabbatarianism, efforts which played a foundational role in the American tradition of consumer activism, have been shunted into other historiographical categories. At the same time, twentieth-century scholars have frequently conflated consumer activism with the 'consumer movement,' the product testing movement on behalf of ordinary consumers that began in the late 1920s, thus cutting off the exploration of important precursors.[3]

Sabbatarians, non intercourse advocates, and free produce proponents supported distinct, and even opposing, causes and advocates of each effort certainly did not see themselves as part of a like-minded coalition. Supporters of these causes neither defined themselves as consumer activists nor saw their cause as fighting on behalf of consumers. Nonetheless, they called on citizens to act in their capacity as consumers and they invented sophisticated and enduring consumerist tactics and philosophies. These movements, to the chagrin of their leaders, neither launched boycotts that damaged the economy of their enemies nor sustained alternative businesses long enough for the greater public to take much notice of them, except as a source of ridicule for the yawning chasm between their bold plans to use commerce in the service of a moral revolution and their short-lived, unprofitable, business failures.

Yet in the late 1820s each of these groups, almost conterminously, developed a form of consumer politics that is recognizably modern. The history of these groups is not a mere preface to modern consumer activism or even its prehistory. Rather these groups constitute what one can call the 'early modern' period of consumer activism. Just as the early modern period of European history set in motion the ideas and practices of modernity, so too 'early modern' consumer activists, in inchoate form, set the terms for the consumer activism that was to follow. Sabbatarians, free producers and advocates of non intercourse should be viewed as 'early modern' consumer activists because their ideologies and actions lie closer to their twentieth-century descendants to whom they were generally unknown – groups such as the National Consumers League and the League of Women Shoppers – than to their eighteenth-century forebears, the Revolutionary boycotters of British goods and wearers of native homespun clothing to whom they paid regular tribute. What their histories reveal is not only that consumer activism existed well before the twentieth century, but that nineteenth-century consumer activists developed a philosophy, practice and vocabulary of consumer activism that twentieth-century (and contemporary) activists, including those in the consumer movement, employed and modified, despite their generally patchy memory of these predecessors. Although it was certainly not their intention, pre-twentieth century groups laid the template of modern consumer activism. These early groups typically failed to achieve their intended goals, whether that was the abolition of chattel slavery, Southern commercial independence, or the protection of the Sabbath from commercial encroachments. But their efforts established a way of thinking about consumption and a mode of action that were themselves enduring, if unintended, achievements. Their understandings of the social consequences of consumption and of the consequent power of long-distance solidarity, while not ends in themselves for these groups, became the means by which modern citizens (and all those who aspired to take part in meaningful political action) believed that they could promote social change. Even as particular movements faded and were forgotten, these means endured as a framework through which future generations conducted their own political efforts.

In the past, most famously during the American Revolution, consumers had been called upon to withhold their patronage from unsavoury merchants who sold goods of British origin as a form of economic and moral protest and to ostracize and even to harass fellow citizens who did. In the new vision represented by these enterprises, consumption was a key pressure point not only negatively but positively; it was not just a stick but a carrot. Not only were consumers asked to boycott certain products or companies, they were also asked to spend their money at morally-sanctioned venues, the 'purchase of that which comes through clean hands,' as the abolitionist newspaper the *Liberator* put it in 1831.[4] This had implications for the ways in which these groups understood the relationship between virtue and sacrifice. With the advent of moral commerce, virtue was no longer automatically twinned with sacrifice, as it had been for the Revolutionary boycotters as well as for abolitionist sugar boycotters. Indeed, the new class of moral entrepreneurs who started free produce stores and other such businesses argued that consumers best enacted their ethical views through the consumption of the goods they sold. By sundering the link between virtue and sacrifice, they opened the possibility for a new kind of ethical consumption. It was now possible to 'buy for the sake of the slave,' one abolitionist urged; others agreed that one could buy rather than sacrifice to enact other ethical commitments.[5]

Free producers, advocates of non intercourse with the North, and Sabbatarians developed a conception of political action in, rather than outside of, the marketplace. Their imagined community of political actors included not only those who avoided products deemed immoral but equally those who purchased the new morally-sanctioned products that they purveyed. Rather than being thought of as a discrete and bounded place, each point of consumption began to be conceived of as a node linking individual shoppers to what was becoming a nation-wide (and, in some cases, even worldwide) web of producers, manufacturers, other consumers, environments and even nation-states. We tend to think of the networked world as a new thing, but the linked nature of the United States, and much of the rest of the world, was a condition that these groups not only posited but around which they tried to build a new politics of solidarity.

These early movements also introduced tensions that continue to exist within consumer activism and occasionally to divide consumer activists, and that continue to get under the skin of their opponents both within and outside of the cause. For example, there were no fiercer critics of the free produce efforts than fellow abolitionists, no angrier opponents of Sabbatarian boycotts than other evangelicals, no harsher denouncers of non intercourse with the North than other Southern nationalists. Their attempts to marry economics and morality, particularly the use of the free market for moral improvement, struck their critics as not only impractical but, in a certain capitalistic sense, immoral. Something about their self-righteousness – a characteristic attributed to each of these groups, and practically all subsequent consumer activists, and which most have borne with pride – which was a product of their magnification of individual action and their belief that buying or boycotting was a performative moral action, meant that they were often singled out for the special scorn society holds out for the sanctimonious. These early consumer activists, like their successors, assigned great power to ordinary consumers, but at the same time generally distrusted the ability of these consumers to exercise such power wisely and justly. Ranting against the unwillingness of consumers to do either what was good for them or what was good for society (a defining characteristic of most twentieth-century consumer activists), has its roots in the frustrations of these pioneering consumer activists, who were the first to recognize the power of organized consumption or non consumption and also the first to believe that ordinary consumers, ignoring the strictures of responsible consumption, undermined their cause through ignorance, indifference, or other moral failings.

Studying consumer activism over the long term not only forces us to look backwards in time but also broadens our conception of what counts as consumer activism and leads us to recognize that this phenomenon is more complex, diffuse and contested than a study of twentieth-century consumer organizations alone would suggest. It reveals that consumer activism is a continuous, not periodic, as well as a contested, not monolithic, political tradition in American history. This long view of consumer activism highlights continuities, transformations and tensions in the theories and practices of consumer activists.

The remainder of this chapter will briefly examine the three antebellum consumer movements, their underlying philosophies, and the criticisms they engendered. It will argue that free produce campaigners, non intercourse advocates, and Sabbatarians, despite their differences, developed the philosophies and techniques and even the vocabulary that continue to guide consumer activism. They also set off a criticism of consumer politics and those who practice it that has not entirely disappeared. Largely forgotten, not only by their heirs in the National Consumers League and other twentieth-century consumer groups but also by historians of consumer politics, these groups are themselves an essential link in the chain of consumer activism.

Sometime around 1826 human nature may not have changed, but around that date a sea-change occurred in the ways in which people believed that they could organize for and promote social change. In 1826, the first free produce store opened in Baltimore. Within two years of this date, the first advocates of Southern 'non intercourse' with the North called for a consumer-driven commercial declaration of independence, and several Northern evangelicals founded the first Sabbath-upholding commercial freight company. Suddenly, in a variety of realms, the two-generation old tactic of the boycott, the withholding of pecuniary support from a business, product, or nation deemed immoral, was joined by another tactic, what we today call the 'buycott': an alternative means of commerce which provided consumers with a positive way to exercise their ethical views. In 1826, a group of Presbyterian Sabbatarians, for example, urged 'all our ministers and church members when traveling, to give preference to such livery establishments, steamboats, canal boats, and other public vehicles, as do not violate' the Sabbath.[6] The ferment of the second Great Awakening produced many similar consumer-based moral reforms, which, by adding the option of purchasing morally-sanctioned goods, offered concerned citizens another choice – fitting for a nascent consumer society – in addition to the boycott, about how to act economically on their moral beliefs. Temperance advocates called for Christians to boycott saloons, and some even opened alcohol-free inns. Advocates of the colonization movement, the campaign to transfer American slaves to Africa, sought to organize a packet line to Liberia. Christian bookstores opened in competition with secular ones. The evangelical reforming brothers Lewis and Arthur Tappan founded a newspaper, the *Journal of Commerce,* that, they announced, would strictly observe the Sabbath and 'avoid all participation in the gain of those fashionable vices which sap the foundations of morality and religion' by refusing to run advertisements for the sale of alcohol or to promote theatrical events.[7]

One of the first observers to take stock of this 'new power brought to bear on society' was the acclaimed Unitarian minister of Boston, William Ellery Channing. In an 1829 essay, Channing highlighted the newness and the underlying similarities, as well as the dangers, of the styles of politics that had suddenly appeared in various quarters of the country in support of a variety of causes. Taking note of the 'immense facility given to intercourse by modern improvements, by increased commerce and traveling, by the post-office, by the steam-boat, and especially by the press, by newspapers, periodicals, tracts, and other publications,' Channing saw that, via this wired infrastructure, the people of a 'whole country' can 'easily understand one another, and easily act together.' No longer was physical proximity the necessary precondition for effective political action. The market revolution had made it possible for 'immense and widely separated multitudes' to unite and act effectively on behalf of causes they held dear. Invoking a military metaphor, Channing observed: 'The grand manoeuvre to which Napoleon owed his victories, we mean the concentration of great numbers on a single point, is now placed within the reach of all parties and sects.' Not only could people from different parts of the nation with no connection other than a shared 'elective affinity' be enlisted 'with the uniformity of a disciplined army' in a new kind of battle, but 'facilities of intercourse' made it possible for them to do so with unprecedented speed. 'So extensive have coalitions become, through the facilities now described, and so various and rapid are the means of communication, that when a few leaders have agreed on an object, an impulse may be given in a month to the whole country.' In noting the ways in which imagined communities of activists acted through the medium of a new infrastructure, Channing taxonomized not only the methods and techniques of the Sabbatarians he disliked but also the many other moral causes which built on this new conception of long distance solidarity.[8]

What Channing left unsaid is that what made these new social movements tick was a vision of the consumer as a powerful moral, political, and economic actor. Sabbatarians, non intercourse supporters, and proponents of free produce were among those who constructed movements built on a new understanding of consumers as what one free produce advocate called 'the original cause, the first mover' of economic activity.[9] This view was most famously promulgated by Adam Smith, who wrote, in an oft-quoted passage from *The Wealth of Nations*, that 'consumption is the sole end of all production.'[10] These groups in the 1820s were the first to attempt to build political movements upon this assumption. In their view, consumers were like billiard players, setting off and orchestrating a chain reaction of economic activity. This vision of the power of ordinary consumers is what sets them apart from previous boycotters, including those of the American Revolution and makes them the founders of modern consumer activism. These activists of the 1820s were also the first to suggest that consumers – rather than agrarian patriarchs, or the producing classes, or, for that matter, elite merchants, the leaders of the non importation campaigns of the 1770s – were the representative citizens and moral centre of the republic. Theirs were the first bottom-up consumer movements, the first to focus on individual consumers as agents of moral and economic change, and the first to use the word 'consumer' in its positive, modern sense, long before most scholars assume that it was coined. The modern-sounding phrase 'conscientious consumer,' for example, originated with the free produce movement.[11] As the phrase implies, these early consumer activists understood consumer power as inevitably moral, since in this worldview consumers were responsible for the far-reaching impact of their actions. They often used the metaphor of a 'chain' to refer to the binding relationships which linked individual consumers to producers of the goods they bought as well as other consumers.[12]

What enabled free produce activists, proponents of Southern economic independence, and Sabbatarians to attribute such power to consumers was their vision of the world and especially the growing part of it connected by market relations to what abolitionist newspapers called 'one connected and dependent whole.'[13] In this interconnected world, since every purchase either rewarded or punished producers of goods, consumers were important political actors and markets provided the political space for them to act. 'Commerce is indispensable to the welfare of society,' claimed L. W. Gause in the *Pennsylvania Freeman*, one of the main organs of free produce sentiment. Although he probably would have agreed with little else said by an abolitionist, a Southerner concurred about the virtues of 'free trade and direct connection between producers and consumers in the common, untrammeled markets of the world.'[14] Unlike many of the market revolution's celebrants, however, these consumer activists did not ascribe morality to the market itself. They believed rather that markets magnified the range and scope of good and bad behavior, since actions that previously might have made only a neighbor unhappy could now spread misery to many more people in distant places. Power inhered in markets but that power could be used for good or for ill. 'Commerce is without a conscience of its own,' is how one Quaker abstainer of slave-made goods put it.[15] Slavery, Samuel Rhoads reminded the readers of the *Liberator* in 1850, 'is sustained by commercial union.' Many Southern nationalists made the same point about the power of the abolitionist North. 'Southern money and Southern labour have indirectly ... bought the Sharpe's rifles, hired the abolition emissaries, and paid the John Browns,' claimed an Alabama editor in 1860. Southern 'dollars to fatten and enrich a set of fanatics whose sole aim and chief delight were to make war upon our institution and rights.'[16] This power to be used for good or ill made the market both powerful and dangerous. The key was to harness the market's power without triggering what Gause called 'unrighteous commerce.'[17] Sabbatarians, free producers, and Southern nationalists agreed that markets did not necessarily make people moral but, if used properly, they provided a powerful engine for moral change.

In his prescient comments, Channing, seizing on the open-ended nature of market relations, pointed out that the 'spirit of association, which characterizes our time,' could potentially empower any cause, including distasteful ones, and warned citizens of the need 'to secure this powerful instrument against perversion.'[18] From Channing's point of view, the Sabbatarian effort to shut down Sunday commerce revealed the dangers of consumer politics. In Channing's estimation, the national network of commerce and communications had provided overzealous moralists not only with a platform but with the ability to attempt to enforce their vision unfairly on the rest of the country. Their claims that people who did not support their boycotts were, in the words of a New York Sabbatarian, 'involved in the guilt' raised the bar of political participation since neutrality or even tacit support for the cause was no longer an option.[19] In the newly-connected world, in which shopping was an invariable social action, from the point of view of Sabbatarians – and it was Channing's signal observation to note that this would be true of all consumerist associations – citizens could not stand on the sidelines of the great social struggles of the age. Rather than soliciting the assistance of a committed minority, Sabbatarians believed that it was their duty to enlist all consumers in their cause, in part by informing those consumers that neutrality was not an option. Since every point of consumption was a node in a national system, an entry point that produced an immediate economic impact, every shopper's purchases were as much a moral mandate as an economic decision. For Lyman Beecher, the founder of the leading Sabbatarian organization, the General Union for Promoting the Observance of the Christian Sabbath, the choice was stark: consumers either sanctioned the 'perpetuation of evil,' or they promoted a worthy cause.[20] In response, the wealthy evangelicals Arthur Tappan and Josiah Bissell set up a Sabbath-observing freight company based in Rochester, New York, the Pioneer Line.[21] Founding this line and asking Christian consumers to support other businesses that obeyed the Fourth Commandment made the option of consuming preferable to the boycott of businesses deemed immoral.

Free produce campaigners also presented consumers with a similar moral binary. They described purchasers of slave-made goods as partners in crime – 'participants,' 'accessories,' 'aggrandizers,' 'enrichers,' 'countenancers,' and 'abettors.'[22] In the words of one free produce supporter:

> It is clear to those who will take the trouble to examine the subject, that the northern merchant who purchases the cotton, sugar and rice of the southern planter ... the auctioneer who cries his human wares in the market, and sell those helpless victims of cupidity ... yea, even the heartless, murderous slave-trader, are each and all of them, only so many AGENTS, employed by and for the CONSUMER in extracting and transferring the products of the unrequited toil, of the poor down trodden suffering slave.[23]

Free produce activists turned the conceit of abolition on its head. The guilty were not the slave-owners but the consumers who kept the slave-owners and his adjutants in business. As an article in the form of wisdom dispensed from a fictitious slaveholder to a Northern consumer declared, 'You don't technically hold the slave, but you give the gold which makes him to be held! We are but your servants!'[24] In this view, the people seemingly far more directly involved in slavery than northern (or British) consumers were, in fact, slaves to them. Free produce shifted the focus away from the South and the slaveholders to the North and its consumers of slave products. As the free produce supporter Henry Grew asked the New England Anti-Slavery convention of 1850, what did 'no union with slaveholders' mean if they themselves were the slaveholders?[25] Abolitionists frequently highlighted the hypocrisy of Northern politicians who compromised with the slave power, but were less used to the charge that, if they purchased slave-made goods which really kept the slave power in business they were hypocrites as well. In claiming, as free produce activists routinely did, that slaveholders were merely the servants of consumers, they analogized northern consumers to the group they most despised, slave-owners, and slave-owners to the people for whom they felt the most sympathy, slaves. Abolitionists identified with the suffering slave, but free produce activists told them they should really identify with the slave-owners if they consumed slave-made goods.[26] Since 'demand is the main prop and stay of slavery,' wrote one free produce advocate, it follows that the 'slaveholder is comparatively innocent.[27] It was the consumer who, to use a favourite word of free produce activists, 'stimulated' the slaveholder to act.[28] This was, to put it mildly, a strong version of consumer sovereignty.

Driven by this understanding of consumer power as the most powerful in a market-based society, these activists set up 'free produce' stores, the first of which opened in 1826 in Baltimore, and which ultimately numbered more than fifty. Most stores sold clothing and dry goods but some also advertised free labour shoes, soaps, ice cream and candy. Quaker Philadelphia was the capital of free produce agitation, but such stores also opened in eight other states (mostly but not exclusively in urban areas) and in England. The last free produce store closed its doors in 1867, two years after the abolition of American chattel slavery.[29] Their goal, similar to Sabbatarians who set up Sabbath-observing businesses, was to make it possible for consumers to act morally while continuing to shop.

Shortly after the first 'free produce' store opened in the North, a group of elite, white Southerners inaugurated a movement similar to it in method and philosophy, if opposite in intent. Underlining the diverse, even antipodal, uses to which consumer activism could be put, Southern proponents of 'non intercourse' with the North aimed to shore up the system of slave labour, while simultaneously weakening the economic and political power of the free-labour North. Employing a topsy-turvy version of the strategy invented by the free producers, and a very different version than the Sabbatarians, they proposed to do this by boycotting Northern goods (included in this category were the products of abolitionist sympathizers in the South as well) and stimulating, through increased patronage, Southern manufacturers and industry. Non intercourse paralleled free produce in duration, during the roughly thirty-five years prior to the start of the Civil War, although it emerged more fitfully than did free produce, spiking dramatically in 1828 (after the tariff crisis), around 1850 (with the crisis of what to do with the lands won in the Mexican war), and again in 1860 (as secession mania began to take hold). Like the free produce movement and Sabbatarianism, its economic impact was minimal, although its political impact in fomenting Confederate nationalism was considerable. Like free produce and Sabbatarianism too, the strategy was criticized as much by presumed allies, other white Southern nationalists, as it was by opponents of slavery.

Although one of the chief claims of non intercourse advocates was that the North was an out-of-control consumer society in which 'Mammonism' ruled (in contrast to the South, which valued traditional, non-commercial values), these white Southerners very quickly came to regard the consumption of Southern goods and services, and the concomitant boycott of Northern ones, as the ultimate act of Southern patriotism.[30] They sought to punish the North not only by boycotting its products, but by establishing 'commercial independence,' which meant, among other things, turning the South into a full-fledged consumer society.[31] Just as American manufacturers turned the non importation movement of the American Revolution into a business opportunity, many Southern entrepreneurs seized on the spirit of non intercourse to attract shoppers. 'The Union May Be Dissolved!,' an advertisement in South Carolina's *Yorkville Enquirer* prematurely declared in November, 1860. 'But whether it is or not, the people will still need such things as are kept for sale by LOGAN and MEACHAM, near the Rail-Road Depot.' The proprietors closed their ad by noting that 'they have now in store a larger and better assortment of GROCERIES than ever heretofore.' A week later the *Enquirer* carried another advertisement that made the secession-as-business-opportunity argument explicit:

> HURRAH FOR THE PALMETTO STATE, Now or Never! Don't let us wait any longer for the wagon, but pitch in at once, and go to KAHNWEILER & BROTHERS' Cheap Store, and buy a WARM SECESSION SUIT, for small sum of FIVE DOLLARS. Kahnweiler and Brothers are determined to sell their stock of READY MADE CLOTHING from now until the first of January, at COST PRICES, and they have made arrangements to manufacture their Clothing in the SOUTHERN CONFEDERACY. And

> being afraid that the Southern and Northern Clothing could not agree together on the same shelves, therefore, we would say that the Northern Clothing must and shall quit the Store. Please call and test the truth of what we say.[32]

The 'Secession suit,' (perhaps a play on one-piece set of underwear, the Union Suit?) was one of many products offered to Southerners the consumption of which was both analogous to and also constitutive of political nationalism, like the 'home manufactured Fatigue Hats' pitched in the *Mercury* early 1861 to the growing ranks of 'regiments or Rifle Companies.'[33] Turning even their founding document into a fungible commodity, advertisements promised that for one dollar Southerners could purchase a lithographed copy of the 'Ordinance of Secession.'[34]

Neither free produce campaigners, non intercourse advocates nor Sabbatarians succeeded in attracting large numbers of like-minded people – abolitionists, Southern nationalists, and evangelicals – to their cause. The result was that their market-based plan of action failed to take root. Consumer activists treated their enemies (slaveholders, abolitionists, non Sabbath-upholding businessmen) as profit-maximizers who would respond to the stimulus of consumers in exactly the same way as other capitalist merchants. 'The slaveholders are not such devoted worshippers of slavery, as to make voluntary sacrifices of their own interests upon her altar,' posited one free produce supporter.[35] Another abolitionist claimed that 'the virtue of self-denial is not potent enough even in South Carolina to hold out long against calculations of profit and loss.'[36] 'Mammon has its own world,' declared a Richmond, Virginia supporter of non intercourse. 'Merchants, as a general rule, no matter what their prejudices will buy and sell in the most profitable markets.' Another Southerner argued that Yankees 'are the last people in the world to persist in a course of action that won't pay.'[37] Sabbatarians too were convinced that they could change 'owners of steamboats, stages, canal boats, and livery stables' by acting 'through the medium of their pockets.'[38] The problem was that these consumer activists, like most of their successors in the twentieth century, did not have enough active supporters to make a dent in the business efforts of their enemies.

Most supporters of their broader causes – abolition, moral reform, Southern independence – rejected the particular consumerist means of these groups as they simply refused to accept the logic that the marketplace should be the locus of political action. 'In commercial matters interest and not feelings governs,' declared a southern cotton factor, explaining his reasons for purchasing the cheapest possible goods, whatever their provenance.[39] Claiming that 'non-consumption is arrant nonsense,' another South Carolina defiantly stated that his principles were 'To buy and sell where we please. If we cannot be supported with Northern goods we will buy British, and where the British are not to our taste, we will take Northern goods.'[40] Similarly, evangelical critics of the Sabbatarians' consumer activism claimed that the boycott was 'contrary to the free spirit of our institutions.'[41] Outside observers made these arguments as well. 'We know, both as a matter of experience and as a matter of history, that the only place in the world in which men do not readily carry out their political and religious opinions is the market-place,' declared the *New York Times*. 'We know that amongst the many follies into which crazes, and theories, and 'isms' drive people, the folly of buying their boots and shirts in the dearest shops is the last to take possession of their minds.'[42]

Critics of these movements also condemned the self-righteousness of the boycotters. Free produce advocates were 'so occupied by abstinence as to neglect THE GREAT MEANS of abolishing slavery,' claimed the country's leading abolitionist William Lloyd Garrison, who declared that since he vigorously pursued these great means, his slave-made purchases should be considered 'innocently used.'[43] Free produce shoppers, he said, had a 'pretext to do nothing more for the slave because they do so much' in the exhausting efforts to find non-slave-made goods and the uncomfortable job of wearing and eating them. Mainstream abolitionist defiance of free produce probably reached its zenith in 1847 when, in response to a free produce motion at an Anti-slavery convention, Wendell Phillips declared that he would be happy to face the 'Great Judgement' attired in slave-made cotton of South Carolina.[44] Members of the Anti-Sabbath Convention used very similar language noting that it was an 'innocent act' 'to indulge in recreation and amusement' on the Sabbath.[45] Calling non consumption schemes 'utterly insufficient to obtain their ends,' a Southern critic accused proponents of 'vapouring and shallow pretention.'[46] The point, critics of all three movements agreed, was that one need not engage in what they deemed the self-important and ineffectual boycotts and buycotts to maintain what one free produce advocate called 'clean hands.'

Sabbatarians, free producers and advocates of non intercourse suffered a seemingly cruel fate. They were largely ignored by their enemies and they annoyed many of their putative allies. They did, however, widely disseminate their views about the moral implications of seemingly quotidian consuming practices. Even though the vast majority of their contemporaries ignored or rejected their view of the moral pre-eminence of consuming practices, these assumptions maintained a steady hold on later practitioners of consumer activism and were recapitulated in very similar form by these successors.

Attending to the history of early nineteenth-century consumer activism does more than fill in a gap in the historiography, the supposed century-long lull between the Revolutionary boycotters and the late nineteenth-century founders of modern consumer activism. Knowledge of the consumer politics of this period helps explain the origins of modern consumer activism and also the shape that it took. A *longue durée* perspective helps us to sort out both the continuities and novelties in the twentieth-century consumer movement.

Several innovations of the free produce movement, non intercourse efforts, and Sabbatarians continue to inform modern consumer politics as well. The most important, perhaps, is the concept of long-distance solidarity, the notion that consumers are responsible for the results of their purchases, however far-reaching and invisible to them they may be at the point of purchase. These 'early modern' consumer activists developed a new conception of causation, which dramatically expanded the concept of responsibility and promoted a worldview in which the idea of an innocent Good Samaritan became unthinkable. In her place was a consumer whose every purchase set off a wave of activity, often criminal, for which she was ultimately responsible. These activists pioneered a politics firmly situated within the market and, indeed, unimaginable outside of it.

Finally, through the innovation of the buycott, these early-nineteenth century groups made an important contribution to consumer activism. The idea that spending money could produce ethical outcomes, challenged the older view, instantiated by the Revolutionary generation, that only sacrifice was virtuous. As one supporter of the free produce movement said, 'We must rival the blood-stained productions in beauty and durability.'[47] Although the language of virtuous sacrifice continues to be the dominant strain of consumer activism through the present, the kind of ethical aestheticism promoted by these early modern buycotters lay at the root of an important minority strain of modern consumer activism, in which buying moral products is as important as eschewing immoral ones. For example, some branches of the anti-sweatshop movement have begun to market 'sweat free' apparel. The 'fair trade' coffee movement, for example, not only warns citizens about the social and environmental costs of corporate coffee, it also offers gourmet alternatives. These contemporary efforts to join consumer culture with political engagement recall the free produce advocates, non intercourse supporters, and Sabbatarians who claimed consumption as social and moral, rather than as personal and amoral. Their efforts to forge a positive politics of consumption provide an important counter-example and corrective to the widespread view of consumer culture as inherently incompatible with political engagement.[48]

Notes

1 Excellent studies of twentieth-century consumer protest include Matthew Hilton and Martin Daunton, 'Material Politics: An Introduction,' in Martin Daunton and Matthew Hilton (eds), *The Politics of Consumption: Material Culture and Citizenship in Europe and America* (Oxford, 2001); Lizabeth Cohen, *A Consumers' Republic: The Politics of Mass Consumption in Postwar America* (New York, 2003). Excellent studies of eighteenth-century boycotts include T. H. Breen, *The Marketplace of Revolution: How Consumer Politics Shaped the American Revolution* (New York, 2004); Woody Holton, *Forced Founders: Indians, Debtors, Slaves, and the Making of the American Revolution in Virginia* (Chapel Hill, NC, 1999); Charlotte Sussman, *Consuming Anxieties: Consumer Protest, Gender, and British Slavery, 1713-1833* (Stanford, CA, 2000).

2 Lawrence B. Glickman, *A Living Wage: American Workers and the Making of Consumer Society* (Ithaca, NY, 1997).

3 Neil McKendrick, John Brewer, and J. H. Plumb, *The Birth of a Consumer Society: The Commercialization of Eighteenth-Century England* (Bloomington, 1982); Charles G. Sellers, *The Market Revolution: Jacksonian America, 1815-1846* (New York, 1991).

4 'Hints,' *Liberator*, 30 July 1831.

5 'Go, Relieve the Sufferings of the Slave,' *Liberator*, 4 January 1839, p. 4.

6 Quoted in Richard R. John, *Spreading the News:The American Postal System from Franklin to Morse* (Cambridge, MA, 1995), p. 180.

7 'The coupling of religious aims with economic enterprise was typical of many evangelical causes,' notes Bertram Wyatt-Brown in 'Prelude to Abolitionism: Sabbatarian Politics and the Rise of the Second Party System,' *Journal of American History*, 58 (September 1971): 316-41, quotation p. 330; John, *Spreading the News*, pp. 180-5, 324 n. 55; Robert H. Abzug, *Cosmos Crumbling: American Reform and the Religious Imagination* (Oxford, 1994), pp. 110-11.

8 William Ellery Channing, 'Associations,' *Christian Examiner*, 34, September 1829, pp. 105-40, (quotations p. 106).

9 The quotation is from an anti-slavery pamphlet by William Fox, 'An Address to the People of Great Britain, on the utility of refraining from the use of West India Sugar and Rum,' (London, 1791), cited in Sussman, *Consuming Anxieties*, p. 41.

10 Adam Smith, *The Wealth of Nations* (1776; Chicago 1996), 2: book 4, ch. 8, p. 179.

11 The quotation is from 'Free Produce Convention,' *Liberator*, 15 November 1839, p. 2. For an example of the scholarly consensus see Richard Ohmann, who argues that 'the very concept and word [consumer] appeared only' in the late nineteenth century. *Selling Culture: Magazines, Markets, and Class at the Turn of the Century* (London, 1996), p. 48.

12 As Elizabeth Clark has noted, the chain symbolized both the shackles of enslaved workers and the 'essence of sympathy' linking people to each other. Elizabeth B. Clark, '"The Sacred Rights of the Weak": Pain, Sympathy, and the Culture of Individual Rights in Antebellum America,' *Journal of American History*, 82:2 (1995): 463-93, quotation p. 482. The purchaser of slave-made goods becomes 'one indispensable link in the chain of causes which perpetuates the system,' according to Lea. W. Gause, 'Free Produce,' *Pennsylvania Freeman*, 2 February 1854, p. 1.

13 'Free-Produce Association–Philadelphia (US)–Extracts from the Last Report,' *Non Slaveholder*, 2 July 1849, p. 109.

14 Gause, 'Free Produce'; 'The Bitter Bit,' *Charleston Mercury*, 29 March 1861.

15 'On the Disuse of Slave Produce,' *The Anti-Slavery Reporter*, 1 January 1847, pp. 1-2.

16 Rhoads, 'Free Produce,' The Alabama editor is quoted in Weymouth T. Jordon, *Rebels in the Making: Planters' Conventions and Southern Propaganda* (Tuscaloosa, 1958), p. 114.

17 Gause, 'Free Produce.'

18 Channing, 'Associations,' p. 140.

19 Quoted in John, *Spreading the News*, p. 183.

20 *Ibid.*, p. 181.

21 Paul E. Johnson, *A Shopkeeper's Millennium*, pp. 85-7.

22 For examples of such language see: 'Address to the Friends of the Anti-Slavery Cause on the Disuse of Slave-Labour Produce,' *Anti-Slavery Reporter*, 1 November 1847, pp. 161-2; Henry Grew, 'Free Labour Produce,' *The Non-Slaveholder*, pp. 162-5; Lewis C Gunn, 'Address to Abolitionists,' in *Minutes of Proceedings of the Requited Labour Convention, Held in Philadelphia on the 17th and 18th of the Fifth Month and by Adjournment on the 5th and 6th of the Ninth Month, 1838* (Philadelphia, 1838), p. 26.

23 Taylor Family Papers. Special Collections, Haverford College.

24 'Prospectus,' *Non-Slaveholder* 1: 1 January 1846, pp. 1-2.

25 Grew is quoted in 'Sketches of the Sayings and Doings at the New England Anti-Slavery Convention,' *Liberator*, 4 June 1847, p. 91.

26 Jean Fagan Yellin, *Women and Sisters: The Antislavery Feminists in American Culture* (New Haven, 1989), p. 32.

27 'The Disuse of Slave Produce and the Abolition of Slavery,' *Non Slaveholder*, October 1849, pp. 196-8. As another free produce activist wrote, slave-labour consumers are 'in a more guilty condition than the slaveholders themselves–inasmuch as the consumer keeps the market open for the products of unremunerated labour.' W. C. B., 'Abolition Consistency,' *National Enquirer*, 1 March 1838, pp. 98-9.

28 See, for example, Sarah Pugh, 'Annual Report of the Executive Committee of the American Free Produce Association,' *Pennsylvania Freeman*, 3 November 1841, p. 4. W.C. B., 'Abolition Consistency.'

29 Ruth Nuermberger, *The Free Produce Movement: A Quaker Protest Against Slavery* (Durham, 1942), p. 119.

30 See Drew Gilpin Faust, *The Creation of Confederate Nationalism* (Baton Rouge, 1988), pp. 42-3.

31 See, for example, 'Commercial Independence of the Confederate States, No. 1,' *Charleston Mercury*, 8 April 1861, p. 1.

32 *Yorkville Enquirer*, 15 November 1860; 22 November 1860. I am very grateful to Aaron Marrs for sharing these advertisements with me and for his remarkable generosity in pointing me toward sources.

33 Aaron Marrs and Brian Fahey brought to my attention the possible comparison with the Union Suit. Williams and Brown of No. 277 King St. produced the 'Charleston Made Fatigue Hats,' *Charleston Mercury*, 16 February 1861.

34 Advertisement in *Charleston Mercury*, 5 April 1861.

35 W. C. B., 'Abolition Consistency.'

36 'Non-Intercourse,' *National Era*, 31 October 1850, p. 174.

37 'The Money Argument,' *National Era*, 1 May 1851, p. 70; 'Will They Persist in This War!,' *Charleston Mercury*, 26 April 1861, p. 4.

38 Johnson, *Shopkeeper's Millennium*, p. 85.

39 A Cotton Factor, 'The Commercial Independence of the Confederate States–No. 1,' *Charleston Mercury*, 27 June 1861, p. 1.

40 Colleton 'To the Editors of the Columbia Telescope,' *Charleston Mercury*, 9 July 1828, p. 2.

41 Johnson, p. 85.

42 'The South and Non-Intercourse,' *New York Times*, 15 February 1860, p. 4.

43 'Slavery Abolished by Abstinence from its Products,' *Non-Slaveholder*, May 1846, 76-78; 'Products of Slave Labour,' *Non-Slaveholder*, April 1847, 84-9 [48, 54].

44 'Sketches of the Sayings and Doings at the New England Anti-Slavery Convention,' *Liberator*, 4 June 1847, p. 91.

45 Alexis McCrossen, *Holiday, Holy Day: The American Sunday* (Ithaca, NY, 2000), p. 31.

46 Leonidas, 'No. V,' *Charleston Mercury*, 18 July 1828, p. 2.

47 D. W. J., 'Free Labour Goods,' *Non-Slaveholder*, April 1848, p. 74.

48 Jim Hightower, 'Dressed for Success,' *Nation*, 24 June 2002, p. 8; Laure Waridel, *Coffee With Pleasure: Just Java* and *World Trade* (Montreal, 2001).

Chapter 2

The Moral Expertise of the British Consumer, c.1900:

A Debate between the Christian Social Union and the Webbs

Julien Vincent

The social, cultural and intellectual history of consumption, already a well-established topic of eighteenth-century historiography, has at last become a favourite focus of historians of late nineteenth-century and early twentieth-century Britain. Most work in this blossoming field of research has been influenced by the history of political economy, theories of civil society, or gender studies. This should hardly come as a surprise. Several developments, characteristic of this period, combined to produce a radical redefinition of the place and role of the consumer in the industrial system and the life of the nation: the demise of classical political economy; the appearance of the 'social question'; the controversy over free trade; the emergence of the 'New Liberalism'; and finally the emergence of a new understanding of woman's place in the family and society at large. British historians have tended as a consequence to identify three 'expert' languages in which the question of consumers was articulated: the language of free trade, which successfully shaped the resistance to protectionist attacks; the language of 'co-operation' and trade unionism, in which possible answers to the social question were formulated; and finally the language of domestic economy, in which women were described as mediators between family and market relationships.[1]

The first language – that of free trade – seems to have been the most influential, penetrating the greatest range of social milieus and most readily adaptable to contemporary questions about consumption. Eugenio Biagini, Boyd Hilton, Anthony Howe, Frank Trentmann and others have rightly stressed the centrality of the idea of free trade, not just for economic policy, but for any general interpretation of British history in the nineteenth century and the early twentieth century.[2] Not only does this idea of free trade explain what had changed for British consumers since the great debates of the eighteenth century on luxury, or on the relationship between 'commerce' and 'virtue',[3] it also accounts – in a not always explicit comparative perspective – for Britain's unique circumstances around 1900. Things were, indeed, very different in Britain from what they were in the US or continental Europe, both of which had espoused protectionism unambiguously towards the end of the nineteenth century. Under attack from Joseph Chamberlain and the tariff reformers from 1903 onwards, the British left united to defend the purchasing power of the lower classes.[4] The consumer is a central figure in this story, for it is through its agency that an abstract political doctrine developed by a handful of individuals – the New Liberalism – became a genuine political force.[5] Balfour's inability to cope with the crisis triggered by the tariff reformers, who were rather on the side of the producers, seems to illustrate not only the need to speak on behalf of the consumer and confer political legitimacy on him, but also the unusually prominent position which the defence of purchasing power assumed in the British notion of the 'common wealth'.

Like any account of a 'national exception', this story of the British consumer in the age of free trade seeks to explain not merely what happened, but also what *failed* to happen. In this case, it is the *absence* of those well-organised and influential 'consumers' leagues', which can be found in the US and in continental Europe before 1914, that made the British situation so exceptional.[6] Because these leagues (which should not be confused with workers' consumer co-operatives) aimed at organising the consumption of the charitable middle class, they appear incompatible with the idea that producers should compete in order to limit production costs. Their failure to establish themselves is not particularly surprising if we acknowledge that British 'consumer experts' were first and foremost free traders. Clementina Black did found a consumers' league in London in 1887 – indeed, it was the first of its kind, a model for similar leagues set up in neighbouring countries in the 1890s – but it did not last long and its founder later repudiated the very idea of an organisation to remind consumers of their responsibilities. Even so, several years after Black's defection, British reformers were still taking an interest in the idea of morally responsible consumption, and a number of them attended the first international congress of consumers' leagues in Geneva in 1908. But attendance by single individuals such as James Joseph Mallon, of the National Anti-Sweating League, could not make up for the absence of any British social consumers' league comparable to those in America, France, Belgium, Germany or Switzerland.[7] It is likely that the leagues failed in Britain because this sort of morally responsible consumerism – an updated version of the old opposition between 'commerce' and 'virtue' – assumed the need for a sort of interference, indeed a boycott, which was contrary to the principles of free competition and free trade in the service of the consumer which dominated the political culture of the time.

However, while there is little doubt as to the dominance of the language of free trade, its consequences for the history of consumption in Britain cannot be determined without a careful examination of the discourses and realities of the practices of consumption. Here, the idea that Britain was an exception with regard to morally responsible consumption can be directly challenged. Around the turn of the century, and outside Clementina Black's consumers' league, there was a movement in favour of a 'responsible' approach to commercial transactions (generally referred to as 'exclusive dealing') and of creating 'white' lists of 'ethical' traders and manufacturers. This movement originally had links with Clementina Black's consumers' league, but remained separate from it and survived its dissolution. Represented in London, Oxford and numerous provincial cities by the Christian Social Union (CSU), it remained active from the early 1890s up to the Great War. It was led by a group of upper- and middle-class morally responsible consumers (of both sexes) who had numerous contacts with contemporary American and European consumers' leagues and shared their aspirations. But since it advocated economic interference in a free-trade country, drew on moral theology in an age of 'secularisation' and used the old language of opposition between individual Christian 'virtue' and the impersonal mechanisms of 'trade', it appears as something of an anachronism if understood within the context of British exceptionalism.

It would be wrong, however, to underestimate its importance in comparison with that of consumers' leagues in neighbouring countries. Certainly the CSU, which was actively engaged in debates on the morality of consumption at the turn of the century, never became a mass movement. But it had a significant influence, not only on the formation of a new social doctrine in the Anglican Church and among the bishops sitting in the House of Lords, but also on public opinion, that erratic but omnipresent entity which some religious thinkers preferred to call the 'social conscience'. The CSU was well up to this task. It had more than 6,000 members in 1905. It was strongly represented in the universities (e.g. William J. Ashley, Hastings Rashdall, Alexander J. Carlyle) and had some support in the House of Commons (George W. E. Russell, Charles F. G. Masterman), on the London County Council, in the publishing world and in the press. Work by members was published by Rivingtons and appeared not only in the *Commonwealth* and *Economic Review* but also in the *Church Times*, the *Guardian* and in a number of major quarterly reviews. Thanks to the charisma and writing skills of public figures such as Brooke Foss Westcott, Bishop of Durham, Canon Henry Scott Holland and the writer and polemicist G. K. Chesterton, and to widespread active support, particularly among middle-class women of both the capital and the provinces, the CSU was able to mobilise a good deal of opinion in public debate, but also to make its influence felt in clubs reserved for the highest (indeed aristocratic) echelons of society into which some of its most eminent members, such as Charles Gore and James Adderley, had been born. Both its methods and the extent of its influence make the CSU's striving in favour of morally responsible consumption look comparable to that of the continental and American consumers' leagues. Like them, the British 'white lists' successfully mobilised not only publicists, economists, researchers and social reformers, but also producers and shopkeepers of 'moral' goods, who were carving out a niche for themselves in the market. For example, CSU members promoted the use of labels by certain producers to indicate their compliance with manufacturing and safety standards such as the use of leadless glaze in certain sorts of ceramic ware. Similarly, Henry Scott Holland and Percy Dearmer did not hesitate to advertise the efforts of the 'New Commerce' to select 'specially recommended' products for their store in central London.

Besides the establishment of these new production and distribution networks, one important aspect of the moral consumption movement around 1900 was the creation of a language that could be used to speak of 'the consumer' in terms that were sufficiently neutral and objective to circulate between different groups and individuals with different perspectives on the commercial world, but also malleable enough to enable them to express value judgements. A consideration of the two sides of this language will bring us to the very heart of what constituted consumer 'expertise' in this period, in either the scientific or the moral sense. Firstly, discussions about consumer behaviour were made possible by certain terms and concepts that were shared by all and permitted disagreements. Secondly, this shared language was understood in different ways according to the particular belief system of any one actor. This can be illustrated by focusing on a single controversy; that arising from a challenge to defend the white lists laid before the CSU by Beatrice and Sidney Webb. Though they shared a similar concept of the consumer's place in the economic system, the Webbs and the leaders of the CSU did not arrive at the same view of its philosophical and moral implications. As early as 1894-5 a debate had been initiated by the more conservative and evangelical wing of the Anglican Church in which the proponents of the white lists had drawn upon theological debates to expound and justify the religious significance of their actions. But by this stage, criticisms of the moral consumer were also emerging from the left. Those who advocated increased government intervention in the economy (such as the Fabians) set out to prove 'scientifically' the inefficacy of the white lists. At the turn of the twentieth century, therefore, it was in the science of economics – a subject whose authority was acknowledged by all contemporary social reformers – that the CSU intellectuals felt bound to locate their arguments.

White lists and the Fabian critique

By 1900 the CSU had been in existence for some ten years, had some thirty branches throughout the country, was still growing rapidly and was beginning to make its doctrinal and practical influence felt amongst the Anglican clergy. In both London and Oxford its members contributed actively to theoretical discussions concerning the science of social reform. In practice, one of its most prominent campaigns aimed to 'moralise' consumption amongst the better off. The CSU seemed destined to become involved in this question: it was, after all, connected with Clementina Black's Consumers' League, of which H. S. Holland had been a co-founder in 1887. It was perhaps from this earlier organisation that the CSU picked up the idea of the white lists, but it adapted them to fit its own set of doctrines: white lists were to become part of a wider campaign for 'exclusive dealing' which aimed to introduce moral criteria into *all* aspects of trade. As such, lists were no mere appeal to virtue in defiance of the laws of trade and economics. The CSU developed a notion of economics no less orthodox than the orthodoxy they could claim in theology. Similarly, the CSU made a point that their information on economic subjects was professional, not amateur. Thus white lists were based on information compiled from trade unions and employers, and from special surveys for which CSU members asked working men to fill in specific questionnaires about working conditions in various businesses and shops in the towns concerned.

Although the CSU had links with the High Church faction of Pusey House in Oxford, an offshoot of the Tractarian movement, it inherited from Broad Churchmen such as F. D. Maurice the idea that 'if the true meaning of the faith is to be made sufficiently conspicuous it needs disencumbering, reinterpreting, explaining'.[8] On the social scene this meant, first and foremost, a confrontation with economics, and that is why the Oxford branch of the CSU founded the *Economic Review* in 1891. But being theologians, they believed too that science neither could nor should replace the message of the Gospels. The works of CSU members, particularly those devoted to moral consumption, aimed to reflect science empirically and conceptually without becoming a mere application of it. Thus their defence of the white lists constantly oscillated between two dimensions: one religious and moral, the other economic and scientific. Indeed, this ability to combine the two proved indispensable at a time when various ideas and practices of social reform were increasingly tending to compete with one another, and questions were being asked not only about their justifiability, but also about their effectiveness.[9]

It was in this context that, in 1897, a year when the social doctrine of the CSU was recognised as a major influence on the Church of England at the Lambeth Conference, the Fabians harshly criticised the system of white lists. Just as it seemed the concept of moral consumption was about to receive the support of the bishops, it was being seriously challenged as a method of social reform. In *Industrial Democracy*, a key text in the economic and philosophical thinking of many social reformers after 1897, Beatrice and Sidney Webb attacked the idea that consumers could 'moralise' the industrial system, as the CSU was claiming and as had been claimed earlier by supporters of Black's Consumers' League. The Webbs, having explained how a long chain of transactions had led to an unequal distribution of wealth, argued that 'paradoxically as it may seem, the consumer is, of all the parties to the transaction, the least responsible for the result.' For them, 'the consumers, as consumers, are helpless in the matter' – 'the matter' being justice and the distribution of wealth.[10]

Although these criticisms were buried in a closely argued treatise in two bulky volumes, they were disseminated in various ways and reached an extensive public. For example, Beatrice Webb repeated them in a more accessible form in 1901, in a contributory volume on social reform intended mainly for women readers. In her chapter – in a work that can be described as ecumenical, since its preface was by Webb's rival Helen Bosanquet – she ironically accused moral (female) consumers of treating harmless penny-pinching as a mortal sin: 'The question remains, can the private consumer do anything in the matter? From time to time we see attempts made, usually by philanthropic ladies, to form "consumers' leagues", the members of which pledge themselves to boycott somebody's matches, to abstain from buying shirts stitched by Tom Hood's garret-sempstress, and, in short, to repudiate the bait of cheapness'.[11] This was an unmistakable attack on the CSU's moral consumers in Oxford, who had compiled a white list of tailors, and were prominent in the campaign against yellow phosphorus in matches, which continued for more than ten years after the Bryant & May strike of 1888.

The consumer in the 'chain of bargains'

The Webbs' hostility may seem somewhat surprising, given that the CSU shared the Fabians' aspiration towards a 'progressive' doctrine which would not contradict generally accepted principles of economics. As with the Fabians, the CSU members were convinced of the 'scientific' validity of their economic world view. Many belonged to reading clubs where they expounded their economic ideas and were assiduous readers of theory, asking of the works of Alfred Marshall, Eugen von Böhm-Bawerk or John Hobson questions sometimes far removed from the less directly practical preoccupations of the authors. This was at a time when university economists were reformulating a theory of consumption that was being made increasingly complex and which must be understood in order to explicate the economic world view held by 'moral' consumers in this period. It was by no means obvious that a distinct theory of consumption was needed, especially in England (whereas in other countries it had long been a separate branch of economics). The matter was debated among theoreticians throughout the 1880s and 1890s, and had at least a symbolic relevance to the question whether the consumer could be represented as an economic agent on a par with the producer, the capitalist and the entrepreneur.[12] The status of this theory had considerable influence on social reformers anxious to match their economic views with those of professional economists. In *The Scope and Method of Political Economy*, the standard work on the subject throughout the English-speaking world from its first publication in 1891, John Neville Keynes, an associate of Alfred Marshall, ably summed up the significance of these debates:

> The truth is that the phenomena of production, distribution, exchange, and consumption, respectively, all so act and react upon one another, that if any one of these classes of facts is given no independent treatment, it must nevertheless come in for a large share of discussion in connexion with the others. Whether all propositions relating to consumption should be arranged by themselves or discussed as they arise in relation to

other topics is, therefore, to a certain extent a mere question of convenience of exposition.[13]

If Keynes could reduce the debate on the specifics of economic theory to a mere problem of classification, it was only because everyone was in agreement, at least on the main idea that all economic phenomena were 'interdependent'. This idea, though updated to fit with the theory of marginal utility, was not very far removed from the old 'economic circuit' idea traditionally associated with Quesnay and his *Tableau oeconomique* (1758).[14] Indeed, the concept of production and consumption as an unending circle was as old as political economy itself, although, as Piero Sraffa has pointed out, this 'circular' interpretation was often challenged, from Ricardo onwards, by a linear interpretation – a 'one-way avenue that leads from "Factors of Production" to "Consumption Goods"'.[15] Over and above their disagreement over the white lists, the Webbs and the CSU shared a vision of industry as an organism in which all economic actions were interconnected by transactions. What exactly was the place of the consumer in such a view? The concept of economic interconnectedness was compatible both with a deterministic account of the economy as a self-regulating system, or with the opposing account, as popularised by historical economists, according to which the economy was capable of moral improvement through individual and corporate action. The notion that acts of consumption and other economic phenomena were interdependent was subjected to strongly contrasting interpretations by the CSU and the Fabians: the former saw moral consumption as the *sine qua non* for moralising the whole industrial system, whereas the latter thought it was mere theory which could never be put into practice. The CSU stressed the importance of individual virtue as a basis for raising the consumer to a position of economic sovereignty; the Fabians, by contrast, denied that consumers could have any power at all.

An important point of reference for this common language, in which disagreement was made possible, was the Austrian economist Eugen von Böhm-Bawerk, a figure frequently cited both by the Webbs and in pamphlets and tracts emanating from the CSU. Böhm-Bawerk, seeking to demonstrate the importance of 'marginal utility' in the theory of capital and interest, described capitalism as a 'chain of bargains' between present and future goods. His *Kapital und Kapitalzins* (*Capital and Interest*), translated with an introduction by the Scottish economist William Smart in 1888, was a major reference for several contemporary studies of consumption.[16] But whereas Böhm-Bawerk saw the exchange of present and future goods as a support for a theoretical argument, the social reformers interpreted it in terms of their own priorities, depending especially on their understanding of the relationships between employer and employee, producers and retailers, buyers and sellers, and on whether they believed that the buyer of a good could, when considering a purchase, gather and analyse sufficient information and so choose the seller judged to be closest to his ideal. The CSU's interpretation of the chain of bargains evidently assumed that the consumer could and should take responsibility. 'In each of these bargains', they claimed:

> A great strategic superiority is possessed by the buyer over the seller. Thus, at one end of the chain the isolated workman cannot make a 'free' bargain with his employer; he has not the same knowledge of the market, and cannot afford to wait. And so on, till at the other end of the chain, the like advantage is possessed by the individual customer, who can buy when and how he chooses, whereas the shopkeeper depends on his quick turnover. The individual customer is thus the ultimate source of the pressure which crushes the small capitalist or the isolated workman.[17]

Böhm-Bawerk's ideas, according to the CSU, suggested that consumers had the ultimate responsibility for the morality of the market. The Webbs, by contrast, interpreted the 'chain of bargains' as limiting the very possibility of moral consumption. The economic interconnectedness, they claimed, was the very reason why consumers would never be able to ascertain the 'morality' of the conditions of production of a particular commodity.[18]

The 'duty to know' and the question of traceability

The Webbs believed the CSU's argument, which summed up the Oxford views on consumption and exclusive dealing at the turn of the century, to be both naïve in its assumption that it was possible to trace the conditions under which every good had been produced, and amateurish in its use of statistics. Moreover, the CSU's argument that the world of trade could be represented as a mere chain of bargains could be stood on its head. Even if one could establish the morality of any particular seller with certainty – a difficult task in itself – this would not necessarily apply to the suppliers, who might owe their position in the market to some kind of immoral competition which they had successfully concealed from their customers. Therefore, the idea that the consumer could exercise real economic sovereignty was a mere abstraction, based on the utopian assumption that the world of bargains was perfectly uncoverable. Since no consumer was omniscient, any attempt to moralise a particular market – i.e. a single link in the chain of bargains – could never lead to a moralisation of the entire chain, and might just as easily shift the weight of competition, exploitation and sacrifice higher up it, relieving one set of economic actors by increasing the sufferings of another. The trouble with the white lists was that they, like other 'relief works', merely palliated the shortcomings of the system without tackling the underlying causes. The Webbs neatly summed up the quandary in *Industrial Democracy* (1897): 'As a practical man, [the consumer] knows it to be quite impossible for him to trace the article through its various stages of production and distribution, and to discover whether the extra sixpence charged by the dearer shop represents better wages to any workman, or goes as mere extra profit to one or other of the capitalists concerned.'[19]

To determine the 'morality' of a seller in a bargain was a very difficult task indeed, which underlined both the theoretical and practical problems of economic research. But, the CSU responded, was it a sufficient reason to abandon the enterprise? This was certainly not the view of those, mainly female members of the CSU, who believed that the moralisation of consumption was above all a question of making adequate economic information available, and who published regular surveys of the conditions of labour in various branches of trade on behalf of their local Branch.[20] A few years earlier one of the CSU's leading 'moral' economists, Wilfrid Richmond, had strenuously defended this kind of research, stressing that there was a 'duty to know' the conditions of production. As far back as 1888, when Black's Consumers' League was in its infancy, Richmond wrote that reliable economic research was a necessary prelude to a moralisation of the economy.[21] Less than ten years later, the Webbs had reinforced the arguments against the white list system and awakened some doubts as to the possibility of individual consumers having economic virtue. But Brooke Foss Westcott countered their clever use of economic theory by adducing the experience of other countries that had consumers' leagues, particularly the USA, where John Graham Brooks and the Church Social Union (an American offshoot of the CSU) had been strikingly successful.[22] In 1899, two years after the publication of *Industrial Democracy*, Westcott again defended the CSU's attitude to consumption in a presidential speech in Liverpool, where he answered the Webbs directly and defended the idea that consumers could have moral expertise: 'In some cases it may be difficult [for consumers to trace the history of what they buy], but experience shows that, even in these, if the information is required it will be forthcoming.'[23] Westcott also countered Beatrice Webb's argument, cited above, that 'ethical' consumers naively assumed that cheapness could be equated with immorality: 'Personal money gain cannot be the controlling motive of either buyer or seller; and it is not cheapness as cheapness which is condemned. Much of that which is cheapest is both good and made under good conditions. Long hours, low wages, bad conditions of labour, do not as a rule produce articles which are really cheap.'[24]

It is certainly true that the publication of *Industrial Democracy* perceptibly changed the tone of CSU publications on the consumer question. From 1897 onwards they took care to explain that working conditions could be 'unknown' even in companies that were on the white lists. They also took more care than formerly to point out the inherent limits of 'consumer responsibility': a consumer could not (they now insisted) 'concern himself with the technical details' of the manufacture of every product on the market. In some cases, government intervention would be the best course.[25] The white list movement survived, however, along with the American and European consumers' leagues, and can be traced right up to the threshold of the Great War. It enshrined a substantial part of the CSU's religious identity and its attempts to reintegrate itself into the social life of the community. Indeed, the CSU's defence of moral consumption in the 1900s went back to theological attitudes that had long existed before the critique.

Christus Consummator

While it is true to say that the CSU theoreticians tackled the same concepts as their Fabian critics, and applied them according to the rules of political economy as understood by contemporary social reformers, the specific ethical and philosophical positions which the Christian thinkers imposed on these shared representations was all their own. They drew on a moral theology dating back to the eighteenth century, in which individual virtue had to be tried and tested in heroic opposition to the mechanisms of trade – quite a different idea from would-be 'scientific' socialism. But it would be simplistic to establish a contrast between a sort of 'Fabian' materialistic socialism, foregrounding the social conditions of economic freedom, and a 'Christian socialist' moral economics centred on individual responsibility. This contrast was introduced retrospectively by the Fabian leaders themselves in order to explain the origins of their society in 1884, but it tends to deny the religious factor in a good many socialist conversions throughout the 1890s and 1900s. Without this factor it is impossible to understand the innumerable attempts to moralise consumption, from the co-ops to quasi-self-governing communal fellowships – not to mention the white lists.[26] Moreover, the Fabians themselves did not exclude ethical considerations. Sidney Ball, who was a member both of the Fabians and of the CSU, published an influential article in 1896 on 'the moral aspect of socialism', which was later distributed as a leaflet through both organisations.[27] Similarly, Sidney Webb was very anxious to secure the support of the Anglican clergy and saw the CSU as an ally.[28] However, while its 'moral aspect' was important, the Webbs' socialism, like Ball's, was first and foremost an economic doctrine focussing on the collectivisation of the means of production, and consumer acts were seen primarily in terms of their economic objectives. Westcott, Gore and Rashdall, on the other hand, put moral responsibility at the heart of their concept of social reform and saw consumer acts in terms of their intentions and possible consequences.

These differing viewpoints point to differing projects rather than a different understanding of the consumer's place in the economic system. Whereas the Webbs were trying to give socialism a scientific underpinning and so strove to break down the traditional opposition between 'virtue' and 'trade', the CSU moralists preferred the latter approach because they considered it essential to uphold the Anglican orthodoxy that salvation had to have an individual dimension. It was this concern for orthodoxy that governed the CSU's insistence on the role of the consumer in social reform. There were, of course, some Anglican theologians in the 1900s who tried to re-cast the opposition between individualism and socialism so as to establish a different perspective on the fit between the Christian notion of moral regeneration and the need for economic and social reform.[29] But these attempts were often accused of being heterodox, if not heretical,[30] and most certainly they belonged to the most 'extreme' current of CSU thinking, which judged the white lists insufficiently radical and advocated clearer support for the Labour movement, which had held seats in the House of Commons since 1906. But most advocates of moralised consumerism, including Westcott, Carter and Rashdall, continued to stress individual Christian virtue in matters economic.

Although the supporters of white lists tended to return to the traditional opposition between virtue and trade, they nevertheless relied on novel theological arguments as a basis for the consumer's 'moral expertise'. These new arguments were developed by CSU theoreticians and, most notably, by the CSU president, Brooke Foss Westcott, Bishop of Durham. Boyd Hilton has commented that Westcott's religious thinking marks the transition from an 'age of atonement', which was pessimistic and obsessed with sin, to a period when British social thinking turned rather towards the notion of Incarnation, more optimistic and more interested in the salvation of the community.[31] From that perspective it is no surprise to find that Westcott was also interested in theories of consumption and expenditure. Though he never explicitly linked his practical CSU writings on consumption with his purely theological writings (because that would have meant interfering with individual Christian consciences), there are unmistakable echoes between these different types of writing, not least the similarity of vocabulary used by this author who, as a philologist in the Ruskin tradition, attributed great moral and philosophical importance to etymology. The 1888 Oxford English Dictionary defined the word *consumption* as inherently ambiguous. It was derived from an Old French word which conflates the Latin *consumere* and *consummare*. Thus *consumption* included the idea of 'finishing', either constructively or destructively and, as such, both etymologically and semantically, it was close to *consummation*. This tension pervaded the writings of the economists, who sometimes saw consumption as the destruction of goods, and sometimes as a derived form of production. Indeed, one could describe all of the CSU's work in favour of white lists as an endeavour to reconcile these two notions, consumption and consummation.

Westcott summed up the central argument of his theology in the title of a series of sermons given at Westminster Abbey in 1885 and published the next year as *Christus Consummator. Consummator*, according to Westcott, meant 'the fulfiller', the one who 'consummates' and 'brings to perfection'. This situated Westcott firmly on the 'catholic' and 'incarnational' wing of Anglican theology. By stressing how Christ perfected and 'brought together' all things (*con-sum*), Westcott set up 'Christus Consummator' against the pessimistic and crucifixion-centred 'Christus Redemptor' who had dominated theological thinking in the first two-thirds of the nineteenth century – and the whole of Protestant thinking before that. Westcott's concept of the *consummator* suggested the way in which economic interdependence and interconnectedness, rather than a reminder of the Fall and of the sin, pointed to the corporate nature of man and to the moral opportunities opened up by modern industry.[32] It was in the light of these ideas that Westcott interpreted the Christian's place in society.

The doctrine of Incarnation and con-summation, as developed by Westcott and his followers, stressed the impossibility of separating the individual and society (although they could, of course, still be distinguished just as the three persons of the Trinity are recognised without their unity being denied). Westcott's theology, together with a growing legal, psychological and theological literature on individual and collective 'personality', suggested a specifically Anglican response to contemporary debates about Individualism vs. Collectivism.[33] Individuals could act in their corporate capacity, and not simply by virtue of their own individual character or by means of the State. To achieve collective moral objectives, however, supposed expert knowledge. Daily acts of economic life had social effects which became a moral problem as soon as a person became conscious of them. Thus we see that the circulation of economic knowledge in the public sphere, via the *Economic Review*, the CSU pamphlets and leaflets, and other economic publications, was an essential component of this realisation of the social nature of man. In his 1894 presidential address to the CSU, Westcott used consumption as an example to illustrate the idea that 'whatever is not faith is sin'. Stressing the link between everyday individual decisions and membership of a human community, he concluded by evoking 'the *consummation* for which we thus look and work and pray, when every nation shall reach its own perfection through the perfection of every part'.[34] Seeing individual actions as links in a 'moral chain' – as it were the moral equivalent of Böhm-Bawerk's chain of bargains – Westcott suggested that the Kingdom of God had the potential to exist in all consumers and was within reach of the community as a whole, and this belief convinced CSU members that their bargains had a particular spiritual importance. The aim of the white lists was not just to attain certain concrete results, but also – and principally – to reveal the spiritual meaning of an idea: the interdependence of economic phenomena. When five years later, in 1899, Westcott was challenged by the Webbs to defend moral consumption, preferential dealing and virtuous expenditure, his presidential address again invoked the notion of *Christus Consummator*. Now he described consumption as fulfilling the moral personality of the individual, and as an effort to assess value and cost from the viewpoint of 'life', as Ruskin would have put it, so to 'create a better type of humanity'.[35] When understood in this way, ordinary acts of consumption recalled no less than 'communion': the consumption of the 'bread of life'. By referring to the moral unity of the economic system, it epitomised the ideal goal of realising, uniting and reconciling all things in one by the divine will.

Conclusion

Who, then, was the British expert consumer of around 1900? This study of the debate between the Fabians and the Anglican reformers of the CSU has enabled a reconstruction of the language of moral consumption, through which it was possible to express diverging opinions on the power of the consumer at that time. This language was oriented around two principal questions. The first related to the 'chain of bargains' and the interdependence of economic phenomena, and asked whether or not it was true that the consumer could, in theory, re-make the economic world in his own image. The second asked whether it was possible, or realistic, to attempt a moral reading of consumer goods and consumer acts, given that this assumed the attainability of reliable knowledge of working conditions at each stage of production, and of the whole process of distribution.

The reconstruction of this language has thrown light on the disagreements between the Fabians and the Anglican supporters of the white lists. Those arguments bore not on free trade, but on a concept of individual and corporate moral responsibility rooted in religion. The failure of Clementina Black's Consumers' League is not, therefore, a uniquely British phenomenon attributable to the unusually strong grip of free trade in that country: to say so would be to project categories intended for political history on to a material culture and a culture of social reform, which were, instead, dominated by a religiosity too all-pervasive as to be reduced to an opposition between free trade and protectionism. Britain did indeed have a committed consumer movement, and it was strongly marked by the theology of 'consummation' in the Kingdom of God. This has some echoes of the influence of social Catholicism, and its theory of salvation through the works of the French *Ligue Sociale d'Acheteurs.*[36] Elie Halévy has rightly drawn attention to the apparent neo-catholic religious convergence between France and Britain towards the end of the nineteenth century.[37] Thus the British consumer expert was not just a free trader, out to defend the workers' purchasing power, but also a clergyman and philanthropist carrying on the age-old debate about the relationship between commerce and virtue.

Notes

1 For an overview see Matthew Hilton, *Consumerism in Twentieth Century Britain: The Search for a Historical Movement* (Cambridge, 2003), Chapter 1. On the three topics see Frank Trentmann, 'Civil Society, Commerce, and the "Citizen-Consumer": Popular Meanings of Free Trade in Modern Britain' in Frank Trentmann (ed.), *Paradoxes of Civil Society: New Perspectives on Modern German and British History* (Oxford, 2000; 2003), pp. 306-32; Martin Daunton and Matthew Hilton (eds), *The Politics of Consumption. Material Culture and Citizenship in Europe and America* (Oxford, 2001); Peter Gurney, *Co-operative Culture and the Politics of Consumption in England, 1870-1930* (Manchester, 1996); Gillian Scott, *Feminism and the Politics of Working Women: The Women's Co-operative Guild, 1880s to the Second World War* (London, 1998) and Margot C. Finn, 'Working Class Women and the Contest for Consumer Control in Victorian County Courts', *Past and Present*, 161 (1998): 116-54.

2 Boyd Hilton, *The Age of Atonement: The Influence of Evangelicalism on Social and Economic Thought 1785-1865* (Oxford, 1988); Eugenio Biagini, *Liberty, Retrenchment, and Reform: Popular Liberalism in the Age of Gladstone, 1860-1880* (Cambridge, 1992); Anthony Howe, *Free Trade and Liberal England, 1846-1946* (Oxford, 1997); Trentmann, 'Civil Society, Commerce, and the "Citizen-Consumer"'.

3 The literature on these two topics is large. See Christopher J. Berry, *The Idea of Luxury: a Conceptual and Historical Investigation* (Cambridge, 1994) and John G. A. Pocock,

Virtue, Commerce, and History: Essays on Political Thought and History, Chiefly in the Eighteenth Century (Cambridge, 1985).

4 Frank Trentmann, 'Wealth versus Welfare: the British Left between Free Trade and National Political Economy before the First World War', *Historical Research*, 70 (1997): 70-98.

5 Michael Freeden, *The New Liberalism: An Ideology of Social Reform* (Oxford, 1978).

6 Hilton, *Consumerism*, pp. 47-52.

7 *Première conférence internationale des Ligues Sociales d'Acheteurs* (Friburg, 1909).

8 Charles Gore (ed.), *Lux Mundi. A Series of Studies in the Religion of the Incarnation* (London, 1889; 1895), p. vii.

9 A. M. McBriar has compared the field of social reform to a sporting competition: see *An Edwardian Mixed Doubles, The Bosanquets versus the Webbs: A Study in British Social Policy 1890-1929* (Oxford, 1987).

10 Sidney and Beatrice Webb, *Industrial Democracy* (London, 1897; 1901), p. 671.

11 Beatrice Webb (ed.), *The Case for the Factory Acts* (London, 1901), p. 16.

12 For an introduction to these debates see e.g. the relevant articles in R. H. I. Palgrave (ed.), *Dictionary of Political Economy*, (London, 1910).

13 John Neville Keynes, *The Scope and Method of Political Economy* (London, 1891), p. 98.

14 A facsimile edition of Quesnay's *Tableau oeconomique* was published by the British Economic Association in 1894.

15 Piero Sraffa, *Production of Commodities by Means of Commodities: Prelude to a Critique of Political Economy* (Cambridge, 1960), p. 93.

16 William Smart himself wrote on 'The Socialising of Consumption' in his *Studies in Economics* (London, 1895), pp. 248-308.

17 *Trade Unions*, CSU, Oxford University Branch, Leaflet No. 29, pp. 1-2.

18 Webb, *Industrial Democracy*, p. 673.

19 *Ibid.*, p. 671.

20 The largest collection of such CSU surveys are kept at the Pusey House, Oxford.

21 Wilfrid Richmond, *Economic Morals* (London, 1888).

22 In his pamphlet on *Expenditure*, Westcott quoted John Graham Brooks, *The Consumers' League: The Economic Principle Upon which it Rests and the Practicability of its Enforcement* (Newton, 1898).

23 Brooke Foss Westcott, *Expenditure*, CSU Leaflet, Presidential Address for 1899, p. 9.

24 Westcott, *Expenditure*, p. 9.

25 Pusey House, Oxford, CSU Archives, CSU Leaflet no. 35, Oxford University Branch, 1901.

26 Kevin Manton, 'The Fellowship of the New Life: English Ethical Socialism Reconsidered', *History of Political Thought*, 24 (2003): 282-304.

27 Sidney Ball, 'The Moral Aspect of Socialism', *International Journal of Ethics*, 6 (1896): 290-322.

28 See, for example, Sidney Webb, 'The Clergy and the County Council', *The Commonwealth*, July 1896.

29 See, for example, James Matthew Thompson, 'The Claim of Christian Socialism', *Economic Review*, 16 (1906): 156-67; William Temple, 'The Church and the Labour Party', *Economic Review*, 18 (1908): 190-202.

30 Ashley Ann Eckbert, 'The Social Thought of the Christian Social Union 1889-1914', (Unpublished Ph. D. thesis, Oxford University, 1990), pp. 116-39.

31 Hilton, *The Age of Atonement*, pp. 294-339, and particularly pp. 330-32.

32 Folke Olofsson, *Christus Redemptor et Consummator: A Study in the Theology of B. F. Westcott* (Uppsala, 1979). See also Brooke Foss Westcott, *Christus Consummator: Some Aspects of the Work and Person of Christ in Relation to Modern Thought* (London, 1886), p. 12.

33 The primary literature on 'personality' is enormous. Let us simply mention here F. W. Maitland's famous 'Moral Personality and Legal Personality', *Journal of the Society of Comparative Legislation*, 6 (1905): 192-200 and, for the CSU, Wilfrid Richmond, *Essay on Personality as a Philosophical Principle*, (London, 1901).

34 Pusey House, Oxford, CSU Archives, Brooke Foss Westcott, *The CSU*, Cambridge, unnumbered pamphlet, 3 December 1894, p. 13 and p. 15. My emphasis.

35 Pusey House, Oxford, CSU Archives, Brooke Foss Wescott, 'Expenditure', Liverpool, 27 November 1899, p. 7.

36 See Marie-Emmanuelle Chessel's chapter in this volume.

37 Elie Halévy, *A History of the English People. Epilogue Vol. 1 1895-1905*, trans. by E.I. Watkin (London, 1929), p. xi.

Chapter 3

Consumers' Leagues in France: A Transatlantic Perspective

Marie-Emmanuelle Chessel

Although American consumers' leagues have been the object of historical study, one is less familiar with the European consumers' leagues created between the turn of the twentieth century and the First World War.[1] As with the American organisations, the European equivalents were mainly (but not exclusively) founded by women in order to promote more 'ethical' patterns of consumption: i.e. they promoted better working conditions for labourers and employees, both male and female alike.[2] In this way consumers' leagues were created in France in 1902, in Switzerland in 1906, and Germany in 1907. Leagues also existed in Milan, Italy, and in Barcelona, Spain, though almost nothing is known about them. Lastly, a league was founded in Belgium in 1911 which, like the Swiss league, continued through the interwar period, but with new nationalistic objectives (it focussed on promoting Belgian products).[3] Generally, European consumers' leagues suffered much during the First World War (the German *Kauferbund*, along with the French *Ligue Sociale d'Acheteurs*, more or less disappeared) and this is why our study concentrates on the period preceding the conflict. We will investigate how the spread of European consumers' leagues occurred and determine to what extent there was a transatlantic 'influence', even an 'Americanisation,' comparable to that which took place in the advertising industry.

During the European interwar period, Americans advertised in Europe and French advertising agencies were inspired by American marketing methods even as they maintained their independence. Did the same thing happen twenty years earlier with 'consumer activism'?[4] As we already know, it is important to examine the nature of the communication and contact which characterised a milieu of men and women reformers, on both sides of the Atlantic, during a period when such exchanges were at their peak. Indeed, the period around 1900 was marked by experiments in different social domains, from social legislation to urbanism, insurance and retirement, both in Europe and the United States. The development of capitalism as it was, with its new consumer goods and new pockets of misery, did not appear as an inevitability but as a social construct. The responses to this development were various (state paternalism, private paternalism, mutualism, socialism, maternalism) and the field of possible reforms was relatively open. Together or separately, in contexts which differed from country to country, men and women discussed the problems and their solutions. This saw the development of a pool of knowledge fed by academic (economic or social sciences) and spiritual (religious knowledge) sources, as well as know-how (social surveys) and plans of action (scientific charity, reform of consumer behaviour, municipal assistance, social legislation). Those we might call 'itinerant reformers' had a major role in facilitating the debates and eventually bringing together solutions by extensive borrowing from science, expertise and experience, in both directions.[5] Among other techniques and as a complement to solutions like social legislation, the transformation of consumer behaviour could be perceived as one way of improving the labour conditions experienced by workers and employees.

This chapter deals with the *Ligue Sociale d'Acheteurs* (LSA) in France and its relationship to American consumers' leagues. Firstly, it will investigate whether or not the creation of the French *Ligue* was modelled on the American consumers' leagues. Secondly, it will describe the nature of the relationships between the promoters of the American consumers' leagues and the French *ligueurs*. And, thirdly, it will detail the courses of action they chose. It will also inquire into the extent of the contribution of consumers' leagues to the emergence of consumer expertise. It is certainly true that terms such as 'expert' and 'expertise' were absent from the reformers' vocabulary at the beginning of the twentieth century. Nevertheless, such a notion, although somewhat vague, has the advantage of allowing us to describe the different kinds of knowledge and know-how which were being developed and debated at the beginning of the century in relation to reform practices and the controls exercised by sponsors such as the state.[6]

Consumers' Leagues and 'Atlantic crossings'

Even before she created the first French consumers' league, the *Ligue Sociale d'Acheteurs*, Henriette Jean Brunhes (née Hoskier) presented a report in 1901 to a small Catholic meeting in Paris on the American consumers' leagues which had been created in New York in 1891 and federated as the National Consumers League in 1898. In this report, she analysed the American example with some precision, cited articles by Josephine Shaw Lowell and John Graham Brooks, the tracts of the Philadelphia and Brooklyn consumers' leagues, and the annual report of the New York league and the National Consumers League (1900 and 1901). She detailed the objectives of these leagues (the moral instruction of consumers), the timeline of their creation, the professions they targeted for protection, and their proposed tools of social action (surveys, 'white lists' of department stores and the labelling of industrial goods).[7] How she came to discover this movement and obtain all the necessary documentation will help to understand more concretely how the transfer of association, participation and commitment took place.

Several elements must be mentioned in order to understand how such transfers took place. Firstly, we must emphasize the importance of cultural mediators. Foremost among them was Thérèse Blanc, pseudonym for Thérèse Benzon, a French woman of letters and specialist in American literature who translated English novels and was a novelist and chronicler in her own right. She contributed to making American culture known in France, particularly that promoted through women's initiatives. In 1899, she attended a conference by Maud Nathan in London and reviewed it for a French journal. It happens that she knew Henriette Brunhes well: they both participated in a women's group called *Action Sociale de la Femme*. Thérèse Benzon would become one of the first members of the French LSA.[8]

Secondly, we must highlight the role of conferences and World Fairs as venues for exchanges between reformers and hubs of information which facilitated transfer from one country to another. The Paris World Fair of 1900 played a major part: the Pavilion of Social Economy included a presentation by American consumers' leagues.[9] One could read about the leagues and look at photographs of sweatshops and model factories. In 1901, Maud Nathan was the guest of the International Congress of Women in Berlin.[10]

Finally, we must point out that transatlantic transfer was rarely simple and direct (from the United States to a single European country). Instead, information about American initiatives was in general circulation throughout Europe. We have seen that Thérèse Blanc translated a conference paper given by M. Nathan in London. But information on consumers' leagues also came to Paris via Germany: Henriette Brunhes translated a German article from the *Frankfurter Zeitung* dated 4 August 1900, on the American consumers' leagues which appeared in September 1900 in a Catholic journal entitled *La Justice sociale*.[11]

It was only after gathering such information through cultural intermediaries, World Fairs and the international press that Brunhes wrote her article of 1901. She presented the American leagues as a model which the French should adapt: 'We have a model example to refer to, one that we need not imitate exactly, but from which we must draw inspiration: it is given to us by the consumers' leagues of the United States.' Thus the Paris League viewed itself very much as the 'daughter' of the New York league.[12]

Beginning with the 1901 article and the subsequent publications of the LSA, such public acknowledgement of affiliation was the result of previous transatlantic contact, already established in the first years between the Brunhes couple and several American women, particularly Maud Nathan and Florence Kelley. Indeed, the 1901 article served as a foundation for Jean and Henriette Brunhes on which to build contacts with the American leagues and obtain both additional information and support. Further contact was made with Maud Nathan during her trip to Europe in 1903 (although the exchange of documentation continued, the French did not travel to the United States). Communication took place either in French, which Maud Nathan spoke and wrote well, or in English, which Jean and Henriette Brunhes read well.[13]

Yet this transfer was anything but obvious or necessary. If Henriette and Jean Brunhes seized on the example of the American consumers' leagues it was because those organizations proposed adequate solutions for a group of women in search of practical social action.[14] Henriette Brunhes retained certain elements of the American example which provided answers to her personal research into social action and which she shared with a group of Catholic women. The first element involved distinguishing between workers on the one hand and those who received aid on the other: the consumers' leagues sought to help the former and not the latter. Such a distinction was crucial: among other matters, this Catholic woman sought to keep her distance from charity work. By helping the 'workers' (and not the 'poor'), the women founders of the *Ligue* in Paris wanted to participate in the reform of the capitalist world just like the unions; they did not see themselves as 'healers' of a situation which was foreign to them.[15] Through the consumers' leagues, they also introduced the principle of 'scientific charity', promoted most notably in the United States by Josephine Shaw Lowell (founder of the Charity Organization Society and first president of the New York Consumers' League). Other reformers in the United States or Great Britain also distinguished between the 'poor' and the 'workers', among whom they found the 'respectable' unemployed who deserved compensation. In other words, the women of the consumers' leagues participated in debates which were more general and which aimed to distinguish the future beneficiaries of social protection from those who would be excluded from the existing system of assistance.[16] The second element retained from the American example and which follows from the first, concerned what Henriette Brunhes termed a 'progressive and highly methodical' procedure: to act first on the conditions experienced by saleswomen in retail stores, and then expand to other areas. Such a limitation of activities to just a few campaigns in order to achieve concrete results was considered a contribution of the American example, as were acts of consumer education and surveys.

This development, fostered by Catholic women, had strong support from a body of men present in those university and reforming institutions from which women were absent. Such was the case for lawyers or economists who tried to establish themselves as the undisputed experts in the development of 'labour law' and advocated the need for state intervention in society.[17] As in the United States where a new school of economists belonging to different intellectual currents bolstered the National Consumers League (Arthur T. Hadley, Richard T. Ely, Henry Carter Adams, Edwin A. Seligman, for example), several economists and jurists supported the creation of the *Ligue Sociale d'Acheteurs*. Refusing 'laissez-faire' and pushing for state intervention in the face of the partisans of liberalism, jurists such as Georges Blondel, Eugène Duthoit and Raoul Jay became involved in the LSA.[18] In addition, certain teachers of the *Collège Libre des Sciences Sociales*, a private institution created in Paris in 1895, became members of the LSA around

1905; the secretary of the *Collège* was also the secretary of the LSA. About 20 per cent of the regular teaching staff of the *Collège* were in fact members of the LSA, among them Jean Brunhes, Pierre du Maroussem, Barthélémy Raynaud and Max Turmann.[19]

A number of distinct groups within the Catholic community acted outside educational institutions to provide support for the LSA. There were Catholic intellectuals who called themselves Christian-democrats and who advanced a definition of social Catholicism. Furthermore, the LSA was a site where certain Catholics sought to declare themselves the legitimate representatives of Pope Leo XIII and the translators into French of the encyclical *Rerum Novarum*: Jean Brunhes and his brothers during the 1890s, for instance. The approach of Georges Goyau and Henri Lorin was somewhat different: here were two Catholics who turned from the academic path and chose the activity of 'publicist,' that is, becoming literary journalists who attempted to define and defend a 'social Catholicism'. Finally, there were the cases of two Catholic lawyers who were very involved both in the *semaines sociales* (an itinerant university designed to promote 'Social Catholicism') and in the LSA after 1909: Jacques Tourret in Lyon and Maurice Deslandres in Dijon. The organisers of these courses met a network of economists and jurists to create a rhetoric focused on anti-liberalism, which was at one and the same time political, religious and economic.[20] Such an encounter took place notably with respect to the LSA. The LSA was thus a site for the expression of a different kind of expertise which, rather than basing itself only in the academic sphere, also sought another kind of legitimacy, that of the world of the educated, of journals such as the *Revue des deux mondes* and of the Catholic hierarchy. Professors, teachers in peripheral institutions, publicists and lawyers came together in different institutions – and in the LSA – to promote the ideas and initiatives of social Catholicism and social reform.

Surprisingly, for some of these Catholics, the United States represented a 'model' of cohabitation between the Catholic Church and the Republic and between the Christian Faith and modern society in general. This was notably the case for Jean Brunhes and Max Turmann, both committed supporters of the 'Americanist' movement.[21] It is precisely this crucial coexistence of different religions within the actions of the consumers' leagues that distinguished the LSA from other Catholic associations of the time. The official texts and the correspondence of the French *Ligue* demonstrate such a conviction. Henriette Brunhes turned to Charles Gide, for example, a Protestant economist and promoter of consumer co-operatives, in order to convince him to support the cause: 'Should we not always follow the example of the Americans who bring together Catholics, Salvationists, Jews, Free-thinkers, etc.?'[22] Affirming the 'neutral' character of the LSA, meaning it did not declare itself exclusively Catholic although it was led by Catholics, was a defining mark in France: this choice was criticised by other

Catholics who preferred purely confessional action. The American influence was likewise denounced by the adversaries of the LSA who criticised it for creating an association which was not exclusively and openly Catholic and which, on the contrary, imported a Protestant association.[23]

In this way, the example of the American consumers' leagues provided a small group of women with a type of feminine social action judged to be scientific and which allowed it to distance itself from charity work. It also offered Catholics, men and women alike, with a means to display a kind of Catholicism more open to other religions. The LSA thus appeared as a forum to 'test' new discourses and new knowledge. Economists and lawyers, promoters of the nascent 'social sciences', met Catholic 'publicists' attempting to define a 'social Catholicism' and make known a public view concerning the definition of social Catholicism in France. At the turn of the twentieth century, the American consumers' leagues, more influenced by Protestantism, thus offered a 'model' for a small group of Catholic men and women and provided them with the tools necessary to carve out a new space for word and action.

The Americans did not deliberately attempt to export their model: it was the French who 'sought out' the American Leagues. Yet, the ties existing between Americans and Europeans in this nebulous reform network obviously favoured such exchanges and, indeed, exchanges of ideas and methods took place in both directions.

American reformers in Europe

If the consumers' leagues experiment made the Atlantic crossing in 1900, it was not only due to a demand on the part of French reformers searching for a new kind of practical social action. It was also because Americans were sustained by a connection with Europe from which they borrowed ideas and projects. The promoters of the consumers' leagues, notably those with whom Jean and Henriette Brunhes corresponded, Maud Nathan and Florence Kelley for example, were familiar with European writings and experiments: they travelled often to Europe, had studied there in some cases, and some of them continued to go there regularly to attend world fairs or conferences in Germany or in France.[24]

The Americans willingly acknowledged that they borrowed the initial idea of consumers' leagues from England. The English reformer Clementina Black was in fact the originator of the first league, though it only lasted from 1887 to 1890; she quickly abandoned the idea in favour of legislative lobbying designed to encourage the establishment of the minimum wage. The hostility of Black and the Fabians Sidney and Beatrice Webb to consumption as a means of action was known to Florence Kelley. According to her, the co-operative movement, the unions, and the English Women's Trade Union League together covered the same territory as the National Consumers League did in the United States, excluding the area of retailing. Consumers' leagues did not develop in England since activism concerning women's work was carried out by other associations like the National Anti-Sweating League or the Women's Industrial Council, while consumption as a means of social action was picked up and developed by the Christian Social Union.[25] The consumers' leagues, like 'casework', a method of individualised social aid, thus travelled first from England to the United States before returning to France.[26]

Subsequently, American reformers continued to borrow ideas from Europe. For example, Maud Nathan was very much impressed with 'sweatshop exhibits', such as those which took place in Britain and Germany.[27] She took up the method in New York: in 1909, the members of the league could borrow all necessary materials to put on an exhibition (photographs, pictures, objects made in sweatshops, objects bearing the label of the NCL) and the league even offered to provide a key-note speaker.[28] When an exhibit was organised in 1908 in Geneva in the context of the International Conference of Consumers' Leagues, she sent a trunk of materials and documents.[29] In 1915, she went to Cleveland, Ohio, to sell linen products and hand-crafted dolls produced in Lyon by women impoverished by the war. Such products were created with the guarantee of the French LSA based in that city.[30]

Of course, the relationship between American consumers' leagues and France was not exclusive: Florence Kelley, Maud Nathan and the secretary of the Boston league, Mary Higgins, had various contacts in all European countries. Just before the First World War, for example, Mary Higgins established ties with Emma Pieczynska-Reichenbach, the president of the Swiss League, getting a description of her activities there. She also received a letter from the founder of the Spanish league, who wrote to her on behalf of a French league member (J. Tourret) to ask her for information on the American leagues. During and after World War I, Florence Kelley and Mary Higgins tried to find out how matters stood for the European leagues through their correspondence with the baroness T. Osy de Zegwaart, of the Belgian League, or to Emma Pieczynska-Reichenbach. We can see then that there was no lack of transatlantic communication between league members.[31]

If the leaders of the consumers' leagues were sustained by a European idea of social action based upon consumption, they also benefited from the creation of new leagues in Europe. This allowed them to spread news of their own activities. In France, the LSA did not content itself only with asking the American leagues for information: it translated and publicised initiatives coming from overseas. In addition, the Americans were proud to learn that their ideas were being disseminated in Europe. Maud Nathan informed the press of this diffusion, emphasising the various countries involved and their contacts with the academic world.[32] What is more, travelling Americans also asked for information regarding the working conditions of French shop assistants or dressmakers. It is true that well-to-do American women often came to buy *haute-couture* (sometimes asking for the reproduction rights); they also made purchases in department stores. The league members therefore asked for the 'white lists' of French dressmakers and manufacturers of Swiss chocolates.[33]

Despite this undeniable interest in European initiatives, the American leaguers did not feel qualified to take part in the organisation of European leagues. For example, Maud Nathan wrote to Henriette Brunhes in 1903: 'I very much doubt that I can come to your aid regarding the work of the LSA since the conditions are naturally quite different between France and America'.[34] In 1904, observing the development of leagues overseas, the American leagues set up an international committee of the NCL, directed by Francis McLean. The stated aim of this committee was to extend the activity of the NCL to other countries and ask the European leagues for their suggestions. In reality, its activities seem instead to have been restricted to gathering information and ideas coming from the European leagues, and making a few comments. For example, Francis McLean produced a short report in 1913 on the European leagues: it was simply made up of letters from France and Germany which she reproduced and upon which she commented.[35]

It was Europeans, not Americans, who took the initiative to organise the two pre-war international conferences on consumers' leagues. Indeed, the Brunhes couple organised the first international conference of consumers' leagues in Geneva in 1908; the second conference took place in Belgium in 1913. These conferences were a means to discuss modes of action for consumers' leagues on both sides of the Atlantic.[36]

Social reform through consumption

The LSA counted 250 members in Paris in 1904 and only 600 in 1908. Having become a national organisation in 1909, by 1914 it claimed to have 30 chapters throughout the entire country and 4,500 individual members.[37] In contrast, the New York league or the first leagues in Boston or Philadelphia had several thousand members when they were founded, and the NCL claimed to have 15,000 in 43 states in 1916. But the number of French members was not insignificant and can be compared to that of the NCL. Indeed, the latter can be considered a relatively 'small' organisation next to the Woman's Christian Temperance Union, for example, which counted 150,000 members in 1892.[38] In both cases, rather than mass organisations, the leagues were small groups of men and women who sought to instruct themselves (as reformers or consumers), to instruct consumers, but also to act in different arenas such as social legislation. The means deployed by the consumers' leagues were therefore diverse and evolved over time. In this context, both men and women took part and developed different kinds of knowledge and expertise.

The Parisian league took its inspiration from the New York league and the two organisations compared well during the first years of the 1900s. The first advice to league consumers which appeared in American cities and in Paris was almost identical. Such advice was diffused via newspaper articles, tracts or posters. In New York in 1897, and in Boston in 1908, consumers' leagues encouraged customers to refuse to pay bargain prices, shop after 5 p.m. or have their purchases delivered in the evening. Consumers were also encouraged to refuse to shop on Saturday afternoons and they were told to behave courteously toward shop assistants. Such advice was frequently reiterated by the NCL, especially during the Christmas period.[39] In the same way, during the holiday season in 1904, the Parisian LSA advised shoppers to avoid making purchases on Saturday afternoons, or on weekdays after 5pm; last-minute purchases were also to be avoided. Consumers continued to receive such advice in 1910 in Lyon, Dijon, Rennes and other French cities.[40] The French league also proposed 'white lists' for dressmakers, comparable to the lists of shops created in the United States in order to by-pass the ban imposed by boycotts. The method for establishing the white lists was the same used in New York for the large department stores: the women of the LSA conducted surveys and determined certain criteria that dressmakers had to agree to respect.[41] While in New York the stores were listed, in Paris it was the names of the dressmakers themselves who appeared on the white lists. Very often, these dressmakers still worked directly for women customers (and not for the stores), since the French clothing industry was less standardized than that of Americans at the turn of the century. The activism of the LSA was thus adapted to the artisan nature of the clothing industry in Paris, in particular with regard to dress making.[42]

It is certainly true that the American leagues, and notably the NCL, took an interest in the textile industry, but this involved cloth manufacturing (and not *haute-* or middle-*couture*) dispersed throughout New York and in different surrounding states. The existence of the NCL thus made action possible both in New York and elsewhere. This choice of economic sector and the arrival of Florence Kelley pushed the NCL to use labels rather than lists, since consumers did not go to the factories. Surveys were carried out in underwear workshops and a label was created for 13 companies held to produce their merchandise 'in clean and healthy factories, and in good conditions' without employing children and without giving work to be completed at home. In 1908, around 60 factories used the label in 13 states.[43] The label was abandoned in 1914 by Kelley in order to avoid competition with trade union labels, particularly during World War I. Use of the label was planned in France, but did not go beyond the stage of a preliminary study. In 1908, during an international conference, the question of competition with union labels caused the idea to be dropped before it could be put into place.[44]

Added to this French and American interest in the clothing industry was the fight against sweatshops (either home-work or not). Home-work saw a considerable expansion in France at the turn of the century, in part due to the growing regulation of workshop production. One finds the same rhetoric and the same images condemning sweatshops on both sides of the Atlantic: the fear of disease which could be transmitted by clothing illustrates the link between methods of production and objects of consumption. From a hygienist perspective, the product became the symbol of a potentially harmful relationship between the social classes. 'Buying clothes whose cost of production and origin are unknown, always favours the exploitation of the take-home workers: it is also even tantamount to purchasing tuberculosis, diphtheria, scarlet fever and bringing them back home' declared one French tract.[45] Contrary to the Americans who sought to 'abolish' home-work, the French appeared more cautious about prohibiting something which would cost women workers their jobs. Debates on this subject took place during a conference in 1908.[46]

Little by little, the LSA spread throughout France (until it became the *Ligue Sociale d'Acheteurs de France* in 1909) and extended its activities beyond the department stores and the textile sector. The number of trades studied and affected by the league increased, though there remained a close tie with the urban context, the small shopkeepers and craftspeople.[47] Francis McLean of the Committee on International Relations of the NCL noticed such expansion in France and Germany in about 1913. This illustrates the high number of campaigns in which leagues became involved in those countries, at the risk of a certain amount of dispersal.[48] No campaign in France was concerned with rural life (although the majority of the country was still rural) or with the world of industry. Certain campaigns were motivated directly by the daily experiences of the women founders: improvement of housing conditions for domestic servants, for example, or for baggage handlers during journeys.[49] They also dealt with the world of crafts and small-scale production, for example that of bakers or butchers from Paris to Amiens.[50] With regard to small businesses and services, surveys targeted laundries, hairdressers, cafés and restaurant waiters. These were then followed up with tracts and posters which always incited consumers to change their purchasing habits.[51]

In moving beyond these diverse campaign tactics and printed advice literature, we will now focus on the involvement of the women who were the principal investigators in these social surveys. These women developed, expertise through their activity as social researchers. Henriette Brunhes was the first to advocate the 'program of constant research'. She suggested a kind of instruction manual to league members for conducting surveys: the 'group leader' had to bring together collaborators, research the available literature on the question, divide up the research work and put together an initial file. Henriette Brunhes prepared such files herself. This was to be followed by the actual investigation which involved going out to 'question' people directly about the targeted work conditions, most often with the aid of questionnaires. The group leader was then supposed to put together the final report, composed of 'facts and figures substantiated by serious references'.[52] In this way, several surveys were launched in Paris about the '*marmitons-patissiers*', but also about laundries and servant housing. The main investigation regarded clothing workshops and finally led to the establishment of a 'white list'. In taking the survey as a preliminary step before action, the leaguers were drawing from the Leplaysien movement, and more precisely the monographic and empirical method of investigation brought up to date by Pierre du Maroussem. A doctor in Law, trained at the '*Ecole des Voyages*' of Frédéric Le Play, and the administrator for the *Société d'Economie Sociale*, du Maroussem was the first Leplaysien sociologist to gain recognition within the university milieu as a professor at the *Faculté de Droit de Paris*. He stands as an interesting example of those intellectuals at the cross-roads of the academic world of law and the nascent social sciences. Freeing himself from the pure monographic method, he insisted on the complementarity of documentary research and field investigation through visits and interviews; and we find exactly such diversity in the investigative method of Henriette Brunhes and the LSA.[53] In November 1903, the LSA asked du Maroussem to teach a course at the *Collège Libre des Sciences Sociales* in Paris on 'the education of the consumer by survey'. Primarily concerned with the clothing, food and housing industries, this course included theoretical methods, discussions and social visits. Such investigations were significant for the history of sociology since these women chose and strengthened an empirical approach to sociology in the face of the more theoretical durkheimien sociology coming into existence at that time. As such, they set the foundations for what would later become the discipline of Labour Sociology. Finally, these inquiries transformed their perception of the world of employment, of women workers and servants, and legitimised their outspoken stance on transforming consumer behaviour.[54]

Once they identified the social problems, the women of the LSA used their new knowledge to propose solutions by reforming their own behaviour as consumers. Their advice was tied to another kind of expertise, acquired during their experience as middle-class women. For example, league member Mrs Klobb recalled that practical knowledge varies and that each women of the LSA had a specialisation at their disposal: 'Mrs Georges Piot knows how to make stale bread look and taste fresh; Mrs Georges Blondel has made a rule that the plates will only be changed once during the Sunday meal so as to lessen the amount of dishes to be washed. The idea is to publish a manual about stuff on Sunday'. Generally, such advice also promoted behavioural norms of the bourgeoisie: one must plan ahead and be able to buy in advance (several months in advance for large purchases or Christmas presents, or a few days so as to avoid shopping on Saturday afternoon). This means that social action at the LSA was also a way to codify, rationalise and protect the practices of women from the high middle class and the aristocracy who refused 'bargain shopping', good buys and the 'democratisation' of consumption.[55]

Besides its investigations and advice for transforming consumer behaviour, did the LSA evolve, like its American counterparts, into a legislative lobby? American historiography traditionally distinguishes between two phases in the history of consumers' leagues: the first, which privileges white lists and labels, stretched from the foundation of the leagues up until 1908; the second concentrates on legislative efforts after 1908, a time when the American leagues (and notably the NCL) called into question the effectiveness of white lists and labels, and subsequently placed less emphasis on the responsibility of the individual. Instead, greater emphasis was placed on collective work with the aim of setting up and respecting social legislation.[56] This distinction is in fact more complex, since consumers' leagues were interested from the beginning in legislation, both on a local level and at the level of the state. Furthermore, it is on this basis that F. Kelley extended the legislative action of the NCL to cover several states. In addition, the state leagues and the NCL did not completely abandon the label and the white lists between 1908 and 1914. Finally, the rhetoric of moral consumption and of consumer responsibility continued to be used, even when the first means of action were abandoned.[57] Thus in the United States, the leagues were not content to simply investigate and give advice to consumers. They were involved in additional activities which sought a legal basis. To achieve this, they used the social surveys which played such a crucial role in the development of legislation.

From the beginning, the French LSA also conceived of its activity as a 'complement to the law', thus following again the American model. It sought 'the vital union of consumer, producer and law-maker'. Between 1900 and 1910, the LSA took part in various movements in France aiming to regulate working hours.[58] One of its first campaigns involved designating Sunday as a day off. The LSA participated in the campaign for the 'reinvention' of Sunday, launched by Catholics, then by hygienists, philanthropists and the Unions.[59] Once the law of July 13, 1906 (which gave weekly time-off) had been passed, the LSA joined with the *Ligue Populaire pour le Repos du Dimanche* (Popular League for Sunday Rest), created in 1889, to verify its correct application. The second campaign concerned the length of the working day and night-work. Along with the employers' federation of bakery workers, the LSA supported the initiatives of deputy Justin Godart on night-work in the baking sector.[60] It thus backed the movement against night shifts (night-work for dressmakers) and its activity culminated in 1910 in a decree limiting night-shift conditions (limiting the working day for women to 10 hours and eliminating work after 9 p.m.). Finally, the LSA defended the minimum wage, after having first been very wary, as the debates and the conference of 1908 show. But after 1910, in the context of the movement against sweatshops, it favoured the preparation of the law of 10 July 1915 on the wages of home workers in the clothing industry. This law was debated for several years before being passed, and its adoption was encouraged by the First World War.[61]

Contrary to the United States where the NCL acted in a 'direct' fashion by inciting states to pass 'protective' legislation on women's labour and then defending such laws when attacked in a state's Supreme Court, the LSA seemed to act more indirectly.[62] In fact, the women of the LSA were not recognised by the State or any other power in their capacity as 'experts', a title which Josephine Clara Goldmark did hold in the United States in the context of the 'Brandeis Brief' (in the trial 'Muller vs Oregon' of 1908). Such 'indirect' action took place firstly via the men of the LSA who also belonged to other reforming institutions: they fed these other institutions with the ideas of the LSA and brought back fresh debates to the LSA. We must point out the essential role of such male reformers, especially (but not exclusively) the social Catholics, who were also members of the LSA: they were active through other institutions like the *Association Nationale pour la Protection Légale des Travailleurs* (the French Association for Labor Legislation) or the *Société d'Etudes Législatives* (for example: Raoul Jay, Paul Cauwès or Raymond Saleilles). The second indirect influence occurred via investigative activity. While their role may not seem as important as in the United States where empirical surveys were used to defend the legitimacy of legislation on women's work, French surveys nevertheless played a part, for instance in the birth of the regulation of home-work in 1915.

Conclusion

As we have seen, if the American consumers' leagues strongly influenced the genesis of the European leagues, and in particular the French league, the latter maintained their autonomy even as they cultivated communication with their counterparts. On the one hand, it is in the context of French reform that the women of the LSA acted. It was a milieu where men monopolized the reforming institutions and where Catholic women were isolated in the face of other feminine and feminist associations. These women consolidated a body of knowledge of their own, thanks to their research and inquiries into the social consequences of their behaviour. This allowed them to develop their own position as Catholic women. On the other hand, the LSA furnished male reformers with the means to display the expertise they had established elsewhere in the professional sphere or in other discussion-oriented and reforming institutions. The demand for recognition by jurists or economists dovetailed with the itinerary of Catholic intellectuals promoting *fin-de-siècle* Christian democracy, who were likewise seeking to make their voices heard on a wide scale and make use of the 'social question' in order to define their identity as social Catholics.

We are thus a long way from (what could be called) the 'Americanisation'[63] of the French consumers' associations and the conclusion that it preceded the American influence on sales and publicity techniques. In fact, it is the French who took the initiative in the transfer because consumption offered answers to questions posed by both men and women in a specific French context. The Americans accompanied this transfer, since it allowed them to develop their initiatives and to learn about European projects. Whatever the differences were between the modes of action utilised by the American and French leagues, acting on consumption prompted the genesis of new expertise in men and women alike. We can conclude then that the birth of consumers' leagues seems to be closely linked in France to, firstly, the participation of certain women in the development of the social sciences and particularly empirical sociology, secondly, the increased autonomy of social economists and jurists who proposed their services to the state in the context of a process of professionalisation and, thirdly, the affirmation of social Catholics, whose institutionalisation of a place of instruction in the form of the *semaines sociales* was a significant step. In all these ways, the United States constituted a surprising model: these Catholic women and men looked overseas and sought in a distant land an example that would make their own world more progressive.

Translated by Erik Haakenstad

Notes

1 Parts of this article were presented at the international conference 'Au nom du consommateur' (Paris, June 2004) and during the seminar 'Genèse de la protection sociale' (EHESS, Paris, April 2005). I want to express my profound thanks to all the participants, especially Alain Chatriot, Nancy Cott, Laura Lee Downs, Patrick Fridenson, Odile Join-Lambert, Matthew Hilton, Claire Lemercier, Paul-André Rosental and Christian Topalov.

2 See for instance, Louis Lee Athey, *The Consumers' Leagues and Social Reform, 1890-1923* (Unpublished Ph. D. thesis, University of Delaware, 1965); Landon R. Y. Storrs, *Civilizing Capitalism: The National Consumers League, Women's Activism, and Labor Standards in the New Deal Era* (Chapel Hill, 2000); Lawrence B. Glickman, 'Consommer pour réformer le capitalisme américain. Le citoyen et le consommateur au début du XXe siècle', *Sciences de la société*, 62 (2004): 17-43.

3 Véronique Pouillard, 'Catholiques, socialistes et libres penseurs: les porte-parole des consommateurs en Belgique (1880-1940)', in Alain Chatriot, Marie-Emmanuelle Chessel and Matthew Hilton (eds), *Au nom du consommateur. Consommation et politique en Europe et aux Etats-Unis au XXe siècle* (Paris, 2004), pp. 262-76.

4 Marie-Emmanuelle Chessel, *La Publicité: naissance d'une profession (1900-1940)* (Paris, 1998); Clark Eric Hultkuist, 'Americans in Paris: The J. Walter Thomson Company in France, 1927-1968', *Enterprise & Society: The International Journal of Business History*, 4:3 (2003): 471-501. See also Victoria De Grazia, *Irresistible Empire. America's Advance through Twentieth-Century Europe* (Cambridge, MA, 2005).

5 Daniel T. Rodgers, *Atlantic Crossings: Social Politics in a Progressive Age* (Cambridge, MA, 1998); Christian Topalov, *Naissance du chômeur 1880-1910* (Paris, 1994). On circulation, see also Pierre-Yves Saunier, 'Circulations, connexions et espaces transnationaux', *Genèses*, 57 (2004): 110-26.

6 Christiane Restier-Melleray, 'Experts et expertise scientifique: le cas de la France', *Revue française de science politique*, 40:4 (1990): 547-85.

7 Musée social, Henriette Jean Brunhes, 'Les ligues de consommateurs', Rapport présenté à la Réunion des Revues sociales catholiques, Paris, 16 April 1901.

8 Joan M. West, 'Americans and American Literature in the Essays of Th. Bentzon: Creating the Image of an Independent Cultural Identity', *History of European Ideas*, 8:4-5 (1987): 521-35.

9 Louis L. Athey, 'From Social Conscience to Social Action: The Consumers' League in Europe, 1900-1914', *Social Service Review*, 52:3 (1978): 362-82; Anne Rasmussen, 'Les congrès internationaux liés aux Expositions universelles de Paris (1867-1900)', *Mil neuf cent*, 7 (1989): 23-44.

10 Anja Schüler, ''How Advanced America is!' The National Consumers League and German Social Reform' (unpublished paper, 2003).

11 Henriette Brunhes, 'Les associations d'acheteurs en Amérique. (La responsabilité du consommateur)', *La Justice sociale*, 371:8 (September 1900).

12 Archives Nationales (AN), Paris, 615 AP 76, letter from H. Brunhes to F. Kelley, 28 February 1903.

13 AN, 615 AP 73, correspondence between Jean and Henriette Brunhes and Florence Kelley and Maud Nathan, 1902-1905.

14 Sylvie Fayet-Scribe, *Associations féminines et catholicisme, 19e-20e siècles* (Paris, 1990).

15 Bonnie G. Smith, *Ladies of the Leisure Class: The Bourgeoises of Northern France in the Nineteenth Century* (Princeton, 1981).

16 Topalov, *Naissance du chômeur*, 229-39.

17 Jean-Pierre Le Crom (ed.), *Les acteurs de l'histoire du droit du travail* (Rennes, 2004).

18 Bruno Dumons and Gilles Pollet, 'Universitaires et construction de l'Etat-providence: la formation économique et juridique des élites françaises (1890-1914)', *Revue d'Histoire des Facultés de Droit et de la Science Juridique*, 20 (1999): 179-95; Christian Topalov (ed.), *Laboratoires du nouveau siècle: la nébuleuse réformatrice et ses réseaux en France, 1880-1914* (Paris, 1999).

19 Joseph Bergeron, *Le Collège libre des sciences sociales: ses origines, son fonctionnement* (Paris, 1910); Christophe Prochasson, 'Dick May et le social', in Colette Chambelland (ed.), *Le Musée social en son temps* (Paris, 1998), pp. 43-58.

20 Christian Ponson, *Les catholiques lyonnais et la Chronique Sociale (1892-1914)* (Lyon, 1979); Philippe Lecrivain, 'Les semaines sociales de France', in Denis Maugenest (ed.), *Le mouvement social catholique en France au XXe siècle* (Paris, 1990), pp. 151-515.

21 Albert Houtin, *L'américanisme* (Paris, 1904), p. 225; Jérôme Grondeux, *Ecrire et faire l'histoire: la pensée catholique sociale de Georges Goyau jusqu'en 1914* (Unpublished Ph. D. thesis, Université de Paris IV, 1994), p. 345.

22 AN, 615 AP 67, draft letter from H. Brunhes to C. Gide, n.d. [1903].

23 Marie-Emmanuelle Chessel, 'Catholicisme social et éducation des consommateurs: la Ligue sociale d'acheteurs au coeur des débats (1908-1910)', in Marie-Emmanuelle Chessel and Bruno Dumons (eds), *Catholicisme et modernisation de la société française, 1890-1960* (Lyon, 2003), pp. 19-39.

24 Axel R. Schäfer, *American Progressives and German Social Reform, 1875-1920: Social Ethics, Moral Control, and the Regulatory State in a Transatlantic Context* (Stuttgart, 2000); Kathryn Kish Sklar, *Florence Kelley and the Nation's Work: The Rise of Women's Political Culture, 1830-1900* (New Haven, 1995).

25 See the essay by Julien Vincent in this volume; Matthew Hilton, *Consumerism in Twentieth-Century Britain: The Search for a Historical Movement* (Cambridge, 2003), p. 48; Jacqueline Kay Dirks, *Righteous Goods: Women's Production, Reform Publicity and the National Consumers League, 1891-1919* (Unpublished Ph. D. thesis, Yale University, 1996), pp. 42-3.

26 Nicole Fouché, 'Le casework: circulation transatlantique et réception en France (1870-1939)', *Revue Européenne d'Histoire Sociale*, 11 (2004): 21-35.

27 AN, 615 AP 76, letter from M. Nathan to H. Brunhes, 26 May 1906.

28 Schlesinger Library, Harvard University, Cambridge (MA.), Maud Nathan Scrapbooks, A57-4, Special Notice, 27 March 1909.

29 AN, 615 AP 76, letter from M. Nathan to H. Brunhes, 6 July 1908.

30 Schlesinger Library, Maud Nathan Scrapbooks, A57-7, 'Destitute Women of Southern France to be Aided by Consumers', *Leader*, 31 October 1915.

31 Schlesinger Library, Consumers' League of Massachusetts, B24, box 24, folder 382, letters between Mary Higgins and women from European consumers' leagues (Emma Pieczynska-Reichenbach, Baroness T. Osy de Zegwaart and so forth), 1912-1920.

32 Schlesinger Library, A57-2, Maud Nathan Scrapbooks, Maud Nathan, 'The Consumers' league in France', n.d. [1903].

33 AN, 615 AP 82, letter from M. Nathan to H. Brunhes, n.d. and 615 AP 76, M. Nathan to H. Brunhes, 26 May 1906.

34 AN, 615 AP 76, letter from Maud Nathan to Henriette Brunhes, 12 July 1903.

35 Schlesinger Library, CLM, B24, box 24, folder 382, National Consumers League, F. McLean, Report of the Committee on International relations, n.d. [1913].

36 *Première Conférence internationale des Ligues Sociales d'Acheteurs, Genève, Rapports et vœux, 24-26 Septembre 1908* (Fribourg, 1909).

37 AN, 615 AP 67, letter from J. Bergeron to H. Brunhes, July 1, 1905; 615 AP 81, 'Observations de la LSA relatives à la loi sur le minimum de salaire dans l'industrie à domicile, présentées à la commission sénatoriale le 6 février 1914', 1.

38 Dirks, *Righteous Goods*, p. 2.

39 Schlesinger Library, Maud Nathan Scrapbooks, A57-1, 'Help for Shop Girls', January 1897; CLM, B24, Box 16, folder 254, Catechism, The Consumers' League of Massachusetts, juin 1908; CLM, B24, Box 11, File 173, Florence Kelley, 'Shop Early', *Charities*, 1907.

40 Maurice Deslandres, *L'acheteur, son rôle économique et social: les ligues sociales d'acheteurs* (Paris, 1911), pp. 87-8; AN, 615 AP 71, Poster of the LSA, Lyon, [1910].

41 Deslandres, *L'acheteur*, p. 31, p. 78.

42 Nancy L. Green, *Ready-to-wear and Ready-to-work: A Century of Industry and Immigrants in Paris and New York* (Durham, London, 1997).

43 Kathryn Kish Sklar, 'The Consumers' White Label Campaign of the National Consumers League, 1898-1918', in Susan Strasser, Charles McGovern, and Matthias Judt (eds), *Getting and Spending: European and American Consumer Societies in the Twentieth Century* (Cambridge, 1999), pp. 17-35.

44 Maxime Leroy, *La coutume ouvrière: syndicats, bourses du travail, fédérations professionnelles, coopératives* (t.2, Paris, 1913), pp. 134-44; 'Résumé de la discussion

sur le label', *Première conférence internationale des Ligues sociales d'acheteurs*, Fribourg, 1909, 134-44.

45 Bibliothèque Marguerite Durand (BMD), Ligue Sociale d'Acheteurs, Tract n° 5, 'Si vous avez le souci de l'hygiène', mai 1906.

46 Judith Coffin, *The Politics of Women's Work: The Paris Garment Trades 1750-1915* (Princeton, 1996); Athey, 'From Social Conscience to Social Action', pp. 375-6.

47 Geoffrey Crossick and Heinz-Gerhard Haupt, *The Petite Bourgeoisie in Europe, 1780-1914: Enterprise, Family, and Independence* (London, New York, 1995).

48 Schlesinger Library, Consumers' League of Massachusetts, B24, box 24, folder 382, National Consumers League, F. McLean, Report of the Committee on Inter-national relations, n.d. [1913].

49 BMD, Tract no. 7, August 1906; Deslandres, *L'Acheteur*, 52-4.

50 'La fermeture des boucheries le dimanche: une intéressante expérience à Amiens grâce aux ligues sociales d'acheteurs', *Bulletin des Ligues sociales d'acheteurs* (1912).

51 AN, 615 AP 71, poster from the LSA de France (1912).

52 AN, 615 AP 82, letter from H. Brunhes to Mrs Audollent, July 10, 1903.

53 Antoine Savoye, *Les débuts de la sociologie empirique: études socio-historiques (1830-1930)* (Paris, 1994); Janet R. Horne, *A Social Laboratory for Modern France: The Musée Social and the Rise of the Welfare State* (Durham, London, 2002).

54 Antoine Savoye, 'Les enquêtrices sociales, pionnières de la sociologie empirique [France, 1900-1914]', in J. Carroy *et al.*, *Les femmes dans les sciences de l'homme* (Paris, 2005), pp. 91-106; Françoise Battagliola, 'Femmes auteurs de monographies ouvrières', *Les Etudes sociales*, 138 (2003): 55-72.

55 Marie-Emmanuelle Chessel, 'Aux origines de la consommation engagée: la Ligue sociale d'acheteurs (1902-1914)', *Vingtième siècle: revue d'histoire*, 77 (2003): 95-108.

56 Schlesinger Library (MC 403, Box 1, Folder 3), Margery H. Ennis, *The Rise and Decline of the Consumers' League* (Senior Honors thesis, 1964), 28.

57 Dirks, *Righteous Goods*, 9.

58 Patrick Fridenson and Bénédicte Reynaud (eds), *La France et le temps de travail, 1814-2004* (Paris, 2004).

59 Robert Beck, *Histoire du dimanche de 1700 à nos jours* (Paris, 1997).

60 *Bulletin de la LSA*, 1909 and 1910; Annette Wieworka (ed.), *Justin Godart: Un homme dans son siècle, 1871- 1956* (Paris, 2004).

61 Athey, 'From Social Conscience', 368-9; Marie-Emmanuelle Chessel, 'Consommation et réforme sociale à la Belle Epoque: la conférence internationale des Ligues sociales d'acheteurs en 1908', *Sciences de la société*, 62 (2004): 45-67.

62 See for instance Theda Skocpol, *Protecting Soldiers and Mothers: The Political Origins of Social Policy in the United States* (Cambridge, 1992).

63 Dominique Barjot, Isabelle Lescent-Giles and Marc de Ferrière Le Vayer (eds), *L'américanisation en Europe au XXe siècle: économie, culture, politique. Americanisation in 20th Europe: economics, culture, politics* (Lille, 2002).

Part 2
Consumer Expertise in War and Peace

Chapter 4

Educating Consumers, Representing Consumers:

Reforming the Marketplace through Scientific Expertise at the Bureau of Home Economics, United States Department of Agriculture, 1923-1940

Carolyn M. Goldstein

In the late nineteenth century, as the economic function of American homes shifted toward the buying of goods and the rendering of services, a group of middle-class women – and a few men – launched an educational reform movement to guide homemakers in this transition. Widely known as 'domestic scientists,' in 1899 they organized a meeting in Lake Placid, New York, to propose a new field of study that would prepare women to perform domestic work more efficiently and manage household budgets more economically: 'home economics.' For the next ten years, a diverse group of educators, writers, and scientists gathered annually to formalize an academic discipline to teach these principles in the nation's schools and universities. The discipline they created reflected a shared a moral conviction about the superiority of white Anglo-Saxon Protestant culture, a belief in scientific and technological progress, and an optimistic faith in the ability of experts to improve social conditions that was characteristic of many early-twentieth century American reform initiatives. In December 1908 they established the American Home Economics Association (AHEA) to promote a vision of private family life that was predicated on a public role for a new group of scientifically trained women.[1]

In their struggle to shape American consumer society, home economists carved out academic and professional niches for themselves as experts about consumer products and consumer behavior in the first quarter of the twentieth century. With support from educational and agricultural leaders, home economics administrators and professors created a distinctive place in the curriculum at public land-grant colleges and many private universities, where they established their field as the '"science" of consumption.'[2] Here they created a distinctly female realm of expertise in the name of the consumer. University college home economics programs allowed women graduates to create vocational avenues for themselves not only as teachers, but also inside institutions that manufactured and marketed food products, domestic appliances, and other household goods. The AHEA's membership, which included mostly women working in the field, reached 15,000 by the early 1940s. By virtue of their ubiquitous presence on the national scene, home economists – as elementary and high-school teachers, college professors, government researchers, agricultural extension agents, representatives of consumer-products companies, women's magazine editors, and recipe and cookbook writers – served as the nation's primary consumer experts in the interwar period. Through their work in business and government, home economists transcended their role as educators to become what I call 'mediators' of consumption. Like the 'brokers' historian William Leach describes, these mediators helped to formulate the modern notion of the 'consumer' as an individual who purchased mass-produced commodities. Unlike advertising agents and salespeople, home economists had a secondary relationship to the market; even those employed in business did not see themselves as mere servants to commercial enterprise. By facilitating communication among manufacturers, retailers, federal officials, and women consumers at a time when many consumer goods were new and many of the structures of consumer capitalism were in formation, home economists played an important technical and cultural translating role in shaping consumer products and their meanings.[3]

This essay examines the efforts of a small group of about 50 home economists working inside the United States government to use scientific expertise to reform the marketplace for consumer goods during the interwar period. Beginning in 1923, officials in the United States Department of Agriculture (USDA) created a Bureau of Home Economics to support a larger program designed to modernize agricultural production and family farm life. Home economists brought an ambitious set of reform and professional goals to this institutional context. Seeking to promote a rational consumer society and develop expertise in consumer products and consumer behavior, they constructed an information clearinghouse to serve the public interest as well as home economists' own identity as experts in the marketplace for consumer goods. The bureau's research program aimed to help women consumers – in cities as well as in rural areas – by providing them with information they needed to be 'intelligent buyers' of agricultural and manufactured goods. At the same time, bureau home economists advocated for the consumers they sought to influence. In informal exchanges and formal negotiations with manufacturers seeking to understand the 'woman's viewpoint,' they stood in for the preferences and needs of 'typical' consumers.[4]

For bureau home economists, reforming the marketplace for consumer goods was an investigative and educational project that promised to bring about social, economic, and cultural change. Although they saw themselves primarily as professional – rather than political – actors, the technical work that home economists performed as civilian government employees often took on a political significance. Without any binding regulatory authority, these home economists operated as some of the first official government advisors to, and representatives of, citizens as consumers. The absence of a clearly articulated federal policy concerning matters of consumption gave this elite group of home economists a chance to equate their vision of rational consumption with good citizenship. Emerging in the 1920s in the context of an economy based on business and government cooperation, and a state agricultural policy that endorsed home economists' special expertise in consumption, the Bureau of Home Economics pioneered in the federal government's discovery of consumers and their place in the national economy. Home economists' identity as consumer representatives continued in the 1930s when New Deal reformers articulated a more explicit political understanding of consumers in a planned economy. Consumer education often blurred into consumer advocacy, and bureau home economists had a confused and contradictory relationship with American homemakers. Still, their attempts to influence the marketplace point to the importance of experts in defining consumers' identities and establishing new products as necessities in the United States in the interwar period.

A woman's profession and the science of consumption

In 1921, Miss H. E. Brennan, a young woman from rural Virginia, was having trouble determining what kind of oil stove to buy for her family's kitchen. So she wrote Minna C. Denton, the Assistant Chief of the Office of Home Economics in the United States Department of Agriculture, for help. Brennan lived six and a half miles from Manassas, a distance too far for her to travel to shop around for stoves. Yet she wanted to know which stove best suited her needs. She expressed frustration at being 'dependent on mail order houses' for information and pleaded for Denton's assistance: 'Housekeepers all around us are half sick from over work. A few real conveniences would stop much of this, take off last straws at any rate ... The farmer's wife seldom know[s] just what to get, where to get it and what it costs ... If you can help us perhaps you will be helping our neighbors too.'[5] Through this inquiry, Brennan summarized a dilemma of many rural women in 1920s America. Although she believed in the promise of labor-saving technology and subscribed to an ideal of 'intelligent' spending, she lacked adequate information to confidently navigate an unfamiliar marketplace.

Home economists identified this dilemma as early as the 1890s, and they staked their identities as teachers and reformers on using science to elevate the status of women as consumers. As participants in the larger women's political culture, early-twentieth century home economists were divided on the issue of women's suffrage, but shared concerns about consumption with groups such as the Housewives' League and the National Consumers League and worked with them to campaign for pure food and against child labor. Home economists' emphasis on the home, rather than politics *per se*, as a site for social change, led them to focus on material conditions, however. Leading university and college professors developed a full-blown curriculum designed to 'train' women such as Brennan to function as what I call 'rational consumers.' By preparing young women to make purchasing decisions according to cost-benefit analyses, they sought to shape middle-class culture according to values of efficiency, economy, sanitation, and health.[6]

By 1920, home economists had won support from the federal government for this educational program and a research agenda to inform it. At first the focus was on food. Inside the USDA, several home economists had played a key role in the first human nutrition investigations in the United States and prepared recipes to help home cooks understand food in quantitative terms. With the establishment of the agricultural extension service and the Office of Home Economics in the 1910s, many home economists traveled throughout rural counties as home demonstration agents reiterating this message about nutrition and promoting labor-saving technologies. New federal funds for teacher training allowed home economists to extend their reach in high-school and college classrooms. During World War I, home economists gained public visibility while playing leading roles in the United States Food Administration (USFA)'s campaign to promote food conservation and won legitimacy from director Herbert Hoover's endorsement of their expertise. Although Minna Denton and her colleagues at the Office of Home Economics were not prepared to answer Brennan's question about oil stoves, they had begun to broaden their investigations to include household equipment and other manufactured consumer goods.[7]

Secretary of Agriculture Henry C. Wallace's decision to elevate home economics to the status of a bureau in 1923 stemmed from an understanding that living conditions on American farms would improve if women like Brennan had assistance in assuming their new roles as consumers, and that home economists were the professional group to provide that help. In responding to a deepening depression in American agriculture and the growing importance of women's organizations in rural life, Wallace charged the bureau with a dual mission. First, its most direct responsibility to the USDA was to help create markets for agricultural products through research into their 'utilization.' Second, as researchers for the Extension Service, staff members were to supply home demonstration agents with ways to improve living standards in rural homes.[8] The USDA's mandate favored modernization in broad terms, but otherwise left it open for home economists to determine what constituted 'improvements' to the domestic lives of America's families.

With the choice of Louise Stanley as bureau chief, Wallace placed the Bureau of Home Economics under the direction of a nationally prominent home economist with a doctoral degree in biochemistry from Yale University, strong ties to rural women, and a commitment to serving consumers through research.[9] Stanley was an astute institution builder and strategist. She led the bureau's development with a keen eye to enhancing the status of home economics as a woman's profession, much as Julia Lathrop had directed the Children's Bureau in the Department of Labor in what historian Robyn Muncy calls a 'female dominion.'[10] Just as Lathrop created an environment to train a cadre of women social workers and reformers to extend women's maternal role into government programs, Stanley similarly built the Bureau of Home Economics as a training ground for young women scientists to develop a specialized research niche around consumption, an esoteric body of knowledge with which she and her fellow home economists could make a unique contribution to American social reform.

Stanley put women in charge of broadening the scope of investigations beyond the emphasis on foods in the Office of Home Economics. In the foods and nutrition division, Stanley herself replaced Charles Ford Langworthy – the former dean of the USDA's human nutrition investigations – as chief and filled the top new foods and nutrition positions with younger women holding doctoral degrees in scientific fields.[11] Although the study of food remained the backbone of the bureau's research program, Stanley hired two dynamic women in their thirties to carve out new research areas in home economics. Textile scientist and consumer activist Ruth O'Brien took charge of a textiles and clothing division which sought to derive science-based criteria analogous to food values by which consumers could judge fabric quality.[12] With graduate training in the 'economics of consumption' and in social survey techniques, Hildegarde Kneeland directed the economics division which studied the efficiency of household production but increasingly turned its attention to family buying habits.[13] On the eve of World War II, the BHE employed nearly seventy scientists, including forty home economists, thirteen chemists, seven physicists, two physiologists, and one bacteriologist. Stanley's success in filling most of these positions with women made the Bureau of Home Economics the single largest employer of women scientists not only in the federal government but in the United States.[14]

As bureau chief from 1923 to 1943, Stanley used the Bureau of Home Economics to strengthen home economics as a research field that generated new knowledge about the rapidly expanding scientific and technological content of the home. Bureau home economists used technical, scientific, and social scientific inquiry to evaluate a wide range of products in terms of their utility to homemakers and their place in family budgets. Questions about what goods consumers purchased, how production processes and product features related to performance, and how care and maintenance affected a product's qualities typified bureau home economists' approach to consumption. Agricultural goods, of course, were often a priority. At the same time, they sought to investigate the expanding cornucopia of mass-produced goods available to middle-class Americans. Throughout the interwar period, bureau home economists investigated cooking methods, sewing techniques, fiber and fabric properties, consumption habits, nutrition guidelines, measuring cup tolerances, meat palatability, child-rearing practices, and family accounting systems. By defining domestic material life in terms of measurable terms and categories, Stanley and her staff established the bureau as an information clearinghouse about consumer goods. Together with similar home economics research programs conducted at colleges and universities, this clearinghouse established home economics as a gender-based science of the user's perspective, a science that both reinforced contemporary understandings of consumption as a feminine activity and at the same time challenged the image of women as passive victims of advertising and irrational desire.

Influenced by Herbert Hoover, with whom they had allied in World War I, home economists perceived a mutuality of interests between consumers and producers. In the 1920s, with Hoover's appointment as Secretary of Commerce and later his election to the presidency, his vision of an 'associative state' reinforced managerial liberals' faith that products, merchandising systems, and consumer behavior could be fine-tuned to yield a more smoothly running market that met the needs of all. The staff at the Bureau of Home Economics sought to facilitate a 'closer fit' of production and consumption by shaping consumer behavior, on the one hand, and on the other hand, representing consumers to manufacturers and retailers of various goods.[15] Bureau home economists assumed that most homemakers, like H. E. Brennan, were rational consumers who wanted to make 'intelligent' purchases, and that they needed better facts to compensate for the paucity of information available through modern merchandising practices. At the same time, home economists posited an ideal producer who was committed to satisfying the needs and demands of these ideal consumers. Rather than manipulating consumers, ideal producers educated them. They competed on quality as well as price, and communicated honestly with consumers about the value of their wares and how to use them most effectively. As an extension of their commitment to consumers, bureau home economists sought to supply 'good' or 'progressive' companies with information about homemakers' preferences so that they could design better products and label them with useful, factual information. By using science to explain products to women in understandable terms and to explain women's needs to producers, home economists in the bureau mediated among agricultural producers, industrial manufacturers, retailers, and American homemakers.

Educating consumers

Conducted on behalf of the public interest, the bureau's user-oriented research elevated the significance of women's roles as consumers to the level of public policy and provided an institutional means to address their needs. The bureau's research program sent a message that consumption was an important economic activity, significant enough to merit attention from a government science program, and that a woman's role as manager of her family's household budget was a public responsibility. The Bureau of Home Economics instructed homemakers about specific products, but most significantly it taught them that to be a consumer in modern America was to be in communication with, and guided by, a new group of experts. With home economists as its official spokeswomen, the government told homemakers that consumption was a matter of facts and research, a process that required the work and guidance of home economists themselves.

Institutionalization in Washington endowed home economists' messages about consumption – wise purchasing, rational living, trained consumers – with official governmental status. Through the scientific and systematic study of fibers, foods, and household appliances, bureau home economists aimed to establish consumption on a rational basis. Although the bureau was a key player in the USDA's overall strategy to modernize the lives of farm families, it did not merely promote consumption *per se*. The bureau's research program sought to redirect homemakers' attention away from manipulative advertising which tapped into 'her primitive instincts,' and toward a more utilitarian, practical framework with which to evaluate the offerings of the commercial marketplace.[16] With science, these government scientists spoke in an alternative voice about the meanings of consumption in interwar America. They used the bureau to project an identity for consumers that challenged cultural constructions of female consumers as vain, emotional, and irrational. At the same time, by using science to quantify the kinds of qualitative changes they wanted to bring about in American domestic life, bureau home economists established 'standards for better living' which promoted values of health, nutrition, economy, and sanitation as hallmarks of middle-class identity. They projected the material features of urban, white middle-class life as the goal for all families, particularly those in rural areas.

By providing a platform for home economists' scientific and cultural agenda, the federal government endorsed the idea that rational consumption was a matter of good citizenship. During the World War I food conservation campaigns, Herbert Hoover's embrace of home economists' expertise had allowed them to make explicit connections between nutritional eating and patriotism. After the war, home economists' confidence that consumers and consumer products could be understood and controlled appealed to a wide range of government officials, politicians, social critics, and reformers concerned about the problem of mass-consumption. In the 1920s, Hoover's campaigns against waste provided a context for home economists to equate 'intelligent buying' with civic duty.[17] Although New Deal reformers challenged the assumptions about the mutuality of interests between producers and consumers held by home economists and Hoover's fellow managerial liberals, their increased attention to the consumer infused bureau home economists' educational agenda with a new sense of legitimacy and kept the bureau in the public eye throughout the 1930s.[18]

Throughout the 1920s and 1930s, the Bureau of Home Economics occupied the center of an extensive communication network. Home economics faculties at agricultural land-grant colleges in each state, home demonstration extension agents in most rural counties, home economics high-school teachers, and editors of women's magazines all recognized the bureau as the nation's authority on practical matters regarding domestic consumption—particularly food and nutrition—and they disseminated the bureau's findings. Bureau home economists used these channels and the bureau's own published bulletins, live radio programs, and traveling exhibits to promote rational cost-benefit analyses as a part of homemakers' daily lives and decision-making processes. Offered free of charge or for a small fee, the bureau's bulletins covered a wide range of topics including stain removal and laundry methods, efficient kitchen arrangements, and cooking instructions. These publications reached an enormous audience. In the 1927 fiscal year alone, the bureau distributed copies of its twenty-seven bulletins to more than two million people. Responding to the bulletins, 'Aunt Sammy's' radio programs, or concerns of their own, homemakers wrote letters to the bureau seeking all kinds of advice on household matters. In the late 1920s, the bureau received fifteen thousand letters annually.[19]

Although the USDA's primary objective was to improve the living standards in rural homes, Stanley and her staff targeted both farm and city families. The bureau's bulletins addressed a wide group of homemakers, many of whom made things at home, but many of whom did not. On the whole, however, bureau home economists assumed that the 'average' consumer was broadly 'middle class' and they directed readers and radio listeners toward an urban ideal.[20] At the same time, the Great Depression led the bureau to shift its educational emphasis to support relief programs aimed at individuals and families enduring serious economic hardship. Democratic leaders formed two new agencies – the National Recovery Administration (NRA)'s Consumer Advisory Board (CAB) and the Agricultural Adjustment Administration (AAA)'s Consumers' Counsel – to advocate for consumers. Both relied on the BHE for information about consumer products and consumer behavior. The Bureau of Home Economics worked with the Consumers' Counsel on a number of projects, including a study of the nutritional value of dried skim milk and a campaign to promote this new food product among low-income families. In addition, the bureau supplied articles on food values, household purchasing, and other topics for this agency's *Consumers Guide.* Intended to explain to consumers why food prices were increasing as a result of government production controls, this publication also listed retail prices of various goods and provided information about grades and standards. According to historian Lizabeth Cohen, the *Guide* became by the mid-1930s 'almost a service organ of the consumer movement.'[21]

By providing practical information about consumer products in support of both Hooverist and New Deal initiatives, by the mid-1930s the Bureau of Home Economics earned a reputation among many Americans as a 'consumers' bureau.'[22] After all, the bureau proved a more neutral alternative to the Good Housekeeping Institute and other 'institutes' operated by newspapers and women's magazines allied firmly to advertisers. However, the bureau's alliance to the agricultural establishment too often kept staff members closely focused on farm products and sometimes prevented Stanley and her colleagues from making objective statements about them. In addition, bureau home economists faced significant constraints on the information they could provide to consumers. Stanley and her staff lacked the resources to investigate the marketplace as comprehensively as they wanted to; the government's publicity operations simply could not compete with the enormous advertising and marketing apparatus that private corporations had at their command. The result was a rather piecemeal, fragmented publications program that failed to embrace the full range of household products available. Besides, not all consumers wanted to consume rationally or master the technical aspects of these products that home economists taught. For those like H. E. Brennan who did, bureau home economists had no legal means of publicizing the complete results of the comparative tests they conducted. As USDA officials, they could report only on the general results, without mentioning specific brands. When homemakers requested information on specific brand names and products, bureau home economists were not allowed to share it.[23] Bureau home economists made repeated, public calls for a change in this government policy, but nonetheless drew criticism from reformers such as Frederick J. Schlink's, co-author of the bestselling *Your Money's Worth* (1927), who soon established Consumers' Research, a private organization which succeeded in providing comparative testing along more specific, but also quantitative, lines.[24]

Schlink's critique, the success of Consumers' Research, and the political economy of the New Deal raised questions about how the bureau's research program served consumers, who those consumers actually were, and the limitations of locating a bureau in the service of those consumers within the USDA. Home economists' strong ties to Hoover and the Republican Party kept Louise Stanley and the bureau's leadership on the margins of political discussions about a government bureau for consumers after Roosevelt's election in 1932. Still, New Deal political and economic leaders drew on home economists' alternative discourse about consumption and on their technical expertise about specific products. President Roosevelt's National Emergency Council invited Ruth O'Brien to write 'Present Guides for Household Buying', which synthesized and summarized, for the first time, the consumer guides to quality grades developed by the USDA and other government agencies. Consumers' county councils distributed copies so widely that O'Brien and her colleagues revised the publication two years later and printed another popular edition. Soon O'Brien's team developed a series of 'quality guides' for assisting consumers in buying ready-made items such as blankets, towels, dresses, coats, and hosiery. By translating technical terms into plain language, these guides assisted homemakers in making rational purchasing decisions.[25] By promoting a cultural language about consumption based on the values of efficiency, economy, sanitation, and health, and providing women with a set of technical criteria and quantitative measures by which to exercise their buying power, bureau home economists critiqued the status quo of consumer capitalism even as they helped to reinforce it.

Representing consumers

For bureau home economists, educating consumers and representing consumers were inextricably linked. Seeking to create a marketplace where the information required to make cost-benefit analyses of purchasing choices was readily accessible, home economists used the bureau's research program to reform not only consumers, but also manufacturers and retailers. Bureau home economists forged cooperative relationships with industrial producers and distributors of a wide array of manufactured goods, and presented themselves as official spokeswomen for 'typical' consumers. They provided informal advice about product development and marketing, and they also participated in more formal collaborations aimed at standardizing manufactured goods and promoting them in scientifically derived terms.

'Standardization' was the order of the day in the 1920s. Hoover and his fellow managerial liberals saw standardization as a way to reduce waste in industrial production; he directed the Department of Commerce's Bureau of Standards to work with the American Engineering Standards Committee (known after 1928 as the American Standards Association [ASA]) to establish voluntary standards for various manufactured goods. Technocratic progressives such as Frederick Schlink and Stuart Chase, Schlink's co-author, led many of these efforts.[26] Home economists, too, viewed standardization as a way to simplify the marketplace. They believed an excess array of goods overwhelmed consumers and reduced purchasing choices to whims motivated by manipulative advertising techniques. Standardization, Stanley and her colleagues hoped, would limit the problem of 'too many designs' and help consumers distinguish among them.[27] Asserting that homemakers both wanted and needed standards to guide them in selection of foods, clothing, and household appliances, bureau employees served on many of the ASA's technical committees. In this capacity, they encouraged industrial managers to consider design criteria that home economists believed were important to women users, to grade their products according to tests, and to provide labeling information.

Two examples – the bureau's refrigeration studies and Ruth O'Brien's efforts to standardize the production and distribution of textiles and clothing – provide a window on the terms in which bureau economists' spoke on behalf of consumers in the 1920s and 1930s. Both examples illuminate the constraints that bureau home economists confronted both inside the government and among commercial actors, as well as the limitations of their influence over production and distribution processes. Still, the efforts of bureau home economists to use science to represent consumers reveal how two contrasting political economies relied upon home economists' relatively unique technical command over textiles and food preservation standards from the perspective of users. O'Brien's activities further suggest that bureau home economists' standardization efforts in the 1920s generated a technical language which enabled them to contribute to the more explicit politicization of consumers' identities in the 1930s.

In one of the bureau's major initiatives, chief Louise Stanley collaborated with members of the ice and electrical industries to promote a new, modern idea of 'constant cold' based on values of health and sanitation. Bureau home economists understood all types of refrigeration as critical to safe food preservation. With funding from trade associations in the competing industries, Stanley and her team studied the use of household refrigerators and produced a series of widely distributed publicity posters that alerted homemakers to the minimum temperatures that any box should maintain in order to keep milk and meat in good condition. The bureau's participation in this project positioned its staff to serve on ASA committees in the late 1920s and to convince manufacturers to establish design specifications and a 'score card' or grading system for ice refrigerators and ice blocks. Although few manufacturers chose to adopt the labels, Stanley and her team used their experience to advise the Tennessee Valley Authority's Electric Farm and Home Authority on standard specifications for low-grade refrigerators to be installed in homes built by this New Deal government program. The bureau's refrigeration studies had only modest success in establishing standards for ice refrigerator boxes and ice blocks, but did much to define all types of refrigeration (ice, mechanical, and electrical) as necessary to the modern household.[28]

As head of the bureau's division of textiles and clothing from 1923 to 1954, Ruth O'Brien drew on her background in textile chemistry, her experience with consumer activism, and her legal training to help consumers make sense of the mind-boggling array of fabrics available on the market. After World War I, consumers witnessed the emergence of new manufactured cellulosic fibers such as rayon and acetate alongside the usual naturally grown fibers of cotton, wool, silk, and linen. The poor quality of many of the rayon fibers, the lack of a standard nomenclature for them, and their resemblance to natural ones created a confusion about how to distinguish one fiber or finish from another, how to decide which type of fabric was preferable for what purpose, and how to care for and maintain fabrics once purchased.[29] To remedy this problem, O'Brien prepared bulletins to teach women how to judge the composition and construction of various types of cloth to determine their durability and how to use and care for them. But O'Brien's emphasis was on creating a new set of standards and specifications for fabric quality that would enhance consumers' abilities to make 'intelligent selections' without having to master too many technical terms. To determine minimum standards of quality, she studied staple textile commodities, analyzed existing specifications used by manufacturers, and correlated these specifications with performance under actual use.[30] Simultaneously, O'Brien worked through the American Home Economics Association and other committees to encourage fiber and textile producers to establish a system of grading fabric quality and labeling fiber content. In spite of years of hard work, O'Brien failed to overcome manufacturers' fears that her suggested specifications and labeling schemes would undermine the branding of their products.[31] O'Brien's vision for fabric identification labels was only partially realized with the passage of the Textile Fiber Products Identification Act in 1960.

O'Brien's efforts to standardize garment sizes were similarly ambitious yet frustrating. Men's sizes had been relatively standardized since the Civil War, but as manufacturers brought ready-to-wear garments for women and children onto the market in the early twentieth century, consumers found an erratic array of clothing sizes and shapes that bore little resemblance to actual bodies. Retailers faced great expenses in returns and exchanges as well as dissatisfied customers, and, by the mid-1920s, some of them began to look into standardizing measurements and sizes for ready-to-wear for women and children. Encouraged by these retailers, O'Brien outlined a plan to conduct body measurements to serve as the basis for standard sizes for women's and children's ready-to-wear clothing. Yet O'Brien had trouble finding the financial resources with which to fund her study. The Bureau of Standards endorsed it, but USDA officials opposed bearing its whole cost because they viewed it to be more valuable to commercial interests than to consumers. Several garment producers and retailers expressed support for the project, but none came forward with the necessary funds. In the late 1930s O'Brien won support for the body measurement project from Roosevelt's Works Progress Administration (WPA), but she failed to convince the women's garment trade to adopt these measurements as the bases for a system of standard sizes. The ASA organized a procedure to establish size standards on the basis of the data collected by the bureau, and mail-order companies adopted some of these standards. But overall, O'Brien's work seems to have had little impact on women's clothing sizes, which still are not standardized today.[32] Standardizing garment and pattern sizes required reforming a large number of small and medium producers who operated in a relatively disorganized, decentralized industry over which the Bureau of Home Economics had very little influence.

The bureau's standardization efforts lost momentum in the 1930s, but as the Great Depression and President Franklin Delano Roosevelt's New Deal programs brought a new level of attention to the consumer, home economists found support for encouraging the 'more effective consumption' they had long sought to promote. Under Roosevelt, correlating production with consumption became an imperative of economic policy, and political leaders and policy makers turned to the Bureau of Home Economics to represent consumers on technical committees. Although the NRA's CAB did not include home economists in its mix of academic men and female labor reformers, O'Brien, Stanley, and a number of other AHEA representatives served as consultants and provided testimony at specific code hearings to formulate quality standards for consumer goods. Ultimately, the CAB did little to set up NRA codes to safeguard consumers and the NRA itself was disbanded by the Supreme Court within two years, but this group's reliance on home economists demonstrated the continued importance of the bureau as a center of expertise about consumption.[33]

Conclusion

Throughout the interwar period, home economists used the Bureau of Home Economics to both educate and represent homemakers in the marketplace for consumer goods. Whether or not American consumers were interested in the bureau's educational messages, staff home economists did not hesitate to speak for them as a group and try to influence the design of many products based on their assumptions about what homemakers needed and wanted. To realize their vision of a more rational consumption system than the free market afforded, home economists used science to facilitate communication among manufacturers, retailers, and consumers. Bureau home economists' research was infused with white, middle-class values of health, sanitation, economy, and efficiency. The communication they facilitated occurred through this filter and was an indirect and, sometimes quite secretive, process.

Bureau home economists' attention to the technical and material aspects of the expanding consumer culture had the potential to help homemakers leverage purchasing power to their advantage. New products such as stoves, refrigerators, cellulosic fabrics, and ready-made clothing occupied the center of daily life for many Americans, and understanding them required users – and potential users – to acquire a new level of scientific and technological proficiency. Yet the rapid change in the technical content of these goods required mastery of concepts and terminologies that not all consumers were interested in achieving. Bureau scientists were pressured to develop ever-increasing levels of specialization to maintain their expertise. Although they attempted to embrace in their investigations the full array of products and services available, the enormity of the task made it beyond their limited resources – and the mission of the USDA – to complete. In addition, bureau home economists' emphasis on the products themselves often limited their ability to advocate for the needs of American families from a broader perspective.

Ultimately, Louise Stanley, Ruth O'Brien, and their colleagues at the bureau were more influential in shaping cultural values about consumption than they were in reforming the marketplace for consumer goods. In spite of limited success in their efforts to standardize commercial goods, improve their quality, or rationalize family buying practices, bureau home economists nonetheless served as pioneering consumer advocates. In their dual capacity as consumer educators and consumer representatives, they did much to shape the way government officials, agricultural producers, manufacturers, retailers, and consumers understood one another. Bureau home economists' efforts to frame consumption in rational terms in the 1920s generated both a technical and a cultural terminology – of efficiency, economy, and sanitation – which other groups drew on as they fostered a political strategy in the 1930s. Bureau home economists' struggles to rationalize the production, distribution, and consumption of manufactured goods challenge historians' understandings of women and consumption in the 1920s, and point to the important role this female professional group played in the development of consumer capitalism in the United States in the decades before World War II.

Notes

1 Laura Shapiro, *Perfection Salad: Women and Cooking at the Turn of the Century* (New York, 1986); Emma Weigley, 'It Might Have Been Euthenics: The Lake Placid

Conferences and the Home Economics Movement', *American Quarterly*, 26 (March 1974): 79-96.

2 Faith McCauley, 'The "Science" of Consumption', *Journal of Home Economics* (JHE), 12 (July 1920): 317-8.

3 Carolyn M. Goldstein, 'Mediating Consumption: Home Economics and American Consumers, 1900-1940' (Unpublished Ph. D. thesis, University of Delaware, 1994); and *The Science of Consumption*, forthcoming with University of North Carolina Press; Carolyn M. Goldstein, 'Part of the Package: Home Economists in the Consumer Products Industries, 1920-1940', in Sarah Stage and Virginia Vincenti (eds), *Rethinking Home Economics: Women and the History of a Profession* (Ithaca, NY, 1997), pp. 271-96; Carolyn M. Goldstein, 'From Service to Sales: Home Economics in Light and Power, 1920-1940', *Technology and Culture*, 38 (January 1997): 121-52; William Leach, *Land of Desire: Merchants, Power, and the Rise of a New American Culture* (New York, 1993), pp. 10-12.

4 Goldstein, 'Mediating Consumption', Chapters 2 and 3; Records of the Bureau of Home Economics and Human Nutrition, RG 176, National Archives, Washington, D.C., (RG 176); Paul Betters, *The Bureau of Home Economics: Its History, Activities and Organization* (Washington, D.C., 1930); T. Swann Harding, *Two Blades of Grass: A History of Scientific Development at the United States Department of Agriculture* (Norman, 1947), Chapter 12; Helen Finneran, 'Louise Stanley: A Study of the Career of a Home Economist, Scientist, and Administrator, 1923-53', (Unpublished Master's dissertation, American University, 1965); and Margaret Rossiter, *Women Scientists in America: Strategies and Struggles to 1940* (Baltimore, 1982), pp. 223-9.

5 H. E. Brennan to Minna Denton, 9 February 1921, Folder: Home Economics Conference Suggestions, Box 989, Entry 17, Records of the Secretary of the United States Department of Agriculture, RG 16, National Archives, Washington, D.C., (RG 16).

6 Kathryn Kish Sklar, 'Historical Foundations of Women's Power in the Creation of the American Welfare State, 1830-1930', in Seth Koven and Sonya Michel (eds), *Mothers of a New World: Maternalist Politics and the Origins of Welfare States* (New York and London, 1993), pp. 43-93; Goldstein, 'Mediating Consumption', Chapter 1.

7 Harvey Levenstein, *Revolution at the Table: The Transformation of the American Diet* (New York, 1988), Chapters 4, 9, and 11; Rossiter, *Women Scientists in America*, pp. 120-121; Betters, *The Bureau of Home Economics*, pp. 30-40; Goldstein, 'Mediating Consumption', Chapter 1.

8 Betters, *The Bureau of Home Economics*, p. 41-3.

9 Finneran, 'Louise Stanley'; Rossiter, *Women Scientists in America*, pp. 229, 233; Marie Dye, *History of the Home Economics Department, University of Chicago* (Chicago, 1972), pp. 195-6; 'Louise Stanley', *JHE*, 46 (September 1954): 454; *Notable American Women: The Modern Period*, s.v. 'Stanley, Louise.'

10 Robin Muncy, *Creating a Female Dominion in American Reform, 1890-1935* (New York, 1991).

11 Betters, *The Bureau of Home Economics*, p. 43; 'Dr. Stanley Discusses New Bureau of Home Economics', 24 September 1923, Folder: Home Economics, Box 989, Entry 17, RG 16; Ruth O'Brien, 'Bureau of Human Nutrition and Home Economics Celebrates a Quarter Century of Service', *JHE*, 40 (June 1948): 294; Gladys L. Baker, 'Women in the U.S. Department of Agriculture', *Agricultural History*, 50 (1976): 195-9; Rossiter, *Women Scientists in America*, p. 229; *Report of the Chief of the Bureau of Home Economics (RCBHE)* (1926): 2.

12 'Ruth O'Brien, Expert on Textiles, U.S. Aide', *Washington Post* (13 March 1976), Section E, p. 6; 'Miss Ruth O'Brien appointed Assistant Chief, Bureau of Human Nutrition and Home Economics'; 'Personal Information About Ruth O'Brien' (1956); and 'Notes About Ruth O'Brien', all in AHEA Foundation Files, AHEA Archives, American Association of Family and Consumer Sciences, Alexandria, Virginia (AHEA); Helen Pundt, *AHEA: A History of Excellence* (Washington, D.C., 1980), pp. 30, 41-2, 212.

13 "Kneeland," Folder: Kneeland, H., Box 550, RG 176; Hildegarde Kneeland, 'The Field of Research in Economics of the Home', *JHE*, 17 (January 1925): 15-19; 'Bureau of Home Economics', *JHE*, 16 (April 1924): 229-30; Ronald Kline, 'Ideology and Social Surveys: Reinterpreting the Effects of 'Labor-Saving' Technology on American Farm Women', *Technology and Culture*, 38 (April 1997): 355-85; and Goldstein, 'Mediating Consumption', Chapter 2.

14 *RCBHE* (1929): 2; Betters, *The Bureau of Home Economics*, pp. 73-6; Helen Atwater and M. Heseltine, 'The Home Economist in Public Service', *Women's Work and Education*, 11:1 (February 1940): 1-5; Ruby Worner, 'Opportunities for Women Chemists in Washington', *Journal of Chemical Education* 16, (1939): 584; Rossiter, *Women Scientists in America*, pp. 228-9.

15 Ellis Hawley, 'Herbert Hoover, the Commerce Secretariat, and the Vision of the Associative State', *Journal of American History*, 61 (June 1974): 116-40; Ruth O'Brien and Olive Hartley, 'Selection: An Analysis of Consumers' Facilities for Judging Merchandise,' Excerpt from the Report of the Subcommittee on Purchasing Procedures of the Committee on Household Management of the President's Conference of Home Building and Home Ownership, 1931, unpublished typescript, Widener Library, Harvard University, Cambridge, Massachusetts, 12; *RCBHE* (1926): 1.

16 Ruth Van Deman, 'Books and Literature', *JHE*, 15 (December 1923): 717-18.

17 Janet Hutchison, 'American Housing, Gender, and the Better Homes Movement, 1922-1935', (Ph. D. thesis, University of Delaware, 1990); Kendrick A. Clements, *Hoover, Conservation, and Consumerism: Engineering the Good Life* (Lawrence, 2000).

18 Lizabeth Cohen, *A Consumer's Republic: The Politics of Mass Consumption in Postwar America* (New York, 2003), pp. 18-61; Persia Campbell, *Consumer Representation in the New Deal* (New York, 1940); Kathleen G. Donahue, *Freedom From Want: American Liberalism and the Idea of the Consumer* (Baltimore, 2003), pp. 198-275; *RCBHE*, (1935): 1.

19 Susan Smulyan, 'Radio Advertising to Women in Twenties America: "A latchkey to every home"', *Historical Journal of Film, Radio and Television*, 13:3 (1993): 306-7; Ruth Van Deman and Fanny Walker Yeatman, *Aunt Sammy's Radio Recipes Revised* (Washington, D.C., 1931); Josephine Hemphill, 'Broadcasting Home Economics from the Department of Agriculture', *JHE*, 19 (May 1927): 275-8; *RCBHE* (1933): 13; *RCBHE* (1927): 10-11; Betters, *The Bureau of Home Economics*, p. 67; letters to the bureau are organized alphabetically by author in RG 176.

20 Goldstein, 'Mediating Consumption', Chapter 2; Ruth O'Brien to Louise Stanley, 27 September 1924, Folder: Ruth O'Brien, Box 600, RG 176; Folder S, Box 705, RG 176.

21 Cohen, *A Consumers' Republic*, p. 29; Campbell, *Consumer Representation in the New Deal*, pp. 65-6, 194-261; *RCBHE* (1934): 13; *RCBHE* (1936): 2; and Box 554, RG 176.

22 Helen Atwater, 'Guides to the Efficient Choice of Household Goods', in *International Congress For Scientific Management* (London, 1935), Box 13, Wilbur Olin Atwater Papers, Wesleyan University Library, Middletown, Connecticut.

23 Anita Newcomb McGee to the Bureau of Home Economics, October 10, 1936, Box 216, RG 176.

24 Charles McGovern, 'Consumption and Citizenship in the United States, 1900-1940', in Susan Strasser, Charles McGovern, and Matthias Judt (eds), *Getting and Spending: European and American Consumer Societies in the Twentieth Century* (Cambridge, 1998), pp. 37-58; Lawrence Glickman, 'The Strike in the Temple of Consumption: Consumer Activism and Twentieth Century Political Culture,' *Journal of American History*, 88 (June 2001): 99-128; Hazel Kyrk, 'The Selection of Problems for Home Economics Research', *JHE*, 25 (October 1933): 686.

25 *RCBHE* (1934): 10-11; *RCBHE* (1935): 13; 'Present Guides for Household Buying', *USDA Miscellaneous Publication* (1934); Bess M. Viemont, Margaret B. Hays, and Ruth O'Brien, 'Guides for Buying Sheets, Blankets, Bath Towels', *USDA Farmers Bulletin*, 1765 (1936).

26 *Annals of the American Academy of Political and Social Science* 87 (May 1928); Robert Westbrook, 'Tribune of the Technostructure: The Popular Economics of Stuart Chase', *American Quarterly*, 32 (1980): 387-408.

27 Louise Stanley, 'The Development of Better Farm Homes', *Agricultural Engineering*, 7 (April 1926): 130; Jessie V. Coles, *The Standardization of Consumers' Goods* (New York, 1932).

28 Goldstein, 'Mediating Consumption', Chapter 3.

29 David A. Hounshell and John Kenly Smith, *Science and Corporate Strategy: DuPont R&D, 1902-1980* (Cambridge and New York, 1988), pp. 161-168; Mary Schenck Woolman and Ellen Beers McGowan, *Textiles: A Handbook for the Student and the Consumer* (New York, 1913).

30 Ruth O'Brien, 'The Program of Textile Research in the Bureau of Home Economics', *JHE*, 22, (April 1930): 281-87; Ruth O'Brien, 'Textile Buying Problems of the Consumer', Rough Draft of Talk to be Given at Kansas Farm and Home Week, February 6, 1930; and 'Problems the Homemaker Meets at the Dry Goods Counter,' Radio Talk—W.R.C., February 14, 1930, both in Folder: Committee—Standardization of Textile Fibers, 1927-30, Box: Consumer Standardization, (AHEA); 'Selection of Cotton Fabrics', *USDA Farmers Bulletin*, 1449 (1926); Betters, *The Bureau of Home Economics*, p. 69.

31 'Recent Work of the Committee on the Standardization of Textiles', *JHE*, 12 (March 1920): 101-9; 'Textile Section', *JHE*, 15 (October 1923): 550-2; Ruth O'Brien, 'Textile Committee Report', *JHE*, 16 (September 1924): 502-3; Ruth O'Brien, 'Textile Standardization: An S.O.S. from the Textile Section', *JHE*, 19 (September 1927): 519-21; Betters, *The Bureau of Home Economics*, pp. 53-4; O'Brien and Hartley, 'Selection', pp. 29-30.

32 Goldstein, 'Mediating Consumption', Chapter 3; Ruth O'Brien, Meyer A. Girshick, and Eleanor P. Hunt, 'Body Measurements of American Boys and Girls for Garment and Pattern Construction: A Comprehensive Report of Measuring Procedures and Statistical Analysis of Data on 147,000 American Children', *USDA MP*, 366 (1941); 'Asks Propaganda For Boys' Styles', *New York Times* (13 July 1939); Patricia Wen, 'Size Often An Immeasurable Problem,' *Boston Globe* (23 December 1998), pp. A1, A14-15.

33 Campbell, *Consumer Representation in the New Deal*, pp. 49-53; *RCBHE* (1934): 10; 'The Consumer and the NRA', *JHE*, 26 (January 1934): 30-32; 'The Consumer and the New Deal', *JHE*, 26 (February 1934): 102-3.

Chapter 5

The Enemy Within:
Food, Nutrition Experts and Consumers in French-Speaking Switzerland, 1900-1946

Joëlle Droux

During the Second World War, the complex problems linked to the quality and quantity of food ingested by the Swiss population gained an unforeseen degree of urgency. While the majority of European people were trying to survive various degrees of malnutrition, Switzerland generally avoided the widespread food shortages and the lethal consequences they entailed for neighbouring populations, whether in terms of general mortality or cases of contagious illness registered.[1] Set up as early as the autumn of 1939, the Swiss wartime food organization was able to distribute the available nutritional stocks adapted to the precise needs of time, space and the biological profile of consumers (based upon age, gender and work).[2] Based on a complex system of cards (coupons), it arranged that consumers would only be given access to actually existing foodstuffs, contrary to what occurred in France.[3] Furthermore, the expert support of nutritional scientists was pivotal in building this organisation: not only were they responsible for the composition of Swiss rations, but they were also summoned to broadcast the new gospel of nutritional hygiene which backed it up.

This paper examines how Swiss nutrition experts acquired their experience as specialists of food reform during the interwar years, and how it shaped their subsequent strategies to change the consuming habits of their fellow citizens from 1939 onwards, urging them to adopt a healthier diet. Admittedly, they acquired a long sought-after official position during wartime, devotedly arguing about the necessity of eating better while having to eat less. But to what extent did they really try to ally with the consumers, especially women, during those six long years of dearth and physical hardship? And where did the consumer's health and well-being register on their professional agenda, compared to the possibility of challenging the microbiological paradigm's dominant position on the medical marketplace? Finally, we will try to establish whether their enthusiastic crusade in favour of food rationing, and the way they presented it, did much to improve their position as consumers' experts and advisers.

Food reform in the interwar years: crucial discoveries, limited audiences

At the end of the nineteenth century, the food question seemed to top the list of the scientific agenda. Indeed, as early as the 1850s, many physiologists had succeeded in identifying and synthesizing the basic components of food deemed necessary for a normal functioning of the human machine (carbohydrates, fats, proteins).[4] Yet, in spite of spectacular achievements of the food industry (meat extracts, canned food, etc), the physiology of nutrition still stumbled against the invisible components present in natural food products, and could only register the fact that life could not be maintained when one replaced these elements by their artificially devised counterparts.[5] The role played by the 'unspecified dietary' (*indéterminés alimentaires*), later called vitamins, which provided no energy but were nonetheless essential to normal life, would be clarified from the 1910s onwards. Before that, the food question also attracted microbiological expertise against adulterated products, which developed into one of the most useful applications of germ theories in the public sphere as early as the 1890s.[6] At the same time, the question of infant feeding motivated scientific research and led to the elaboration of new milk formulas devised for normal or sick children. In Switzerland, the local industry (Nestlé, Guigoz) quickly provided standardised formulas (*farines lactées*), which would finally contribute to the diminution of infant death rates.

And yet, in spite of these achievements, food experts failed to convince the medical hierarchy of their impeccable scientific status, at least in Switzerland. This was due to three reasons: first, most of them were related to new specialisations such as paediatrics, still a newcomer in the medical galaxy;[7] second, the food question remained more or less a gendered issue, which did little to improve its scientific status among the male-dominated medical elite;[8] and, third, certain newly devised food products (milk formulas as well as artificially malt-enriched products) were still established on an empirical basis: no one could yet explain, let alone prove, why these products did (or did not) work.[9] For the time being, the medical hierarchy remained sceptical of these nutritional 'facts', and only admitted the usefulness of nutritional expertise in a much reduced range of medical cases (metabolic dysfunctions such as diabetes, obesity, gout or chronic digestive pathologies). This marginalized status of dietetic expertise, in spite of intense lobbying, was clearly displayed in hospitals, where nutrition experts remained under the clinician's guidance.[10] It was not until the 1930s that academic positions in nutrition were created in French-speaking Switzerland.[11] Until then, compared to the microbiological disciplines which were reigning supreme in the medical field, dieticians could only claim minor academic posts, revealing the rift that was being widened between the old continent and the US experience with regards to the scientific status of nutrition experts.[12]

This modest spectrum of dietetics achievements may very well explain why nutrition experts had to turn to new partners outside of the academic hierarchy for public recognition: first of all, they found scientific patronage within the booming agro-alimentary or pharmaceutical industries (Nestlé, Roche, Wander, Maggi,

Guigoz, Knorr), which were eager to attract their expert knowledge and experience. Indeed, scientific experiments in nutrition were often financed by private industry.[13] This alliance gave birth to a new kind of mass consumption, launching new kinds of standardised products on the food market (synthetic vitamins or items artificially enriched with vitamins, minerals, amino-acids and hormones), with a growing use of advertising in the medical and general media.[14] From then on, the science of nutrition was reaching new territories: since life had been clearly proved to be both fuelled by energetic supplies and by tiny vitamin contributions, new physiological researches were launched to establish the minimum amount of food necessary to survive for each and every category of human being, according to climate, gender, type of work and age (plus, later, the possible doping effects of vitamins-enriched products). This combination of new scientific and industrial expertise related to nutrition led to a new ambition, that of creating a wholly scientific food ration, providing both energy and vital components, while helping build a better race, stronger and resistant to infection.[15] Indeed, some nutrition experts clearly expressed these promethean goals, making them clearly palatable for political movements thriving on the degeneration/regeneration obsession.

Establishing a healthy diet: a *Lebensreform* objective

Not only was the food question at the top of the agenda of large-scale business corporations, it also inspired new ways of coping with health and illness.[16] Since the beginning of the twentieth century, alternative therapies strongly associated with food reform had begun to develop. At a time when the medical marketplace had evolved into something of a giant microbiological network of laboratory research, practitioners such as Dr Bircher in his Zurich sanatorium developed a combination of alternative therapies to attract their clients, linking hydrotherapy or physiotherapy to food reform mostly based on vegetarian and non-cooked dishes (like the famous *Birchermuesli*). Often, the professional support that nutrition experts failed to muster within the academic world, was found instead within such alternative or *Lebensreform* milieus, which were developed from the eugenicist debates from the end of the nineteenth century. As elsewhere in Europe or the USA,[17] the question of infant protection, and notably the infant feeding problem, figured prominently among their preoccupations, which explains their early contribution to the popularisation of vitamins' therapeutic or preventive effects (against rickets especially).[18] Besides, their regard for food questions fitted neatly into a political agenda bent on reforming the Swiss citizen's modern way of life. Swiss families, according to such nutritional experts, were on the verge of moral and physical degeneration, largely due to the effects of the mass consumption society.[19] The consumption practices of young people were especially frowned upon by these moral entrepreneurs, both as symbols of their delinquency and of their falling victim to a materialistic way of life promoted by the modern consumer economy: induced to drink, have fun, and gobble down unhealthy food, these hedonistic consumers ignored or disregarded the consequences of their individualistic mindset. Young mothers were the main targets of these criticisms, especially when they indulged themselves in leisurely activities which impinged on the time dedicated to their babies' needs: 'To sacrifice her child's health for the sake of her pleasure is a crime,' was a credo consistently preached by many social hygiene specialists.[20] Besides, this exploded *Lebensreform* network carried in its wake a wide range of alternative groups (vegetarian propagandists), sectarian movements (Theosophy) or heterodox medical practitioners (homeopathy), all of which found in the food reform experiments ideas to back up their strident appeals to purity, simplicity and harmony, which were, in turn, deeply embedded within an overt anti-modernism.[21] Thus, a reaction against modern consuming behaviour appeared as early as the 1920s as a common ground for these hitherto scattered pressure groups.[22]

Since the end of the First World War, the food market in urban Switzerland had been transformed by the development of modern department stores and the growth of cooperative organizations.[23] Even if the level of poverty was still threatening large groups of working and lower middle-class families, the twentieth-century consumer was nevertheless dazzled with new consuming opportunities. This may well have been especially true for rural migrants attracted to regional capitals such as Geneva and Lausanne: in town, they benefited from much more diversified food products than in the countryside, where a monotonous and highly imbalanced diet of potatoes and indigenous vegetables, brown bread and bacon by-products – all washed down with a generous amount of alcohol – was still the rule.[24] Besides, a growing number of consumers were enjoying the new range of products offered by the food industry, such as refined sugar and sweets, white bread, various kinds of meat, pasta and ready-made tinned food: financially attractive, easy to shop, cook, and preserve, hygienically controlled by their household experts, these radically new forms of foodstuffs soon conquered a rather wide clientele in the urban environment, especially overburdened working mothers.

It was precisely these developments which incensed the morally prurient advocates of social hygiene. As early as the 1920s, their special 'healthy food' committees began to lobby against what they considered a lack of common sense that pushed modest families (and especially working-class mothers) to indulge in unhygienic food habits (eating white instead of brown bread, abandoning vegetables for canned foods and pasta, indulging children in their 'irrational' need for sweets). This was the crucial point at which the special expertise from the new science of nutrition was eagerly sought after and confidently given.[25] Indeed, nutrition experts offered scientifically-corroborated evidence of the potentially harmful effects of the new habits of the urban consumer. The bread question particularly acquired a symbolic status, as science could prove that refined white bread contained fewer of the vitamin components that played a crucial role in the assimilation cycle of other micro-nutriments essential in the fight against infectious disease.[26] Thus, individuals indulging in modern refined food were labelled as guilty contributors to a weakening national racial stock.

Besides, the nutrition experts of the 1930s were extremely keen on underlining their new motto of *équilibre alimentaire* (balanced diet), pointing out the delicate balance necessary to human survival and well-being.[27] This notion of *équilibre alimentaire* soon gained a special aura in the discourse of social hygiene groups. Indeed, it fitted most conveniently within a *Weltanschauung* asserting the cardinal values of bourgeois moral order and philanthropic rationale: balance, reason, restraint, harmony, order, stability and most of all, self-control (*versus* faults traditionally associated with the popular masses' pleasure-seeking instincts). On the eve of the Second World War, scientific arguments on proper food hygiene were deeply integrated into the general framework of social hygiene propaganda, offering an expert legitimation to their mixture of moral restraint and social discipline. Among many other consequences, it should be emphasized that this scientific support was pivotal in arguing for the reinforcement of housework training for young girls, a project traditionally cherished by social hygiene advocates but hitherto only partially achieved.[28] Since the end of the 1930s, the scientific evidence gathered around the crucial importance of rationalised cooking to the necessary preservation of vitamins supplied a new rationale for the necessity of *enseignement ménager* for young girls and teenagers, future caretakers of the family's nutritional balance. Scientific cooking thus became a vital prerequisite for a steady nation's health. Indeed, if Swiss people were suffering from latent malnutrition, the blame was not to be entirely attributed to their economic circumstances (even if the after-effects of the 1930s crisis were not totally ignored), but also to the mothers' lack of knowledge of nutrition.[29] A partial consensus was thus built up around the cure to be applied against ill-mannered motherhood and its pathological aftermath: the option was to re-educate the public (women and mothers first), to abandon their unbalanced food habits and return to the mythical austere food of the ancient Swiss farmer. Swiss consumers had to be convinced that self-inflicted rationed food would prove beneficial to their health.

This kind of dietary orthopedics nevertheless fell short of reaching its intended target. In the wake of pre-war economic recovery, mass consumption did not show any signs of going away. Indeed, for a majority of consumers, emerging from a twenty-year crisis of unemployment and daily struggle, the immediate benefits of industrial food-products easily outnumbered hygienists' threats. Actually, social hygienists failed to achieve any general implementation of their austere ideals: except for cooking manuals used to educate schoolgirls during the 1930s, the 'balanced diet' obsession, in Switzerland as elsewhere, only prospered in those *Lebensreform*-minded middle-class families who could afford it.[30]

Besides, outside certain social hygiene circles, no such specialist consenus existed on food reform and malnutrition, especially when some alarmist nutrition experts pleaded for a general supply of vitamins in order to compensate for the (over) estimated diet deficiencies which were supposedly ruining the nation's strength. For these experts, some of them associated with industrial firms producing vitamin-enriched products, the extent of the nation's deficiencies was so large that it would prove useless to try to fill them by a simple return to raw food and adequate cooking. They looked across the Atlantic towards the United States, in order to develop a pragmatic solution to the diet problem: instead of calling for a hypothetical change of food habits (a process which might well prove to be unpopular, long and unsuccessful), US experts had chosen to supplement the new industrially-produced and refined food (first of all white bread) with a mix of standardized synthetic vitamins.[31]

But this solution was strongly opposed by many Swiss experts. First, the opposition to systematic distribution of synthetic vitamins stemmed from the 'balanced diet' experts and their social hygiene allies, who feared it would deter a majority of consumers from altering their poor eating habits, thus ruining their reformist strategy. They stuck to their balanced diet ideal, which was supposed to offer a natural supply of micro-nutrients. In addition, the efficiency of vitamin prescriptions was subject to strong doubts in the medical world, since nutrition experts were not even able to reach agreement on crucial matters such as the actual extent of vitamin-deficiency.[32] Also, the question as to which method it was best to use to detect a vitamin deficiency was still unclear, since no easy-to-implement methods of diagnosing vitamin deficiencies were available.[33] All this undoubtedly fed a widespread scepticism towards vitamin therapies among the medical elites.[34]

On the eve of war, nutrition expertise was deeply divided as to the best strategy to be adopted towards a food reform deemed inevitable: those associated with *Lebensreform* or social hygiene milieus advocated a puritan doctrine of balanced diet implying a radical change of food consuming and producing, while others favoured a supplementation tactic, either within the free market or endorsed by sickness funds.[35] At the same time, outside of their own expert circles, nutrition reformers were challenged over their seemingly unconvincing data, their inner dissensions or their sectarian profile, while politicians trusted in the food industry to guarantee the consumer's safety.[36] As for the general public, it knew little about these nutrition experts before the war, although circumstances in the 1940s would provide the advocates of the balanced diet with an unexpected medium to spread its credo.[37]

Testing the diet: the experience of war

When the Second World War broke out, the Swiss population was told it had to brace itself for shortages and to be prepared to rely on its indigenous food products. Prior to 1939, consumer needs had been widely met by mass importations, but the war prevented the continuation of this situation. Food had to be rationed not only along strictly calculated proportions, but according to the capabilities of national food production: thus, potatoes became a prominent feature in the nation's diet, while rarefied cereals had to be distributed sparingly. The story of war rations in Switzerland has already been told elsewhere, and the question which arises here is not so much that of the nature of rationing than of its justification according to the facts and knowledge relating to nutritional science.[38] Indeed, whereas the Swiss rations had first been dictated by quantities of national produce, it was their dietary quality that would be mostly advertised to the public. Thus, the enrolment of nutrition experts within the system of wartime controls was crucial to the elaboration of consumers' rations along the lines of minimal energy (calories) and protective value requirements (vitamins, minerals, hormones), especially since science was to be enrolled to sustain the nation's morale: this may very well explain why the federal wartime food administration put the 'balanced-diet' experts at the forefront of dietary resistance, instead of their 'supplementation' counterparts.

Indeed, 'balanced-diet' experts, familiar with restraint-oriented arguments, were stridently vocal in standing up for the official rations. As early as the end of 1939, whether on their own initiative or following an administrative mandate, they publicly championed the cause of the war diet, relentlessly celebrating the 'desirable restrictions'.[39] Pointing out that Swiss food rations held no less than 3000 calories, (well above those offered by neighbouring countries) they dutifully spread a confident gospel towards administrative efficiency and foresight: 'Let us not complain ... the starvation spectre is definitely removed, even if the war should long last'.[40]

Their names, hitherto rather hidden from the media, would soon become familiar to many readers. Nutrition expertise was beginning to permeate the whole spectrum of local media (general, military, feminist, cooperative), popularising its interwar nutritional terminology perfectly embodied in the Swiss war rations: 'Our food is now much better balanced than before the war'.[41] This prolific striving to convince Swiss consumers about the value of their everyday diet provided no room for any doubt: whenever a question arose that could not be solved in a reassuring way, nutrition experts either switched to an incomprehensible jargon (artificial sugar might be dangerous because of its *méthémoglobinisant* effect) or eluded the question enitrely.[42] Asked about his opinion as an expert, one such nutrionist curtly informed his audience in 1941 that the daily intake in micro-nutrients 'must be in keeping with nutrition laws' exigencies'.[43] It seems as if what they stood for during the war was not so much the food rations themselves but the 'natural' and balanced version of nutrition expertise they had previously promoted during their interwar activities. In many papers published in much the same vein during the war, Swiss citizens were thus given an unrelenting lesson on their eating habits, which strictly followed the lines implanted during the interwar years by former pioneers of food reform: 'Let us eat less, but let us eat better'.[44]

The gospel of traditional good food (brown bread, dairy products and vegetables, 'everyday menus of our dear old Swiss ancestors'[45]) was enthusiastically recited in every possible variation by professional experts and their allies, among whom, not surprisingly, the social hygiene movement leaders figured prominently.[46] Indeed, the blaming of pre-war irrational food consumption now acquired a patriotic glaze that served the interests of both experts still trying to impose themselves upon food policy and eugenicist movements, eager to acquire administrative mandates for the re-education of the masses (particularly women, who 'must draw their inspiration from the science of nutrition, well advanced in our country, and carry out its diffusion').[47] Nutrition experts collaborated in this food orthopaedics ambition in words and deeds: not only was their advice on rational food hungrily sought after, but they helped some hitherto dormant *Lebensreform* lobbying groups to perform their patriotic mission, for example in setting up dressing, drying, and preserving demonstrations. Indeed, the art of hygienic cooking, essential for the preservation of micro-nutriments, rapidly reached an unexpected degree of urgency: given the level of inflation, it appeared vital to teach housewives how to maximize the daily rations by learning how to fight food waste, while preparing and preserving non-rationed and vitamin-rich domestic vegetables and fruit. This seemed especially true for working-class women, for whom middle-class feminine associations were eager to drill according to the 'balanced diet' credo of their expert allies.[48]

The implementation of this rational attitude towards food nonetheless came across a myriad of impediments, which nutrition experts failed to admit even when social anxieties or actual pathologies eventually emerged. First, experts refused to publicly admit that social status could have any effect on nutrition: if a family (and above all a working-class mother) could not make do with her allotted ration, it could only prove that she was a bad cook and poor patriot. Concluding an investigation on popular diets directed by the federal administration for war economy, a young female social worker sternly noted that: 'During our investigation, some criticisms have been made against the rationing system, but we have considered them neither serious nor grounded. Besides, these people could very well realize by themselves that their rations were adequate '.[49] No hint was ever given about the fact that some poor families could not afford indigenous raw vegetables or fruit, non-rationed but too costly. What is more, the practical problems that many people encountered when trying to adapt to this new mode of eating were systematically brushed away. For example, nobody seemed to be aware that leguminous vegetables (highly-celebrated by experts because they were rich in vitamins) had to be cooked for quite a long time, in a time of severe coal rationing, by working-class women already overburdened with the privations of a war economy. Despite the increasingly apparent reality that almost everyone was losing weight at an alarming rate no comment from nutrition experts ever appeared in the public newspapers other than a complacent *satisfecit:* chorusing in the local media, nutrition experts rejoiced that their dreams had come true with the swift eradication of obesity, dental troubles and cardiovascular diseases.[50] Even more striking, they failed to be true to facts concerning the gradual decrease of the ration, from the 3000 calories of 1939 to 2400 in autumn 1942, then 1440 calories in March 1943; for some experts, the remaining 1000 calories could easily be found if people drew from the indigenous vegetable and fruit stocks. But the physiological fact that raw vegetables and fruit or non-refined bread, if eaten in too large quantities, badly prepared or inadequately washed (not to mention adulterated food), could cause digestive troubles or even intoxications (mostly through intestinal parasites) was not given the publicity it should have deserved for the consumer's sake. Finally, when rations had to be seriously cut to the extent that they no longer even contained the basic *équilibre alimentaire* and harmonious proportions so praised by the nutrition experts, some of them still provided reassuring data about the inter-changeability of the rations' components ('the current augmentation of non-refined cereals in our food ration will bear absolutely no ill effects on our health').[51]

This deliberate downplaying by the 'balanced-diet' experts of the possible ill-effects of rationed food was by no means the rhetoric adopted by all. When communicating through the professional media,[52] they did make mention of such topical issues as the digestive troubles caused by massive raw food consumption,[53] especially for young children,[54] the general loss of weight caused by deficiencies in food intake,[55] and the alarming dietary status of the working class.[56] Moreover, some experts asserted that a massive supplementation of synthetic vitamins was highly desirable for fragile people,[57] and knew that such treatments were already available (in the army[58] and in some schools[59]). The pre-war breach between 'balanced-diet' experts and their 'synthetic supplements' colleagues began to reappear: indeed, some of the latter volunteered advice on vitamin supplements, for example in presiding over conferences including informative/advertising films lent by the Swiss pharmaceutical industry.[60] Still, they refused to let their wringing scientific doubts or most worrying medical data slip into the mainstream media.

How did the general population react to these controversial issues? Nobody could ignore the fact that the nation's health did not quite match the levels proclaimed by the nutrition experts. For one thing, many people fell ill during the war, especially from 1944 onwards.[61] Traditional infectious diseases were visibly gaining ground, due to a weakening of peoples' natural immune defences. This spectacular breach in the nation's health could hardly pass unnoticed, especially for families whose children were easy prey to infectious onslaughts.[62] Most of them finally recovered (the mortality rate did not fall in any notable way during the war), but the personal experiences of this malnutrition-related morbidity, even if minor compared to neighbouring countries, may well have provoked alarm in the ordinary citizen. Understandably, many of them tried to resort to the black market, the fraudulent activities of which boomed during the war (65,000 offences were registered for 1942, and more than 100,000 for 1943[63]). But police controls and money sanctions were severe. Given the circumstances, it is no wonder that families went to their general practitioner to get medical exemptions to the war ration.

Table 5.1 Medically prescribed supplements granted for Geneva canton (1943-1945)

	Sugar, rice, pasta, leguminous vegetables, flour, butter, oil, cheese, bread, meat (kg)	Milk and cream (litres)	Eggs (pces)	Coffee, meat, chocolate, cheese (points granted)
1943	35,927	149,991	-	-
1944	27,839	178,754	8,191	7,046,400
1945	28,971	221,195	10,524	24,279,500

Source: 'Rapports annuels de l'office cantonal de l'économie de guerre', published in the annual *Rapports du Conseil d'Etat* (Genève, 1939-1947).

Indeed, rank-and-file physicians did not hesitate to transgress the rules set by their nutrition expert colleagues, sometimes at the cost of provoking reprimands[64] ('the need of quantitatively more abundant rations is infinitely less than these exaggerated demands for dietary supplements would make believe'[65]). The experts had undoubtedly failed to convince both general practitioners and consumers, probably because they would not drop their monolithic argument of the beneficial side of scientifically balanced rations, at a time when people experienced daily physical hardship induced by nutritional dearth.

Facing these unwavering certitudes, consumers finally chose to cheat the rationing system, be it with GPs' complicity or simply with consumerism. Indeed, another resource to compensate for the limitations of the food ration (even if cooked according to scientific guidelines), was to resort to the offers available on the drug market. The growing amount of advertising for vitamin-enriched items, both in scientific and general journals,[66] as well as the recurring mention that they were not rationed, tends to show that the balanced diet was not the only solution available to panicky consumers. Supplemented products, whether under their classical brand name (Nestlé, Roche, Wander) or in the numerous marked-down parcels sold in cooperative shops, attracted a new clientele during wartime, underlining the general scepticism (to say the least) towards the welcome effects of this balanced diet.

Beyond the wartime diet: nutrition experts and the post-war Swiss mass consumer

This chapter has outlined the field of wartime nutritional expertise from the historical background of the interwar years, when certain nutritional scientists began to incite their compatriots to graciously submit themselves to a stricter diet. Facing new challenges created by a burgeoning mass consumer society on the one hand, and by the reconfiguration of the medical marketplace after the pasteurian revolution on the other, some nutritional experts had begun to ally themselves to the social hygiene movement. This alliance largely benefited the eugenicist-minded new philanthropic lobbies, who eagerly welcomed any scientific rationale that would support their crusade for national purity, social harmony and cultural traditionalism, such as was contained within the newly established nutritional concept of the balanced diet. But while this alliance met with limited success in the 1930s, largely due to the lack of consensus between nutrition experts, nevertheless, as soon as the war broke out, food specialists were finally given the large audience they had so consistently looked for. Indeed, from the fall of 1939 onwards, the national media would eagerly ask them to contribute to the superior patriotic mission of enlightening the Swiss citizen on food issues.

But this expert position which opened up new avenues of public legitimacy for the 'balanced-diet' food experts also led them to a radical dead-end when it came to their credibility in the eyes of ordinary consumers. Strongly associated with a monolithic defence of the scientifically-based rations they had helped formulate, the nutrition experts had to face the growing discontent and scepticism of families no longer convinced (if they ever had been) that scientific rationing would make them happier and healthier. Moreover, instead of distancing themselves from social and moral hygiene movements pursuing their own puritan agenda during the war, they tied themselves to a bandwagon of anti-modern phraseology which did not lead them to keep in touch, let alone sympathise with, the consumers' needs or cravings. At the end of the war, these nutrition experts thus found themselves not only cut off from the consumers, but also from the GPs whom they had tried to by-pass during their ambitious climb toward public recognition. Subsequently, in the immediate post-war period, the death knell was sounded for some of the experts' hopes of establishing a preventive medicine based on the balanced diet ideal. Indeed, the discovery of the effectiveness of antibiotics against infectious diseases boosted the microbiological paradigm at the expense of the food-reform alternative to citizen's well-being. In the ensuing years, the pharmaceutical industry put many efficient drugs against metabolic pathologies on the market, at a time when the generalization of welfare systems allowed a vast majority of people to afford them.[67] Balanced diet thus no longer seemed to be the wonder-cure against contemporary disease, and Swiss nutrition experts, as elsewhere in Europe, retreated into a rather obscure academic position.[68] The consumer-patients now preferred to establish their own food habits and to take an appropriate medicine to soothe any occurring trouble, instead of resorting to any preventive food *régime*. In the long-run, nutrition experts most probably proved to have been right about the disastrous effects of over-sugared, over-fat and unbalanced diets on the Nation's health: but their strategy of placing consumers in front of an uncomfortable clear-cut alternative between the benefit of dearth and the curse of abundance, whether in time of peace or crisis, only resulted in the smothering of their arguments amidst the seemingly all-conquering growth of the mass consumer society.

Notes

1 'Etat sanitaire de l'Europe en 1942-1943', *Médecine et Hygiène*, 15 March 1945. For extreme cases of wartime mortality rate in France: Isabelle von Bueltzingsloewen, 'Les aliénés morts de faim dans les hôpitaux psychiatriques français sous l'occupation', *Vingtième siècle*, October-December 2002: 99-115.

2 Jakob Tanner, 'Incorporated Knowledge and the Making of the Consumer: Nutritional Science and Food Habits in the USA, Germany and Switzerland (1930s to 50s)'; paper (cited with author's permission) presented to conference, *Knowing Consumers: Actors, Images, Identities in Modern History*, Centre for Interdisciplinary Research, Bielefeld, February 2004.

3 Paul Sanders, *Histoire du marché noir 1940-1946* (Paris, 2001).

4 H. Kamminga and A. Cunningham (eds), *The Science and Culture of Nutrition, 1840-1940* (Amsterdam, 1995).

5 Lucie Randoin et Henri Simmonet, *Les vitamines* (Paris, 1939), pp. 57-65.

6 Alessandro Stanziani, *Histoire de la qualité alimentaire, XIXe-XXe siècles* (Paris, 2005).

7 In 1946, paediatricians represented only 3.7 per cent of the Swiss medical profession.

8 The paediatrician seems to have benefitted from a much better position in the USA and in France, according to Alisa Klaus, *Every Child a Lion: The Origins of Maternal and Infant Health Policy in the United States and France, 1890-1920* (Ithaca, 1993). Recent studies are more prudent: Judith Sealander, *The Failed Century of the Child: Governing America's Young in the 20th Century* (Cambridge, 2003).

9 Malted products were systematically tried for babies with digestive troubles. At the end of the 1920s, it became clear that in associating B vitamins and flour, these formulas worked to the assimilation of other vitamins present in milk.

10 Dr P. Besse, *Preuves de la nécessité d'un enseignement médical diététique* (Geneva, 1920).

11 In 1934 at the cantonal hospital of Geneva.

12 Fernando Salmon, 'A New Diet, a New Hospital in 1930s Spain', in Kamminga and Cunningham, *The Science*, pp. 259-87. In the same volume, Rima Apple is less optimistic about the status of female experts of nutrition ('Science Gendered: Nutrition in the United States, 1840-1940', pp. 129-54).

13 Many medical papers advertised the use of Nestlé and Wander milk formulas during interwar years.

14 Sally M. Horrocks, 'The Business of Vitamins: Nutrition Science and the Food Industry in Interwar Britain', in Kamminga and Cunningham, *The Science*, pp. 235-58. Adel P. den Hartog, 'Modern Nutritional Problems and Historical Nutrition Research, with special reference to the Netherlands', in H. J. Teuteberg (ed.), *European Food History: A Research Review* (Leicester, London, New-York, 1992), pp. 56-70.

15 Lucie Randoin and Henri Simmonet, *Les données et les inconnues du problème alimentaire* (2 vols, Paris, 1927).

16 L. Margaret Barnett, 'Every Man His Own Physician': Dietetic Fads, 1890-1914', in Kamminga and Cunningham, *The Science*, pp. 155-78.

17 Greta Jones, *Social Hygiene in Twentieth-Century Britain* (London, 1986); Marijke Gijswijt-Hofstra and Hilary Marland (eds), *Cultures of Child Health in Britain and the Netherlands in the Twentieth Century* (Amsterdam, 2003). In Switzerland the '*Cartel romand d'hygiène sociale et morale*' was active in French-speaking areas, and the National Foundation for the Protection of Children (Pro Juventute) at a federal level, with other related associations (Pro Familia).

18 Dr S. Chapuis, 'Quelques mots sur l'alimentation artificielle du nourrisson dans la pratique générale', *Pro Juventute* (1921): 59-66.

19 M. Veillard, 'Pro Familia', *Pro Juventute* (1922): 284-7 denounces the pursuit of luxury and modern conveniences, abortion, divorces, adultery, atheism, licentious habits, egotism, Malthusianism. The question of family disintegration was familiar first to philanthropic and later to eugenics milieus on both sides of the Atlantic: see Sherri Broder, *Tramps, Unfit Mothers and Neglected Children: Negotiating the Family in Late 19th Century Philadelphia* (Philadelphia, 2002); Frank Mort, *Dangerous Sexualities: Medico-Moral Politics in England since 1830* (London, New-York, 2000).

20 Dr S. Kleynmann, *La bonne nurse; manuel de puériculture pratique* (Lausanne), 1938, p. 40.

21 *Force et santé, almanach végétarien et naturiste Suisse*, 1942.

22 The consumer issues were by no means limited to health-related effects: for other developments see A. Chatriot, M.-E. Chessel, M. Hilton (eds), *Au nom du consommateur: consommation et politique en Europe et aux Etats-Unis au XXe siècle* (Paris, 2004).

23 *75 ans de coopération (1868-1943)*, Genève, 1943: 39 per cent of Geneva families were members of the cooperative movements in 1942 (only 19 per cent in 1900).

24 Alfred Gigon, 'L'alimentation à la campagne', *Revue suisse d'hygiène* (1930): 561-569.

25 The Food Committee of the *Cartel romand d'hygiène sociale et morale* gathered 15 medical experts on nutrition (versus 5 lay members).

26 Dr H. Muller, 'Taux d'extraction de la farine et qualités biologiques du pain', *Revue médicale de la Suisse romande* (1939): 560-67.

27 L. Randoin and H. Simmonet, *Les vitamines*, pp. 212- 14.

28 The Swiss foundation for the protection of children, *Pro Juventute*, published numerous papers on this issue from 1920 on.

29 Dr R. Warnery, 'Comment préparer la jeune fille à son rôle de mère?', *Pro Juventute* (1933): 247-52: nowadays 'the children's health and even their life is endangered by their mother's incapacities and ignorance', as some 'young mothers, shaking off every yoke, abandon their offspring to the *Pouponnière* and prefer running to new and always deceiving adventures'.

30 Michael Nelson, 'Social trends in British diet, 1860-1980', in C. Geissler and D. J. Oddy (eds), *Food, Diet and Economic Change, Past and Present* (Leicester, 1993), pp. 101-20.

31 Dr Messerli, 'L'aliment complet', *Revue suisse d'hygiène* (1932): 789-791.

32 E. Burnet, W.R. Aykroyd, *L'alimentation et l'hygiène publique* (offprint of the *Bulletin trimestriel de l'organisation d'hygiène de la Société des Nations* (Genève), 1935.

33 Jeffrey P. Brosco, 'Weight Charts and Well Child Care: When the Paediactrician Became the Expert in Child Health', in A. M. Stern and H. Markel (eds), *Formative Years: Children's Health in the United States, 1800-2000*) (Ann Arbor, 2002), pp. 91-120.

34 Dr G. Bickel, 'Quand et comment faut-il prescrire les vitamines?', *Praxis* (December 1942): 960.

35 The pharmaceutical industry supplied many paediatric services with synthetic vitamins, which then partook of the general feeding routine taught to both middle-class mothers and nurses students (Dr M. Pictet, 'Des vitamines: prévenir vaut mieux que guérir', *Archives du Bon Secours* (Geneva school of nurses) (1932): 1-11.

36 Jim Philips and Michael French, 'Adulteration and Food Law, 1899-1939', *Twentieth Century British History*, 9:3 (1998): 350-69.

37 'Numbers of scientific progresses have been made during the first half of the 20th century, but we lacked time to popularise or implement them', Dr P. Besse, *L'alimentation comme problème national* (Genève, 1937).

38 Joëlle Droux, 'Rationnement et consommation en Suisse (1939-1945)', in Chatriot, Chessel and Hilton, *Au nom du consommateur*, pp. 63-79.

39 'La Suisse au milieu de l'Europe en guerre: restrictions souhaitables', *Le mouvement féministe*, 5 April 1941.

40 Dr H. Muller, 'Ne nous plaignons pas', *Le coopérateur genevois*, 20 August 1942.

41 Dr H. Muller, 'Situation et perspectives', *Le coopérateur genevois*, 31 December 1942.

42 Dr L. M. Sandoz, 'Sucres naturels et édulcorants artificiels', *Le coopérateur genevois*, 30 November 1944.

43 Dr L. M. Sandoz, 'L'alimentation du travailleur', *Le coopérateur genevois*, 25 September 1941. From the same, in *Le mouvement féministe*, 25 September 1943: 'Here in Switzerland, scientific research about tuberculosis risks is more optimistic than elsewhere'.

44 Dr L. M. Sandoz, 'Mangeons moins, mais mangeons mieux', *Le mouvement féministe*, 24 October 1942.

45 Dr H. Muller, 'Le lait, source de vie et de santé', *Le coopérateur genevois*, 28 September 1939.

46 The 'Food hygiene committee' of the *Société genevoise d'utilité publique* organized many conferences and brochures with local nutrition experts from 1939 to 1946.

47 Dr L. M. Sandoz, 'La valeur sociale de l'alimentation', *Le mouvement féministe*, 22 February 1941.

48 'Quelques réflexions sur le dernier rationnement', *Le mouvement féministe*, 21 March 1942, censuring the 'superstition of meat among modest classes'.

49 Catherine Schweizer, *Enquête sur le régime alimentaire actuel d'un groupe de dix familles de condition très modeste* (Geneva, 1943).

50 Dr E. Martin, C. Schweizer, 'Enquête sur l'état de nutrition des enfants genevois de l'âge scolaire, avant, pendant la guerre', *Revue suisse d'hygiène* (1945): 468-72: the current 'nutrition status is much better than in 1918 (flu!) and more balanced than in 1930'.

51 Dr H. Muller, 'Pain et pommes de terre, base de notre alimentation', *Le coopérateur genevois*, 21 January 1943.

52 *Glandes endocrines et vitamines* (Geneva), 1943 (special teaching session at the Medicine Faculty of Geneva).

53 Dr Z. Ali, 'Alimentation de guerre et affections du tube digestif', *Praxis*, December 1943, pp. 889-90. Dr L. M. Sandoz, 'Les crudités et l'enfance', *Pro Juventute*, 1945, pp. 252-5.

54 Dr J. Taillens, 'Faut-il donner des légumes aux nourrissons ?', *Revue médicale de la Suisse romande* (1944): 660-67.

55 Dr L. M. Sandoz, 'Le pain et l'armée', *Revue militaire suisse* (1943): 429-42: 'the population currently receives only the third, or half to the maximum, its daily need of B1 vitamin' (p. 439).

56 Drs A. Fleisch et C. Petitpierre, 'Vitamines et sels minéraux en Suisse avant et pendant la guerre', *Schweizerische Medizinische Wochenschrift* (1945): 680-83.

57 Dr P. Gautier, 'Equilibre alimentaire, vitamines et croissance du nourrisson; cours de perfectionnement organisé par la Faculté de médecine de Genève' (Geneva, 1943), pp. 300-315 ; Dr L. M. Sandoz, 'Le standard de vie de nos écoliers et son influence', *Pro Juventute* (1944): 282-4: 'Today, one can be sure that nine times out of ten, the diminution in calories is associated with imbalance and nutritive deficiencies'.

58 Dr L. M. Sandoz, 'Applications militaires de la diététique et de la pharmacothérapie', *Revue militaire suisse* (1943): 303-17, 355-69.

59 Dr L. M. Sandoz, 'Les carences alimentaires et les restrictions', *Pro Juventute* (1943): 6-18.

60 Hoffmann-Laroche, for example: *Rapport annuel de la Société genevoise d'hygiène publique* (Geneva), 1940, p. 96.

61 11,333 cases of infectious diseases registered in Switzerland for 1941, 72,232 for 1944, 25,121 for 1945 (*Rapport 1945-1946 du Cartel Romand d'hygiène sociale et morale* (Lausanne, 1946).

62 644 children hospitalised in the paediatric services of the Geneva cantonal hospital in 1938, 1,010 in 1942, 1,234 in 1944: *Annual Reports of the Cantonal Hospital of Geneva* (Geneva, 1937 – 1947).

63 'La lutte contre le marché noir', *L'illustré*, 19 August 1943.

64 In Geneva, the local commission of nutrition experts for the war economy was staffed by the same experts who partook in social hygiene lobbying against modern food habits before 1939 (Archives of State, Geneva , Intérieur R2, War economy).

65 *Rapport annuel de la Société genevoise d'utilité publique* (Geneva, 1943), p. 195.

66 See, for example, the advertisements for a drug, 'exact compensator for under-nourishment', inserted in a medical journal for GPs where many papers regarding food-deficiencies were edited ('A propos des carences alimentaires: le TOT'HEMA', *Praxis* (December 1943): 855.

67 Sophie Chauveau, *L'invention pharmaceutique: la pharmacie française entre l'Etat et la société au XXe siècle* (Paris, 1999): 273sqq.

68 David F. Smith, 'Nutrition Science and the Two World Wars', in David F. Smith (ed.), *Nutrition in Britain: Science, Scientists and Politics in the 20th century* (London, 1997), pp. 142-65.

Chapter 6

Shopping for an 'Economic Miracle': Gendered Politics of Consumer Citizenship in Divided Germany

Katherine Pence

Germany emerged from World War II defeated, occupied by foreign powers, and plagued with material shortages. But within a decade, the nation witnessed radical transformation through division into two states and rival 'Economic Miracles'. The competition between capitalist and socialist consumer cultures in the 1950s was particularly emblematic for this reconstruction. With the Cold War division of Germany each state worked to bolster its legitimacy by promising its own 'Economic Miracle' complete with abundance and the pleasure of consumption. As the ones most responsible for subsistence in the postwar years,[1] female shoppers particularly demanded state responsibility for mediating shortage and ushering in prosperity. In return, each state urged loyalty from its citizens and active participation in the economy to help bring about this affluence. At the same time, the black market and eventually smuggling across the new German-German border made this task of forging consumer loyalty especially problematic. Molding responsible consumer-citizens in both East and West entailed constant tension. State policies designed to enlist shoppers as partners with a paternalistic state were coupled with efforts to contain 'deviant' shoppers. Women were empowered as expert consumers, but their power was strictly circumscribed and monitored by vigilant populations and Cold War regimes that scrutinized shopping choices.[2]

Citizenship in this sense is not just a legal category, but also a terrain of practices and subjective identities in which categories of inclusion and exclusion are perpetually enacted.[3] Citizens negotiated their relationship with the state as a social contract articulating their rights and duties for inclusion within the polity. In the twentieth century, the dawn of mass consumption has made consumer policy vital to this social contract.[4] While increasingly pressured to provide consumer affluence for its citizens, states also demanded that shoppers participate responsibly in the economy to make this promise a reality. Individually, shoppers could express political loyalty through private purchases that on their own or in aggregate would fuel their home economy. As organized groups in alliance with the government, what Lizabeth Cohen has called 'citizen consumers',[5] consumer experts could demand consumer protection and guide these masses toward such rational choices. Cohen suggests that in the United States, the ideal consumer in the postwar 'Consumers' Republic' was a 'purchaser as citizen' who served the national interest in a dynamic economy by pursuing personal material desires.[6] The contraposition of rival capitalist and socialist systems in Germany created tension between the mobilization of desire among 'purchasers as citizens' and the ongoing need to constrain and direct this desire for the sake of ideological commitment. This dynamic shaped the particular contours of Cold War German consumer-citizenship as the two Germanys worked to overcome shortage and launch their so-called 'Economic Miracles'.

Legacies of shortage after 1945

The German population reified the end of the war in 1945 as a Zero Hour or radical break with the Nazi past. From 1945 to 1949, Soviet, American, British and French military administrations abolished Nazi state institutions and attempted to democratize their occupation zones. The high political stakes of denazification and increasing Cold War tensions in a context of extreme material deprivation made this period an intensified moment for renegotiating the relationship between state and citizenry. Rationing and shortages made material concerns paramount for the German population after 1945.[7] The right to a better standard of living therefore became central to this new definition of citizenship as new states emerged.

Governmental regulation of consumption through rationing signaled a new era of state responsibility for ensuring a basic standard of living.[8] The rationing systems also reinforced the politicization of consumption by reflecting overt political agendas. At first the military occupiers aimed to keep calorie allotments low to punish the defeated nation. The lowest rations, fluctuating between 1000 and 1550 calories per day,[9] were dubbed 'hunger cards' or 'ascension cards'.[10] By 1947, heightening Cold War tensions transformed consumer policies from punishment to economic restoration and eventual promise of better standards of living.[11] Even the Soviet Zone's productivist strategies were underpinned by promises of consumer satisfaction.[12]

Still, even with the new desire to feed the German population more adequately, supplies were low and rations remained insufficient. The 'rubble women', who performed labour of reconstruction and familial subsistence, dominated the postwar landscape as they undertook the laborious task of standing in line for often up to five hours for scarce commodities.[13] These women, and especially housewives given the lowest rations since they were considered 'unproductive', had to devise means for attaining extra food and supplies. Local governments published recipes suggesting women sacrifice, 'make-do' with *ersatz* foods,[14] or remake worn out underwear remnants into 'pretty' lingerie.[15] One 1949 almanac offered a recipe that told, 'how one can bake a cake entirely without fat, without an egg, and without milk—that still tastes really good'.[16] Consumers could embody rational citizenship through committed sacrifice and extra labour. Consumers combined these recommended strategies with less acceptable subsistence behavior that challenged the official regimes. They traded on the black market, stole, falsified ration documents, and hoarded goods acquired in forbidden trips to trade directly with farmers.[17] German women also fraternized with occupational soldiers, out of love and affection, to gain material benefits, or both.[18] As a whole, these semi-licit forms of trade became symbols of 'deviance' posing a threat to the smooth functioning of the rationing systems and by extension the political regimes.

Perhaps most overtly challenging to political stability was grass-roots protest by hungry consumers. Hunger strikes, whether spontaneous or communist led,[19] took place throughout Germany especially after ration levels dipped in the harsh winter of 1946/47.[20] The United States introduced the Marshall Plan in 1947 to all of Western Europe including western Germany in part to keep such protests from leading to communist revolution.[21]

The mixture of legal and illegal strategies for negotiating shortage in the postwar years set the stage for consumer-citizenship to be defined in tension between dutiful and 'deviant' consumer behavior. Increasingly, each half of Germany promised material abundance in return for the population's loyalty to its economic system. Female shoppers continued to face pressure to conform to responsible models of consumer citizenship when the German Democratic Republic (GDR) in the East and the Federal Republic (FRG) in the West were founded in 1949. The first step toward the foundation of these two separate regimes was a watershed moment marked by spectacles designed to enhance desire for abundant commodities in the new Germanys: the dual currency reforms in 1948.

Consumer-citizens in the West German social market economy

In a Cold War departure from the four occupiers' original plans to make Germany's major economic decisions jointly, the British and American Zones, unified into Bizonia in 1947, initiated a separate Western currency reform in June 1948, which the French Zone also accepted in spring 1949. This reform was meant to revive the economy, eliminate the black market, pave the way for accepting the Marshall Plan, and usher in Economic Council Director and future FRG Economics Minister Ludwig Erhard's social-market economy. Erhard aimed for the West German currency reform to coincide with a miraculous spectacle of abundant goods appearing overnight in shop windows around the country, which made this moment the 'founding myth of West German society'.[22] This sense of rebirth is reflected in some eyewitnesses' descriptions of this 'miracle': 'Over night we were turned from ration coupon shoppers and supplicants into customers'.[23] Newly minted consumers took centre stage at the opening act of a Federal Republic that promoted desire for material goods.

However, new economic difficulties after the currency reform led to protests, during which unions, housewives, and the embryonic state negotiated who would represent consumers. Erhard's release of price controls meant rapid inflation; the return of hard currency and devaluation of savings coincided with unemployment.[24] The bursting shop-windows tormented poorer shoppers. As one housewife complained in an opinion survey, 'Today the shop windows awaken a thousand wishes, for which I have no money'.[25] According to one female critic, abundant but expensive displays could even 'lead to class hatred'.[26]

Driven by such resentment, female shoppers demanded fairer prices from shopkeepers and ultimately from political authorities. In their earliest protests, angry shoppers, mostly women[27] erupted in violent behavior such as 'bombarding the merchants with apples and tomatoes.[28] In the town of Recklinghausen, consumers upended market stands and ruined the seller's fruit.[29] In the American Zone, 'they distributed the much too expensive poultry, without caring about the objection of the merchants'.[30] These 'women's strikes' were mostly unorganized, but sometimes supported by the communist KPD party.[31] Women's grass-roots political activism helped solidify their role as primary consumer-citizen.

In their often violent and unruly manner, these female consumers demanded that economic and political officials respond to their needs. Though women proved their political importance through protest, they were increasingly expected to channel that power into forms that would aid the budding social-market economy. As the initial chaos of the post-currency reform subsided, trade unionists worked to discipline and co-opt this female consumer protest. The trade unions assumed a role as consumer representative to mold undisciplined women into respectable consumer-citizens. In a series of more organized consumer boycotts (*Käuferstreik*) staged after the reform, the trade unions empowered and proscribed women's actions as rational consumers. Now irresponsible women were held accountable for high prices rather than shopkeepers or politicians' economic policies. An image emerged of unreasonable housewives who had embarked on a frenzied buying spree and hoarded goods, thereby increasing demand and leading to inflation. A unionist explained:

> There was a great deal to buy again … It was no wonder that at first, despite all warnings, everyone purchased uncontrollably and without discipline … Who can blame the mother, if she finally buys for her children ... that which she has not only lacked for years, but also that which was also absolutely necessary for construction of the youthful bodies.[32]

This unionist urged respect for impetuous shoppers who only hoped to feed their children but also warned women against undisciplined and uncontrolled shopping. A flyer distributed at a 1948 'shoppers' strike' similarly reflected didactic attempts to control 'reckless' female buying behavior:

> German Housewife! Boycott! You have valuable money in your hands! Your husband worked hard for it with his own sweat! You sin against your family when you pay exorbitant prices! If you don't buy, the prices must fall! German housewife, recognize your power![33]

Thus, rational consumption became a duty and responsibility for the explicitly 'German' housewife commensurate with motherhood and citizenship. Consumer and union protests culminated in the biggest strike of the postwar period, the November 12 work stoppage, where union organizers made price control a key demand.[34] In these protests, the unions valorized women's consumer power, but stepped in as consumer counsel hoping to mold this raw power, instructing women in the complexities of the new market.

New housewives' organizations also vied for the role of consumer representatives, drawing on women's shopping expertise. The Berlin Housewives' Organization, suggested that, 'the Berlin housewife will master these tasks [of shopping in the new market] with proper consideration of the conditions created by the currency reform, since she has proven her flexibility in the postwar years time and again'.[35] This article recalled women's domestic subsistence labour during the rationing period as proof that they could now master these new challenges of the free market. In a new role as expert housewife-consumers they were to contribute to the prosperity of the 'Economic Miracle'.

West German consumer policy evolved in the face of these protests. Erhard's inability to maintain his plans for a free market reflected the power of the grass-roots consumer activists and organized labour in 1948. Erhard was forced momentarily to put aside the free market to institute a stop-gap measure based roughly on the British 'Utility-Program'.[36] Erhard's so-called 'Everyman Program' aimed to help the consumer, not by reverting to controls as strict as rationing, but by using state intervention to channel raw material to industries willing to mass-produce cheap, standardized goods like shoes for sale at low, fixed prices.[37] The unions pushed for a broadening of this program and were particularly critical when the regime failed to deliver on its promises.[38] With the influx of Marshall Plan aid in 1949, Erhard was able to abandon the program, deflate trade union critiques and preserve his neo-liberal free market, which he hoped would sharply distinguish against the increasingly centralized planning in the Soviet Zone.[39]

Erhard weathered the post-currency reform protests and could proceed with his plan for state consumer representation under the banner: 'prosperity for all'.[40] However, since female consumers had been such prominent protesters in the 1940s, they were at the centre of his 'conscious consumer politics'.[41] Co-opting women as consumer experts was in part a way to ally them with the state rather than the unions, who presented a potential challenge to Erhard's neo-liberal agenda. As a cornerstone of his policies he promised women a better array of more modern commodities to help with housework. Erhard launched paternalistic state-sponsored campaigns to promote the purchase of household appliances like refrigerators. In 1953, heralded as the 'year of the consumer',[42] Erhard's Ministry launched a refrigerator campaign to shift perception of these appliances from luxury to necessity.[43] In a 1955 campaign called 'Erhard helps the Housewife' he promoted further 'rationalization in the household', to ease the housewife's burden.[44] A report on this program noted that '[Erhard] wants to ignite a stream of consumption'.[45] In return for this state aid, the consumer was to assume the role of partner to the state, 'to create a consumer-consciousness and thereby to construct a feeling in the consumer for his rights and duties in economic life.'[46]

Erhard's Ministry also enlisted women to serve the economy as expert consumers. In 1953, Erhard established an umbrella organization for consumer representation, the Working Group for Consumer Unions (AgV), composed of a number of groups including housewife organizations. As prominent members of this group, organized housewives guided average consumers with publications designed to make the complex market for new commodities more 'transparent'.[47] Prominent women's leaders aligned with Erhard to promote mutual responsibility between the economy and the housewife[48] and they could also critique state policies. The establishment of the AgV as primary consumer representative also took this power from the trade unions,[49] thereby making the state itself a leading voice for consumer concerns and principal ally of organized housewives.

Thus, the consumers' claims to power during the uncertain years of shortage helped to make consumer issues a key part of the postwar political and economic agenda in West Germany. Within this burgeoning consumer culture, women were to embody responsible consumers molded by such watershed events as the post-currency reform boycotts. Their incorporation into the state as consumer representatives and experts became both a route to power and a containment of their power within appropriate forms of consumer-citizenship. In the development of the Cold War consensus, women's consumer power was increasingly subjected to discipline to instill purchasing choices with a sense of patriotic and ideological responsibility. This focus on discipline and responsibility became especially imperative due to the presence of the competing economic system next door in East Germany.

Planning a 'miracle' for East German consumers

The socialist regime in East Germany hoped to embody a true alternative to capitalism. In reality, consumer culture in the GDR developed according to similar trajectories while it worked to mold female citizens who were both workers and consumers. In the Soviet Zone, the currency reform failed to produce similar spectacles of abundance, but the regime did attempt to convince the population that building socialism would also usher in a new era of prosperity. In 1948 the Soviet Zone launched its first Two-Year Plan to increase production, especially in steel, iron, coal, and transportation sectors.[50] At the same time, the dominant Socialist Unity Party (SED) also claimed a commitment to raising production in consumer industries, especially for much needed textiles and shoes. This promise was constrained by the realities of Soviet industrial dismantling and the subsequent inordinate investment in heavy industry to the detriment of consumer goods production.[51] Despite emphasis on heavy industry, propaganda still attempted to link consumption to socialist ideology. In fact, the SED recognized that alleviating consumer crises and building a viable consumer culture would be one key to gaining and maintaining power.[52] Unlike profit-driven capitalism, consumer culture in the East aimed to educate the shopper about availability of commodities, questions of taste, and also the connection between material culture and the politics of socialism.[53]

Soviet Zone administrators planned an event following their currency reform to serve as an alternative spectacle of abundance inaugurating the birth of socialist consumption: the premiere of a state-run chain of stores in the autumn of 1948 called the People's Trade Organisation (HO).[54] The HO was called 'Free Stores', because it sold goods 'freely' without ration cards. The SED privileged the HO above private shops and consumer cooperatives (*Konsum*) as the true expression of socialist 'selling culture'[55] and a so-called 'instrument of battle in the hands of the working-class'.[56] The communist party organ, *Neues Deutschland,* reported on the HO opening day as an equivalent display of plenty to that in the West, with customers thronging outside the new stores and thrilled to find previously scarce goods.[57] As in the West these newly abundant goods were expensive. Central planners set HO prices just under black market prices to eliminate the currency overhang without enabling speculators to buy all the 'free' goods to resell illegally. Planners aimed to lower these prices incrementally as the black market disappeared and supply increased.

Just as the West German currency reform brought unrest and protest, the population critiqued the discrepancy between the HO's reported displays and the real availability of goods as a symbol of problems with the entire regime. A worker from Brandenburg/Havel protested, 'One shouldn't say "Free Stores", but rather "Free Black Market". The prices are as high as on the black market. It is just the state itself, which rakes in the high profits. The worker can't buy anything with his money, because the prices aren't compatible with his earnings'.[58] The HO faced continual difficulties securing quality stock and setting-up respectable establishments.[59] Although the regime seemed unwilling or ill-equipped to respond to these early critiques, the building sense of frustration in the early years of the GDR culminated in a massive uprising in 1953 that the regime could not ignore. This crisis escalated after intensification of socialist transformation in 1952, such as the forced collectivization of farms and the nationalization of private retailing.[60] When these changes precipitated food shortages in spring 1953,[61] rations were shortened for many basic commodities.[62]

Female shoppers prominently protested against living conditions throughout 1952 and early 1953 by staging small boycotts and strikes. Since the trade unions and civil organizations had been centralized and made party-loyal, organs of the state and party themselves stepped in as the primary consumer advisors and representatives. The SED Central Committee tried to thwart protests by calling on these women to remain committed to the regime. The state's 'regime of thrift' (*Sparsamkeitsregime*) introduced an austerity measure to encourage consumers to take responsibility for eliminating inefficiency and waste through sacrifice.[63] To foster a direct relationship between the citizenry and the state, the SED also gave citizens the right to complain to government officials with petition letters (*Eingaben*).[64] During the 1952 crisis, the SED chose a high-ranking woman in the SED, Elli Schmidt, to field these complaints as head of a special consumer committee.[65]

Average shoppers appealed to Schmidt overtly as the responsible female consumer writ large who would understand their problems finding the goods they sought due to her 'natural' role as housewife/consumer. One letter addressed Schmidt: 'You yourself as a woman will understand what is necessary, like practical clothing material for winter and summer'.[66] Schmidt's commission urged these petitioners to be patient and trust in the regime and the Five Year Plan, to understand the need for price hikes, and to be satisfied with delayed gratification.[67] On the eve of the biggest challenge to the SED regime, it is telling that a woman functionary was given the task of reassuring consumers that the state would fulfill its duty to provide for its citizens. While 1953 was Erhard's 'year of the consumer', this year was more crucial for defining consumer citizenship in the GDR. Unsatisfied by Schmidt's often empty assurances, the June 17 uprising pressured the regime to do more to make good on its promises. Angry protesters demanded a drop in HO prices by 40%[68] and chanted a variety of slogans that reflected consumer dissatisfaction, including 'HO makes us k.o. [knocked out]!'[69]

The regime responded with an intensified 'New Course', a program professing to improve consumption and other aspects of citizens' lives. In subsequent programs throughout the 1950s, the GDR promised to modernize consumption and improve conditions for female shoppers. In 1958, when GDR rationing finally ended, SED chairman Walter Ulbricht declared that overtaking the West in per capita consumption would be the primary economic task of the regime. In accordance with this goal, the regime increased its commitment to producing modern goods like appliances and commodities made of plastic.[70] New programs for increased commodity production included 'The 1000 Little Things of Daily Life and Services and Repairs'.[71] Now the party, industries, retailers, and the whole population were supposed to band together to help increase consumer supply.[72]

East German women's grass-roots consumer activism was even more forcefully channeled into the service of the state than in the West. Post-1945 women's committees were consolidated into a SED-sponsored, mass organization for women: the Democratic Women's Union of Germany (DFD). DFD functionaries interpreted rationing improvements as a gift from the regime directly to women, encouraging them to feel bonded to the state.[73] To cope with shortages the DFD instructed women how to make do with alternative goods.[74] DFD seminars informing its constituents of the latest consumer developments recruited women for membership and participation in brigades designed to aid the HO and Konsum stores with problems in retailing, such as packaging goods, cleaning in stores, and filling in for sick shopkeepers. Drawing on the assumption that 'Trade interests all women, because they do the most shopping'[75] these volunteer efforts brought unemployed women into some form of service to the state. Thus, the DFD instructed women in how to survive the inadequate planned economy through delayed gratification and compensatory labour.[76] Similar to its West German neighbor, the GDR state enlisted female shoppers to serve as loyal consumer representatives. These women would help enact socialist consumer policies would purportedly in turn relieve them of their household burdens and provide prosperity free from capitalist exploitation.

'Deviant' shopping across the East-West border

Both the FRG and the GDR paternalistically offered to 'help' women in return for their service to the state as consumer experts and models of rational, patriotic shopping. However, the coexistence of competing economies in divided Germany unleashed the potential for desiring the goods across the border, thereby making it much more difficult to maintain discipline and loyalty among consumer-citizens. Throughout the 1950s the gap widened between the two German regimes. The lure of commodities across the border presented a unique problem for each regime.

The Berlin Blockade of 1948-9 made the divided city a showcase of the two economic systems and heightened ideological politicization of shopping choices. West Berliners could choose between food airlifted to them by Western Allies or rations offered by the Soviets.[77] Some West Berliners did take the Soviets up on their offer, but most rejected it as political betrayal.[78] Thus, in the Blockade German officials and the global superpowers overtly urged the German population to make shopping decisions reflecting their developing political affinities.

Into the 1950s, border crossing to shop was cast as a traitorous cause of economic disaster. In 1950, when postwar unemployment peaked in West Berlin, shoppers could exchange their West Marks for East Marks at an advantageous rate to shop cheaply in HO stores over the border. Shopkeepers, officials and the general population held female shoppers accountable for such transgressions by producing a poster featuring the silhouette of a West German female shopper heading to the HO with a purse and a shopping bag in her hands, and the words 'unemployment' and 'economic ruin' in her wake.[79] The West Berlin municipal government also sponsored a contest to provide a name for archetypal 'deviant' shoppers who strayed to the East. Entries from average citizens suggested names such as 'Mr. and Mrs. Reason-for-going-broke', 'Mr. Sneak-to-the-East and Mrs. Ruin-the-West', or 'Stalin's Sweet-meats'. Other entries caricatured just the female shopper. One submission included a drawing of a hyena dressed as a woman carrying a shopping bag and a cash envelope, heading from the exchange booth to the HO. Another entry, showed a 'Border Hen' halfway over a fence to get to a bag of 'HO-wheat' on one side (East Berlin) while defecating on the other (West Berlin).[80] With the winning entry, 'Mr. Disgrace and Mrs. Shame', the campaign blamed economic problems on shoppers themselves rather than on government policies.[81] The general population participated in policing shoppers by developing a vocabulary condemning them. This campaign and subsequent laws forbidding shopping in the East, however, failed to stop West German border crossing consumption.[82]

However, border crossing eventually became most problematic for the GDR, as economic fortunes of the two states turned. Early in the decade, GDR officials welcomed Western shoppers as targets for propaganda. However, by 1952 the Marshall Plan began to spur greater economic growth in the FRG. Eventually GDR officials forbade shopkeepers to sell to anyone without a GDR identification card so Westerners wouldn't exacerbate HO shortages.[83] As the 'Golden West' became a seductive spectacle from the mid to late 1950s, East German shoppers often were lured to the West for goods unavailable in the East.[84] GDR authorities tried to control these Westward-bound shoppers through surveillance, police force and propaganda. Border guards checked packages for smuggled goods. GDR citizens tried to escape such detection by, for example, wearing new Western shoes and smearing them with mud to make them look worn.[85] Still, police reports revealed that border crossing and smuggling never ceased.

Shopping in the West signaled discontent with Eastern consumption, but the most extreme expression of dissatisfaction with the GDR regime was permanent flight to the West. A variety of personal and political factors led to flight from the GDR, but expectation of a higher standard of living in the West was one draw across the border. Those who fled often wrote home of great material satisfaction in the West.[86] In a FRG survey of refugee youth, a third said they felt good there due to lifestyle and standard of living.[87] Between 1949 and 1961, reportedly 2.6 million people left East Germany for the West.[88] The limitations of the GDR's ability to foster a sense of loyal consumer-citizenship among its population apparently played a role in this flight. Therefore, the limits of loyal consumer-citizenship also became a factor in the most severe form of containment to stop this exodus, the building of the Berlin Wall in 1961.[89]

Conclusion

The background of ration era shortages and the division of Germany into competing economies shaped consumer-citizenship in the Western social-market and Eastern socialist 'Economic Miracles'. Perhaps more so than in other countries, the political culture of consumption in the Cold War Germanys developed as tension between responsibility and 'deviance'. The question of who would represent the consumer in each state was bound up with this politicized question of Cold War loyalty and responsibility. Each state worked to co-opt responsible female consumers to serve their own economy by participating in consumer organizations, sacrificing during shortages, or assisting and appreciating state-sponsored consumer promotions. However, 'deviant' shopping behavior always remained a space of autonomous behavior that potentially threatened the regimes. This perceived threat is evident in the energy expended on disciplining and monitoring shopping behavior. Whether in active protest like boycotts, in illegal black market activity, or in ongoing smuggling of goods across the border, shoppers claimed power for themselves and directly or indirectly challenged their own political economies. Although such challenges existed in both East and West, this activity increasingly became a greater problem for the GDR when real investment in consumer industries most visibly failed to match promises of a better standard of living there compared to the FRG. This gap was most evident in the 1953 crisis and at the end of the 1950s. 'Deviant' consumption challenged official socialist ideology and the Westward flight of GDR citizens seriously threatened the regime. However, 'deviant' consumer strategies such as smuggling continued to exist despite policing and even after the building of the Wall. In another sense, these strategies may have helped to preserve the GDR's stability by giving the population a means of attaining desired goods even when the planned economy was unable to do so. Semi-licit consumption strategies learned in the immediate postwar years may have helped shoppers grapple with the inadequacies of their regimes so they ultimately did not have to rebel against them. The central promise of an 'Economic Miracle' involved consumers, especially women, in a crucial ideological struggle to fulfill this consumer fantasy in politically loyal forms, but it also unleashed not only such questionable consumption strategies but also desires that could not be contained by the bounds of Cold War consensus.

Notes

1 Elizabeth Heinemann, 'The Hour of the Woman: Memories of Germany's 'Crisis Years' and West German National Identity', in Hanna Schissler (ed.), *The Miracle Years: A Cultural History of West Germany, 1949-1968* (Princeton, 2001), pp. 21-56.

2 Katherine Pence, 'From Rations to Fashions: The Gendered Politics of East and West German Consumption, 1945-1961', (Unpublished Ph. D. thesis, University of Michigan, 1999), Forthcoming as a book.

3 In their recent edited volume on gender, subjectivity and citizenship, Kathleen Canning and Sonya Rose have called for a study of how, 'juridical and legal inscriptions, as well as the unwritten traditions, of citizenship, create subject positions that have meanings for those governing and those inhabiting citizenships, as well as those excluded from citizenship'. Kathleen Canning and Sonya O. Rose, 'Gender, Citizenship and Subjectivity: Some Historical and Theoretical Considerations', in Kathleen Canning and Sonya O. Rose (eds), *Gender Citizenships & Subjectivities* (Oxford, 2002), p. 5. Recent theories of citizenship have paid attention to how 'inclusion and exclusion represent two sides of citizenship's coin'. This dynamic of inclusion and exclusion has particularly been examined in terms of racial exclusion. Ruth Lister, *Citizenship: Feminist Perspectives* (New York, 1997), p. 42. See also Anne M. Cronin, 'Advertising Difference: Women, Western Europe, and "Consumer-Citizenship"', in Maggie

Andrews and Mary M. Talbot (eds), *All the World and Her Husband: Women in Twentieth-Century Consumer Culture* (London, 2000), p. 162-76.

4 For a recent study of consumer politics see, for example: Martin Daunton and Matthew Hilton (eds), *The Politics of Consumption: Material Culture and Citizenship in Europe and America* (Oxford, 2001).

5 Lizabeth Cohen, *A Consumers' Republic: The Politics of Mass Consumption in Postwar America* (New York, 2003), p. 8.

6 *Ibid.*

7 Landesarchiv Berlin Kalkreuthstr. (LAB-K) RG 260 OMGBS 4/8-3/2, Office of Military Government (Berlin) Information Services Control Section, APO 755, US Army, Public Opinion Survey Department, 21 February 1946, Survey No. 12.

8 Belinda Davis, *Home Fires Burning: Food, Politics, and Everyday Life in World War I Berlin* (Chapel Hill, NC, 2000), p. 21; Paul Erker, *Ernährungskrise und Nachkriegsgesellschaft: Bauern und Arbeiterschaft in Bayern 1943-1953* (Stuttgart, 1990), p. 31.

9 Nicholas Balabkins, *Germany Under Direct Controls: Economic Aspects of Industrial Disarmament 1945-1948* (New Brunswick, NJ, 1964), p. 106.

10 Rainer Gries, *Die Rationen-Gesellschaft. Versorgungskampf und Vergleichsmentalität: Leipzig, München und Köln nach dem Kriege* (Münster, 1990), pp. 195ff.

11 Thomas Alan Schwartz, *America's Germany: John J. McCloy and the Federal Republic of Germany* (Cambridge, MA, 1991), p. 31.

12 Mark Evan Landsman, 'Dictatorship and Demand: East Germany Between Productivism and Consumerism, 1948-1961', (Dissertation, Columbia University, 2000).

13 Given the disproportionate ratio of men to women after male soldiers had died at the front, contemporaries pointed to a "surplus of women" in postwar Germany. Sibelle Meyer and Eva Schulze, *Wie wir das alles geschafft haben: Alleinstehende Frauen berichten über ihr Leben nach 1945* (München, 1984), p 93.

14 Charlottenburger Heimatmuseum, Berlin, 'Eiscremepulver hilft Zucker sparen!' in Hauswirtschaftlichen Beratungsstellen des Magistrats der Stadt Berlin Abt. für Ernährung (ed.), *Der Haushalts-Brief: Eine laufende Sammlung zeitgemässer Ratschläge für sparsames Kochen und Wirtschaften* 14, 28 January 1947.

15 'Wäsche vorteilhaft erneuert', *Neues Frauenleben,* 2 (1947):19; 'Ein Unterkleid aus Resten', *Für Dich,* 1:9 (13 October 1946).

16 "Wir backen…' *Illustrierter Telegraf Kalender 1949* (Berlin-Grunewald, 1949), p. 84.

17 Alan Kramer, '"Law-abiding Germans"? Social Disintegration, Crime and the Reimposition of Order in Post-war Western Germany, 1945-9', in Richard Evans (ed.), *The German Underworld: Deviants and Outcasts in German History* (London, 1988), p. 248; Gabriele Stüber, *Der Kampf gegen den Hunger 1945-1950: Die Ernährungslage in der britischen Zone Deutschlands, insbesondere in Schleswig-Holstein und Hamburg* (Neumünster, 1984), pp. 611ff.; John E. Farquharson, *The Western Allies and the Politics of Food: Agrarian Management in Postwar Germany* (Leamington Spa, 1985), p. 64.

18 Maria Höhn, *GIs and Fräuleins: The German-American Encounter in 1950s West Germany* (Chapel Hill, 2002); Katherine Pence, 'The 'Fräuleins' meet the 'Amis': Americanization of German Women in the Reconstruction of the West German State', *Michigan Feminist Studies*, 7 (1992-1993): 83-108.

19 Christoph Kleßmann and Peter Friedemann, *Streiks und Hungermärsche im Ruhrgebiet 1946-1948* (Frankfurt/New York, 1977), p. 49.

20 *Ibid.*, pp. 48-9; Michael Wildt, *Der Traum vom Sattwerden: Hunger und Protest Schwarzmarkt und Selbsthilfe in Hamburg 1945-1948* (Hamburg, 1986), p. 52.

21 Günther J. Trittel, *Hunger und Politik: Die Ernährungskrise in der Bizone (1945-1949)* (Frankfurt/New York, 1990), p. 214.

22 Lutz Niethammer, '"Normalisierung" im Westen: Erinnerungsspuren in die 50er Jahre', in Dan Diner (ed.), *Ist der Nationalsozialismus Geschichte? Zu Historisierung und Historikerstreit* (Frankfurt/Main, 1987), p. 24.

23 Hans W. Richter, 'Traumland aus Kohl und Spinat', in *Mein erstes Geld. Währungsreform 1948, Augenzeugenberichte* (Freiburg, 1985), p. 69 cited in Gries, *Die Rationen Gesellschaft*, p. 331.

24 Alan Kramer, *The West German Economy, 1945-1955* (New York, 1991), p. 147.

25 Jahrbuch der öffentlichen Meinung, 1945-1955. Allensbach, 1956, p. 149, cited in Erker, *Ernährungskrise*, p. 260.

26 Everhard Holtmann, *Politik und Nichtpolitik: Lokale Erscheinungsformen politischer Kultur in frühen Nachkriegsdeutschland* (Opladen, 1989), p. 169.

27 Inge Marßolek, *Arbeiterbewegung nach dem Krieg (1945-1948) Am Beispiel Remscheid, Solingen, Wuppertal* (Frankfurt/Main, 1983), p. 198.

28 Archiv des Deutschen Gewerkschaftsbundes Britische Besatzungszone (DGB BBZ) 11/93, (Protest gegen Preiswucher), Bericht über die Protestkundgebung des Deutschen Gewerkschaftsbundes, Kreisausschuß Münster, auf den Servatiplatz, 11 August 1948. File page 17.

29 DGB BBZ 11/93, An den DGB Bundesvorstand, Düsseldorf, Kollege Stenzel, Letter from DGB Kreisausschuß Recklinghausen, Heussner, 10 August 1948. File page 35.

30 DGB BBZ 11/93, (Protest gegen Preiswucher).

31 See Erker, *Ernährungskrise*, p. 284.

32 DGB BBZ 11/93 (Protest gegen Preiswucher).

33 DGB BBZ 11/93 DGB Kreisausschuß Recklinghausen. August 1948.

34 Gerhard Beier, *Der Demonstrations- und Generalstreik vom 12. November 1948. Im Zusammenhang der parlamentarischen Entwicklung Westdeutschlands* (Frankfurt/Main, 1975).

35 LAB-K RG 260 OMGBS, 4/11-1/23 Women's Affairs, A. Heinicke, 'Währungsumstellung - eine Studie für Hausfrauen', *Wir Hausfrauen*, 1:4 (April 1949): 1.

36 The Utility-System was a British program instituted in 1942 to deal with wartime shortages by controlling production of cheap, standardized goods. France instituted a similar *Systems der utilité sociale* in 1946 and 1947. Erich Egner, 'Das Utility-System und seine Lehren: Ein Kapitel moderner Verbraucherschutzpolitik', in Erich Egner, *Studien über Haushalt und Verbrauch* (Berlin, 1963), pp. 329-353.

37 Ludwig Erhard, '"Marktwirtschaft im Streit der Meinungen," Rede vor dem 2. Parteikongreß der CDU der britischen Zone, Reckinghausen, 28 August 1948', in Karl Hohmann (ed.), *Ludwig Erhard Gedanken aus fünf Jahrzehnten: Reden und Schriften* (Düsseldorf, 1988), p. 146.

38 DGB GVZ 13/11, "Arbeiter, Angestellte und Beamte im Vereinigten Wirtschaftsgebiet. Zur Demonstration des gewerkschaftlichen Willens." Poster proposal, Frankfurt a.M. 6 November 1948, Der Gewerkschaftsrat des Vereinten Wirtschaftsgebietes. File page 139.

39 Rainer Klump, 'Vierzig Jahre Deutsche Mark', in Rainer Klump (ed.), *40 Jahre Deutsche Mark: Die politische und ökonomishce Bedeutung der westdeutschen Währungsreform von 1948* (Wiesbaden, 1989), p. 62.

40 Ludwig Erhard, *Prosperity through Competition* (London, 1958), p. 169.

41 Bundesarchiv Koblenz (BAK) Bundesministerium für Wirtschaft (B102)/37241 Bericht über die Tätigkeit des RAL-Arbeitsausschusses zur Beratung des Einheitsgütezeichenprogramms von Prof. Dr. Müller-Armack erstattet: vom Obmann, Prof. Dr. W. Herrmann. 27 June 1952.

42 Ludwig Erhard, *Deutsche Wirtschaftspolitik: Der Weg der Sozialen Marktwirtschaft* (Düsseldorf, 1962), p. 209.

43 BAK B102/35963 Herrn Dipl. Kfm. Dr. Heinz C. Schade, Karlsruhe - Durlach, Betr: Mehrverbrauch langlebiger Wirtschaftsgüter an Herrn Prof. Müller-Armack. Im Auftrage: Weniger, 28 August 1953; and B102/35963 Vermerk Betr: Konsumfinanzierung von langfristigen Gebrauchsgütern. Bonn, 14 April 1953.

44 BAK B102/35963 Herrn Professor Müller-Armack, Betr: 'Erhard hilft der Hausfrau' from Ockhardt, Bonn, 10 May 1955.

45 BAK B102/35963 Dr. Leitreiter, Vermerk Betr: Konsumentenprogramm, 'Erhard hilft der Hausfrau' Bonn, 11 July 1955.

46 BAK B102/35996 Betr: Verbraucher-Unterrichtung, Signed: Hösel, Bonn, 16 August 1954.

47 BAK B102/35985 Dr. Hillner, Vermerk: Betr: Besprechung der Arbeitsgemeinschaft der Verbraucherverbände bei dem Herrn Minister. Bonn, 19 December 1956.

48 Elke Schüller and Kerstin Wolff, *Fini Pfannes: Protagonistin und Paradiesvogel der Nachkriegsfrauenbewegung* (Königstein/Taunus, 2000).

49 The Deutsche Gewerkschaftsbund (DGB) became the umbrella organization for all West German trade unions in 1949. DGB 24/5283 Merl, An die Hauptabteilung 'Frauen' im Hause Betr: Verbrauchervertretung, Düsseldorf, 18 March 1953.

50 Walter Ulbricht, 'Planmäßige Wirtschaft sichert die Zukunft des deutschen Volkes. Referat vor dem Parteivorstand der SED, 29 June 1948', *Der Deutsche Zweijahrplan für 1949-1950* (Berlin (East), 1948), p. 20.

51 Ina Merkel, *Utopie und Bedürfnis: Die Geschichte der Konsumkultur in der DDR* (Köln, 1999), p. 39.

52 Andreas Malycha, *Die SED: Geschichte ihrer Stalinisierung 1946-1953* (Paderborn, 2000), pp. 200ff.

53 Dz, 'Entwickelt höhere Verkaufskultur!', *Die Konsumverkaufsstelle* 9 (August 1950), 103.

54 Katherine Pence, 'Building Socialist Worker-Consumers: The Paradoxical Construction of the *Handelsorganisation*-HO, 1948', in Peter Hübner and Klaus Tenfelde (eds), *Arbeiter in der SBZ-DDR* (Essen, 1998), pp. 497-526.

55 Schi, 'Wir bauen: 'Stumme Verkäufer', *Die Konsumverkaufsstelle* 6 (1949), 80.

56 Stiftung Archiv der Parteien und Massenorganisationen der DDR im Bundesarchiv (SAPMO-BA) Freie Deutsche Gewerkschaftsbund Bundesvorstand (FDGB Buvo) 0462, Wirtschaftspolitik, Handelsorganisation HO, Verwaltungsrat. Sitzungsprotokolle und Arbeitsunterlagen, November 1948-December 1949. Koll. Göring, FDGB Gewerkschaft der Angestellten, Zentral-Vorstand HA. I, Organisation, Betr: Organisationszugehörigkeit und Gewerkschaftsarbeit in den Freien Läden, signed, Ueberfeld. Berlin, 5 December 1948.

57 '"HO"! Das Tagesgespräch von Berlin: "Gestern wurde der erste freie Laden in der Frankfurter Allee eröffnet"', *Neues Deutschland*, 268 (16 November 1948): 4.
58 SAPMO-BA SED Zentralkomitee (ZK) Abt. Wirtschaftspolitik IV 2/6.02/76 Information über die Reaktion der Bevölkerung zur Eröffnung der 'Freien Läden', 1 December 1948. Arbeiter, 30 Jahre alt, Brandenburg/Havel, Information, Potsdam, 20 November 1948.
59 SAPMO-BA FDGB Buvo 0462, Bericht des Hauptgeschäftsführers der Handelsorganisation-HO, Streit, vor dem Verwaltungsrat, 22 April 1949.
60 Andreas Pickel, *Radical Transitions: The Survival and Revival of Entrepreneurship in the GDR* (Boulder, 1992), pp. 36-7.
61 Manfred Hagen, *DDR—Juni '53: Die erste Volkserhebung im Stalinismus* (Stuttgart, 1992), p. 25.
62 'Fettaufruf für März 1953', *Nacht-Express*, 50 (28 February 1953), reprinted in Peter Jung (ed.), *Verordneter Humor: DDR 1953* (Berlin, 1993), p. 41.
63 Peter Hübner, *Konsens, Konflikt und Kompromiß: Soziale Arbeiterinteressen und Sozialpolitik in der SBZ/DDR 1945-1970* (Berlin, 1995), p. 150.
64 Ina Merkel and Felix Mühlberg, 'Eingaben und Öffentlichkeit', in Ina Merkel (ed.), *'Wir sind doch nicht die Meckerecke der Nation': Briefe an das Fernsehen der DDR* (Berlin, 2000), p. 17.
65 Katherine Pence, '"You as a Woman Will Understand": Consumption, Gender and the Relationship between State and Citizenry in the GDR's Crisis of 17 June 1953', *German History*, 19:2 (2001): 218-42.
66 Bundesarchiv Potsdam (BAP) DC 6/14, Regierung der DDR, Min. HuV, StK HuV, Schriftwechsel Versorgung mit Textilwaren, To: Frau Elli Schmidt Berlin, 12 February 1953.
67 BAP DC 6/14, Min. HuV, StK HuV, Schriftwechsel Versorgung mit Textilwaren, To: Frau Elly Voigt [sic], 27 April 1953.
68 Hagen, *DDR—Juni '53*, p. 62.
69 *Ibid.*, p. 61.
70 Eli Rubin, 'The Order of Substitutes: Plastic Consumer Goods in the Volkswirtschaft and Everyday Domestic Life in the GDR', in David F. Crew (ed.), *Consuming Germany in the Cold War* (Oxford, 2003), pp. 87-120.
71 SAPMO-BA FDGB Buvo 1548 Frauenabteilung, 'Vorschläge des Kreisvorstandes des FDGB an den Rat der Stadt und den Rat des Kreises Jena zur Erarbeitung des Kreisprogrammes für Dienstleistungen und Reparaturleistungen und die 1000 kleinen Dinge des täglichen Bedarfs', November 1959-July 1960.
72 Günter Pawelke et al., *Mehr und bessere industrielle Konsumgüter: Eine Anleitung für die Praxis* (Berlin (East), 1960), p. 75.
73 SAPMO-BA Demokratische Frauenbund Deutschlands Bundesvorstand (DFD Buvo) 296, Sitzungen des Sekretariats des BV, Protokoll Nr. 18/III, 8 January 1951, TO: #6 Aufhebung der Lebensmittelkarten für Erzeugnisse von Getreide und Hülsenfrüchten., 1. Dem Schreiben an den Ministerrat der Regierung der DDR, 23 December 1950 wird nachträglich zugestimmt. Anlage 6 An den Ministerrat der Regierung der DDR, Berlin, From: DFD 1. Vorsitzende (Elli Schmidt) DFD Bundessekretariat.
74 SAPMO-BA DFD Buvo 542, Büro des Sekretariats, Rundschreiben; Der DFD spricht zur Fleischversorgung!, To: Leibe Hausfrauen der DDR!, From: DFD Bundesskeretariat, Abteilung Agitation, 25 April 1951.

75 Demokratische Frauenbund Deutschlands (DFD), 'Schöne Schaufenster gute Waren zufriedene Frauen', DDR 1956. Vgl. SAPMO-BA DFD Buvo 325, Sekretariatssitzung Protokoll Nr. 94, 26 November 1956.

76 Ina Merkel, 'Frauen in der DDR: Vorschläge für eine neue Kultur der Geschlechterverhältnisse', in Hubertus Knabe (ed.), *Aufbruch in eine andere DDR: Reformer und Oppositionelle zur Zukunft ihres Landes* (Reinbek bei Hamburg, 1990), p. 91.

77 Cyril Buffet and Uwe Prell, 'Stabilität und Teilung. Die Berlin-Krise 1948/49 - Auftakt zum Kalten Krieg in Europa', in Uwe Prell and Lothar Wilker (eds), *Berlin-Blockade und Luftbrücke 1948/49. Analyse und Dokumentation* (Berlin, 1987), pp. 42 and 177.

78 LAB-K Rep. 10B Acc. 1888 Nr. 1618. Hildegard Alle, 12 December 1949; Horst Albrecht, 7 July 1950; Gertrud Basse, 13 September 1949.

79 LAB-K Rep. 10A Acc. 2021 Nr. 386.

80 *Ibid.*

81 Katherine Pence, '"Herr Schimpf und Frau Schande": Grenzgänger des Konsums im geteilten Berlin und die Politik des Kalten Krieges', in Burghard Ciesla, Michael Lemke and Thomas Lindenberger (eds), *Sterben für Berlin? Die Berliner Krisen 1948: 1958* (Berlin, 2000), pp. 185-202.

82 Curt Reiss, *Berlin Berlin 1945-1953* (Berlin-Grunewald, 1953), p. 175.

83 Sylvia Conradt and Kirsten Heckmann-Janz, *Reichstrümmerstadt: Leben in Berlin, 1945-1961* (Darmstadt, 1987), p. 97.

84 Rita L., 'Briefe von drüben...' *Die Neue Hauszeitung – Karstadt* 6:5 (February/March 1955/1956), p. 18.

85 US National Archive, HICOG RG 466, Berlin, Foreign Service Dispatch, 'Continuing Purchases by East Residents in West Berlin'. From, Stephen C. Brown, Chief Economic Affairs Division, 17 December 1952.

86 Patrick Major, 'Going West: The Open Border and the Problem of *Republikflucht*', in Patrick Major and Jonathan Osmond (eds), *The Workers' and Peasants' State: Communism and Society in East Germany under Ulbricht 1945-71* (Manchester, 2002), p. 199.

87 Gerhard Schröter, *Jugendliche Flüchtlinge aus der SBZ* (München, 1958).

88 C. Bradley Scharf, *Politics and Change in East Germany: An Evaluation of Socialist Democracy* (Boulder, CO, 1984), p. 182.

89 Major, 'Going West', pp. 190-209.

Part 3
Consumers in the Society of Consumption

Chapter 7

Consumers' Associations and the State: Protection and Defence of the Consumer in France, 1950-2000

Alain Chatriot

'They say we are living in a consumer society. This is true, but we are not yet in a society of consumers. Consumers are the silent extras in a drama in which they are supposed to be the main characters.' The quotation comes not from a militant consumerist but the future president of the French Republic, Valéry Giscard d'Estaing, then the Minister of Finance. In the same speech of 6 October 1972, at the inauguration of the first international consumer exhibition in Paris, he suggested that 'at last the consumer is becoming a full partner in French social life and economic society.' This declaration invites reflection on the shape of consumer policy in France in the second half of the twentieth century. The speech and the context in which it was given both point to a crystallisation of the consumerist wave in France in the early 1970s. At the same time, the style of this speech indicates the manner in which 'consumers' were seen in those days: as a symbolic stake in political struggles. This text also poses the question of the difficulties of mobilising consumers in France. From this standpoint, 1972 is an interesting year because of a scandal around Talc Morhange (a contaminated baby product) that highlighted questions of the safety and protection of consumers. It was also a year of disagreement among consumer organisations after the departure of the *Union Fédérale des Consommateurs* (UFC, Federal Consumers Union, publishing *Que Choisir?*) from the *Institut National de la Consommation* (INC). In 1972, too, an exhibition organised at the outlets of FNAC and the visit to Paris of the American lawyer Ralph Nader both raised the issue of how France was mobilising in comparison with other national experiences. This same year, the Council of European Ministers met in Paris and dealt with the issue of consumption at the level of the Common Market. In December 1972, a law was passed on door-to-door sales that opened the way to a series of major laws on consumer protection. Finally, in November 1972 a meeting took place in Aix-en-Provence between lawyers and business executives to discuss the 'new data for consumer law'.

Political mobilisation, partisan struggle, product scandals, divisions among consumer associations, international models, EC policy, national legislation, and a plan for codification all characterise the diversity of stakes posed by consumption in France in the crisis years of the final third of the twentieth century. The fact that they were concentrated in the year 1972 (four years after 1968) indeed indicates that the forms of social mobilisation and public policy concerning consumption were both at a turning point. French consumers' associations, in all their diversity, were taking on a major role in the face of the State. The French government, comparable to its European equivalents in that period,[1] was trying in effect to associate its public policies with the expertise possessed by these actors in the field of consumption. Therefore, the expertise sought from consumer movements and from those persons designated by consumer councils was, rather classically,[2] simultaneously a request for information, a recognition of their representativeness, and a defense of contradictory interests. The role played by institutions like the Economic and Social Council[3] and those authorities that specialised in consumption issues testifies to the desire of the state to have partners in order to negotiate and advance a series of programmes on matters of consumption. Famous for its centralised state and its technocracy, France in the 1960s nevertheless appeared to be more complex, and so we must qualify its proclaimed Jacobinism.[4] Consumption might even appear as one of the privileged sites of the opening of the state to the aspirations of civil society.[5]

After various institutional experiences and the first major efforts by associations focusing on consumption, the 1970s seemed to be a decade of the entry of the French consumer onto the political and social stage.[6] After an overview of both the French consumerist movement and previously existing institutions, we will be able to appreciate the evolution of the legislative apparatuses set up during those years. The creation of a Secretary of State for Consumption in 1976, a post given to Christiane Scrivener (an Independent Republican) should be interpreted within this new political and social framework. The political break of 1981 with the election of a Socialist President is also noteworthy in the realm of consumption. Strongly marked by the nomination of Catherine Lalumière (a Socialist) to a newly born Ministry of Consumption, this fresh policy was not without limitations, however. Despite real changes, it was still from the vantage point of legislative and regulatory protection that consumption policy was organised. The 1990s, on the other hand, were marked by progressive disinterest in consumption issues from the perspective of social mobilisation, but they revived the whole set of consumer problems first posed in the 1970s and 1980s, especially during the great food crises of the end of the century.[7] Culminating in the publication of a consumption code in July 1993, after more than ten years' preparation,[8] as well as the innovations caused by a gradually impinging European framework, this overview allows us to examine current forms of consumerist mobilisation.

The era of the consumer (1950-1975)

The idea of making the voice of consumers heard by the state in France, among white collar unions and producers, is an old one and was long advocated by social Catholicism.[9] Five major categories of associations of consumers can be found in France in the second half of the twentieth century:[10] associations with a trade union or political inspiration, women's or families' associations, independent associations (devoted only to the defence of the consumer), cooperatives, and specialist associations (particularly in regard to housing).[11] This multiplicity of French associations (among which we must not forget UROCs, the *Unions Régionales d'Organisations des Consommateurs*) is not surprising, contrary to the neo-Tocquevillian assumption that denies the existence of any associative activity in French society. On the contrary, the 1970s were a decade of more general thinking about the place of associations in a democracy, symbolised by a range of debates about the '*cadre de vie*' (living environment).

The 'first generation' of organisations called upon to participate in a new consumption policy was composed of groups that were often family-based, women-specific or co-operative. The *Fédération Nationale des Coopératives de Consommation*, created in 1912, had long spearheaded consumer demands. But after the Second World War, and especially after 1970, the co-operative movement was having its last heyday before gradually losing the pioneering role that it had held.[12] The *Union Féminine Civique et Sociale*, created in 1925, well represents the involvement of women's movements in the reforming nexus. Family movements were also interested in consumption issues, whatever their successive configurations and their doctrinal differences.[13]

The rise of associations of consumers issuing from various union confederations is interesting, for it shows the tensions internal to consumerism. Thus, Gabriel Ventejol, secretary of the trade union *Force Ouvrière* and future president of the *Conseil Economique et Social*, explained in May 1974: 'Our way of seeing problems is not quite that of other consumers' associations. We keep constantly in mind a concern to defend both salaried producers like ourselves and consumers. If we aimed only to defend the consumer, we might be led to fight only for the lowest price, without taking into account a need for the social progress that leads to increasing salaries and social benefits.'[14] The first two organisations were the OR.GE.CO (*Organisation Générale des Consommateurs*), created in 1959 (gathering at the start most of the trade unions, before becoming a link between the CGC – *Confédération Générale des Cadres* – and the CFTC – *Confédération Française des Travailleurs Chrétiens* – with the creation of other associations) and FO-Consommateurs (which became AFOC, *Association Force Ouvrière Consommateurs*) in 1974. They were then joined by the Asseco-CFDT (*Association Etudes et Consommation de la Confédération Française Démocratique du Travail*) and by the Indecosa-CGT (*Association de la Confédération Générale du Travail pour l'Information et la Défense des Consommateurs Salariés)* in 1979, then, in 1984, by the ADEIC *(Association de*

Défense d'Education et d'Information du Consommateur de la FEN, Fédération de l'Education Nationale).

But the major phenomenon of the period was the rise of the UFC-*Que Choisir?* After difficult beginnings, and despite the partnership of the Belgian Association of Consumers, the UFC benefited from one of its mistakes: a lost lawsuit against the Arthur Martin (household appliance) company in 1973 ultimately gave it wide publicity and an image of independence from manufacturers. The position of the UFC in the face of the development of consumers' associations that were issuing from trade unions remained shaky, however. Other researchers, like the sociologist Louis Pinto,[15] have stressed the fact that this consumerist movement was not linked to an independent social mobilisation but rather to activity on the part of a 'technocratic humanism' whose typical exponent was André Romieu, founder in 1951 and president of the UFC, civil servant and member of the cabinet of Antoine Pinay, first secretary of the National Committee of Consumption before being its representative at UNAF. The UFC occupied a special place thanks to its highly regarded periodical.[16]

The centrality of the question of representativeness is well summarised by Louis Pinto on the basis of his sociological observations: 'The mode of legitimation of each of the partners is always vulnerable to disqualifying objections on the part of others: while the spokespersons of associations might be charged with "irresponsibility" or "incompetence" and especially with insufficient representativeness, public agencies can be contradicted in their claim to represent the general interest and so judged to be either subject to the particular interests of "professionals", or as purely and simply useless, ineffective, etc.'[17] Responding to this issue, the state defined the criteria of representativeness and thereby recognised the 'approved consumers' associations'. Approval can be given to local, departmental, regional or national associations for five years and the criteria are linked to activity (one year of existence and proof of effective and public activity with a view to defending the interests of consumers), to numerical representativeness (10,000 dues-paying individuals for a national association) and to independence from all forms of professional activities. These criteria, advanced on the basis of the law of Orientation of Commerce and Artisans (27 December 1973)[18] and its decree of application of 17 May 1974, are today defined by articles L.411-1 and R.411-1 and follow the Consumption Code and decree of 21 June 1998. They are particularly interesting for showing that the state has the power to legitimise these interlocutors, with recognition being realised in the form of public subsidies received by associations and also in the possibilities furnished by sitting on established consultative bodies.

French institutions specifically charged with consumption pre-date the 1970s. Apart from older administrations attached to the Ministry of Agriculture or to the Ministry of the Economy and Finance, we should note an awareness in the post-Second World War period inaugurated by the creation of a 'Bureau of Consumption' at the Economic Programmes Department of the National Ministry of the Economy in 1945. Then, linked with the *Commissariat du Plan*[19] and the

INSEE, the CREDOC (*Centre de Recherche et de Documentation sur la Consommation*) was created in October 1953.[20] An institution that included social partners like the Economic and Social Council was very interested in the themes of informing and protecting the consumer.[21] Successive reports and advice from the Council allow us to understand both the importance of the topic and the possible tensions among social partners (for example, representatives of management distrusted representation from consumers who might be hostile to them, and the confederations of white collar workers disagreed over economic priorities with respect to consumption).

Under the impetus of the Gaullist Prime Minister Michel Debré, the National Consumption Committee (CNC) was created by a decree of 19 December 1960 and then established on 13 February 1961 by Joseph Fontanet, Secretary of State for Interior Commerce. Finally, as proposed by the CNC and on the demand of consumers' associations, and again on the initiative of Michel Debré (now as Minister of Economy and Finance) a law of 22 December 1966 created the *Institut National de la Consommation* (INC).[22] The status of the INC and its gradual exhaustion were sources of conflict. Very soon, representatives of associations accused the INC of conducting its own policy by passing itself off as an organisation representing consumers. Thus the Federal Union of Consumers (UFC) quit the INC's administrative council in 1972, judging that the technical body had proclaimed itself an organisation of consumers without having either that status or independence. Here was a tension that touched all associations: between the demand for recognition and governmental support, and the desire for autonomy.

Consumption seized by policy (1976-1992)

Along with mobilised consumers' movements and a slowly evolving institutional framework, an apparent political break occurred with the nomination in January 1976 of Christiane Scrivener as Secretary of State for Consumption, overseen by the Ministry of Economy and Finance. The press immediately pounced on this new personality, baptising her 'Madame Consumption' while stressing the originality of her training as a graduate of the Harvard Business School. If *Le Figaro* was pleased with this 'ministry for the fourth power', *Le Monde* was more tactical, explaining crisply: 'The creation of a Secretary of State for Consumption has political significance. At a moment when the Opposition is taking greater advantage of demands from organisations for the defence of consumers, it was inconceivable that M. Giscard d'Estaing, who inaugurated the Consumers Salon '72 just three months ago, would leave to the Left a monopoly on these preoccupations.' *L'Humanité* devoted an article to her lack of real political influence, concluding with the blockbuster question: 'In fact, what is she dealing with?'[23] During a press conference of 26 May 1976, Christiane Scrivener announced her policy programme that essentially amounted to preparing a law that was finally tabled in 1977. In line with the new Secretary's plans, the Socialist

Party's 'consumption' group started working in 1975 and embarked on a veritable race in parliamentary proposals.

The draft law was well received in the Senate where it was first presented. The introducer of the bill stressed the precise character of the text: 'At first look, it is difficult not to be struck by the contrast between the evidence of the title – "relative to the protection of and information to the consumer" – and the technical quality of the provisions, sometimes very meticulous, that it contains.'[24] The Secretary of State finally brought to the vote two laws both dated 10 January 1978, one dealing with informing and protecting consumers in relation to certain credit operations and one dealing with the same in relation to products and services.[25] The latter law corrected provisions of the 1905 law on suppression of fraud and falsification, and through its chapter 4 enabled a stronger fight against abusive clauses. In parallel with Mme. Scrivener's drive, the Ministry of Economy and Finance was being reorganised. A new journal, the *Revue de la Concurrence, des Prix et de la Consommation* (*Competition, Price and Consumption Review*) was launched in June 1977 as part of the same effort. Minister Robert Boulin explained that he wanted 'to make relations between the French people and their government easier and more fruitful' and he added that the review marked 'a timely enlargement of the tasks of the Office of Competition and Prices and a modification in the nature of its contact with the public. While its image was previously associated with purely conjunctural and regulatory interventions, now there will be added in-depth activities to foster competition and defend the consumer.'[26]

But the Scrivener experiment did not last long. The 1978 legislative elections spelled the non-renewal of her brief and even its disappearance from the cabinet. The press commented in malicious tones: 'In the end, one may ask if Mme. Scrivener is today paying the price for having acted too quickly and too well. Is the existence of the Secretariat still justified now that its mission is accomplished and what remains is only to "steer" the instrument now in place?'[27] In fact, the post seems to have been offered to a trade unionist but the latter, after having accepted, then withdrew and too late for the post to be offered again to Scrivener.

François Mitterrand had devoted his Presidential campaign's 26th proposition to consumption, announcing: 'Distribution circuits will be reformed, the construction of *grandes surfaces* [hypermarkets] regulated, the powers of consumers strengthened.'[28] The creation of a full ministerial post in June 1981, given under the second Mauroy government to Catherine Lalumière, a Socialist lawyer, seems the symbol of this new voluntarism. However, the situation was a little more complicated. It was not that the Socialists had instrumentalised consumption, but that this ministerial promotion might be better viewed as the departure of the post held by the minister in the first Mauroy government, since the Public Function was supposed to go to a Communist minister. Catherine Lalumière had succeeded, nevertheless, in obtaining some administrative services, notably in taking the Suppression of Fraud away from the Ministry of Agriculture and the Distribution-Services-Consumption department from Finance. While she did not manage to obtain control over Competition and Consumption, which Jacques Delors refused to remove from Finances in a delicate period dominated by the issue of a price freeze, the new minister did obtain real power through the presidency of the inter-ministerial group on Consumption.

Claiming responsibility for this particularity, Catherine Lalumière explained at the time: 'The Ministry of Consumption is effectively and naturally an inter-ministerial ministry, since it protects the consumers of all products – whether industrial, agricultural, pharmaceutical – as well as of both public and private services. So I am more or less interfacing with most of the activities of other ministries.' She took advantage of this interview to differentiate herself from the experience of 1976 to 1978: 'In Mme. Scrivener's day, the Secretariat of State was an integral part of the Finance Ministry. Now the Ministry of Consumption is totally independent. In addition, the Secretariat of State did not have the means to execute its decisions because it was a sort of headquarters charged with preparing a certain number of texts. Once these texts were voted and passed, meaning once its work was accomplished, the Secretariat of State disappeared right after the 1978 legislative elections.' This relative rupture from her predeccessor aroused critiques from both Right and Left.[29]

Among Catherine Lalumière's most discussed measures was the reform of the INC by the decree of 20 December 1982. While the Council of the Administration had since 1966 been composed of 23 members (12 consumer representatives, 6 professional representatives and 5 public representatives), the new one had 27 members: 16 consumers (with the addition of new organisations originating in the trades unions), 8 qualified specialists, and 3 representatives of INC staff. There was also a desire to bolster the scientific study of consumption within the framework of the new research policy launched by the French minister Jean-Pierre Chevènement. But what should be stressed is the role of the Research and Coordination bureau of the Ministry established in 1982, a gamble by the central administration in creating an autonomous ministry to challenge the constantly reasserted control by the Ministry of Economy and Finance. During this same period, one of the symbolic peculiarities of recognising consumers' movements was to grant them seats on administrative councils in the new nationalised enterprises, under a law of 11 February 1982, but these nominations were open to numerous criticisms. Mention might also be made of another important and related debate she launched, over the possibility of 'collective conventions' in consumption that would link producers and consumers, as well as the controversies which emerged over information and price control.

Catherine Lalumière finally proposed a new legislative bill to mark her hold over consumption policy. Passed in July 1983,[30] the text was more restrictive than the preceding one of January 1978, but apart from the creation of the Commission on Consumer Safety, the dominant theme was much the same. As the Socialist who presented the bill in the National Assembly underlined, the declaration of principle put 'a general obligation of safety on a par with the principle of freedom in trade and industry.'[31]

The return to the simple status of Secretary of State in 1983, though little remarked upon, was occasionally scoffed at. But beyond the withdrawal of the ministerial title, one should note that among the various successors to Catherine Lalumière few seemed to make a mark with the exception of yet another woman: Véronique Neiertz at the end of the 1980s, who concentrated on overindebtedness. Other variations on consumption policy were produced in those years, however, and one administrative mutation needs to be mentioned. The General Management of Competition and Consumption (a 1978 result of the transformation of the General Management of Competition and Prices) was combined with the Repression of Fraud Service (formerly part of the Ministry of Agriculture) at the end of 1985 to become the General Management of Competition, Consumption and Repression of Fraud (DGCCRF). And the INC remained at the centre of union and political conflicts, as in the summer of 1985 during a change of director. The Secretary of State Henri Emmanuelli (PS) concluded: 'The INC is a sea urchin, difficult to caress because it has prickles everywhere.'[32] Beyond these administrative and legislative changes, it is difficult to perceive in this period the attitude of the judicial apparatus that was gradually taking over these issues.

The most significant campaign begun by Catherine Lalumière was the project to codify consumption law. The issue of codification is complex and crucial for tackling the question of consumption policy from a perspective other than that limited to consumers' movements and administrative or political institutions. The decision to construct a code from a set of legislative and regulatory provisions is never a neutral or simple operation. The history of the construction of this code is nevertheless rich and sheds light on consumption policy. The task was first suggested by Christiane Scrivener but put into effect by Catherine Lalumière shortly after she arrived. When the final report of the Commission to Codify Consumption Law was handed over in 1990, the new Secretary of State, Véronique Neiertz prefaced it as follows: 'An inventory was necessary but so also was harmonisation, unification, and reflection on everything that existed and also on what a real law on consumption ought to be.'[33] Officially created by a decree of 25 February 1982, the Commission to Codify Consumption Law took over on 9 December 1981 the task given to its president, the lawyer Jean Calais-Auloy. This law professor from Montpellier University had been interested in these matters for a decade already, and had explained his objectives back in 1972: 'The protection of consumers should not take place through a burgeoning of repressive legal texts but through a simplification that would put them within the scope of any ordinary citizen, through the recognised right of consumers' associations to take legal action to force protective legislation to be respected.'[34] The overhauling commission, composed only of lawyers and administrators, met for three years roughly twice a month and wrote two intermediate reports before submitting the final one to Henri Emmanuelli in April 1985.

However, the proposal for a code presented in 1985 was not given to Parliament. Meanwhile, the new 1988 laws on the legal capabilities of consumers' associations and especially the laws of June and December 1989 on cleaning up commercial practices and over-indebtedness required the preparation of yet another report (given to a working group that met a dozen times from May to December 1989). Jean Calais-Auloy again called for the creation of a code: 'Consumption law such as currently present in France – and this is true of other countries – is not satisfactory. It is made up of a multitude of legal texts, written in haphazard circumstances with no thought to coherence, such that the rules are difficult to know and understand, even for specialists.' He defended his attempt: 'Only the text presented here can we call a *Code de la Consommation*. It in no way contributes to legislative inflation; on the contrary, it replaces numerous and complicated laws.' He concluded his presentation as follows: 'Adoption of the Code would allow professionals and consumers to know better the rights that apply to them. It would also allow them to understand their purpose: to establish a balance in the relations between economic partners.'[35] Significant delays and sources of tension with the Higher Commission on Codification (created in 1989) would further delay a final result.

French consumption policy within the European Union (1993-2005)

The law of 26 July 1993, promulgated under the government of the Right, established the Consumption Code and thus substituted a single legal text for over ten laws, ordered into five books: informing consumers and formation of contracts; conformity and safety of products and services; consumer debt; consumers' associations; and institutions. The actual enactment, after more than ten years of preparation and often acute legal debate, passed almost unnoticed.

The construction of Europe was being strengthened at the very moment when this laboriously built edifice went into effect. Its best specialist, Jean Calais-Auloy, could thus wonder in 1993: 'While the creation of a market without internal borders generally favours consumers, the elaboration of European law, as it is happening at the moment, risks aggravating the situation of weakness in which consumers find themselves. The complexity of EEC legislation, the maintenance of differences among national legislations, and the multiplication of cross-border litigation harm all parties, but especially those like consumers who have neither the competence nor the means to deal with it.'[36] Technical debates developed between legal professionals on these subjects.

While we cannot go into detail on the history of the Community's – and then the EEC's – consumption policy,[37] we need to recall a few dates, measures and institutions. A first Committee of Consumer Contact was created by the Commission in 1962 and it underwent many transformations until June 1995 when its reorganisation resulted in a more flexible and less onerous structure. Two programmes had been proposed by the Council of Ministers in 1975 and 1981 on consumption matters. The European Court of Justice was also gradually constructing elements of jurisprudence in this field, like the writ 'Cassis de Dijon' of 1979 or 'Kech and Mithouard' of 1993. The Commission published in

November 1993 a Green Paper on *Access of Consumers to Justice and the Settlement of Consumer Disputes in the Single Market.* In 1995 the General Direction XXIV received a brief for informing and defending the consumer, before in 1997 taking more precise charge of the health and protection of consumers. But we should note that the principle of subsidiarity applies in European law on consumption. Various European groups were representing consumers; the oldest, created in March 1962, is the BEUC (European Bureau of Consumers' Unions). They were rather critical of Brussel's policy.

Without going into detail on very recent events, a report by Deputy Chatel presented in 2003 allows us to grasp the 'strengths and weaknesses of French consumerism' within the European framework.[38] The strengths are those of the law itself: it is a more coherent and more protective law than that which appears in other countries due to the existence of the Code; there is an institutional apparatus that does not leave some sectors outside public regulation; and there exists a legal system that offers solid guarantees of basic principles. But this optimistic overview does not forget to list five weaknesses: institutional fragmentation is a source of confusion for the consumer (the layout of public institutions is overly complex and overly centralised, and the consumerist movement is divided);[39] the drive to institutionalise collective bargaining among professional bodies has not led to concrete results; there is a cultural lack of education and self-protection among consumers; modes of damage reparations are not satisfactory for the consumer; and those who take the consumer into account have poor institutional visibility and an insufficient presence in Brussels.

With regard to the solutions proposed (including the creation of a large *Office National de Protection du Consommateur* that would embrace a foundation and be decentralised by the creation of regional chambers of consumption, or the idea of making the CNC into a 'real parliament of consumption'), one must stress that the report's diagnosis rather correctly belongs to the lineage of tensions manifest over the last thirty tears. The report is quite harsh about institutions such as the INC, characterised by an 'unresolved crisis' that is simultaneously financial (its management was denounced by the Accounting Office and the Inspection of Finances, despite its transformation in 1990 from a public administrative establishment to a public industrial and commercial one) and a crisis of positioning, marginalised as it is between the DGCCRF and the autonomous consumers' associations. This report, typical of the enduring tensions in the consumerist camp, has been badly received by some associations: the INDECOSA-CGT principally criticises the attacks on the great number of associations; the UFC does not hesitate to speak of 'a missed opportunity', stressing that 'informing the consumer does not do everything' and that 'mediation has its limits', while it calls instead for 'more dissuasive sanctions'.

The theme of defending the consumer has recently been mobilised once again by French political rulers. After the declarations of President Jacques Chirac during his New Year's wishes to the nation on 31 December 2004, various projects were proposed. An initial law has been passed, but it is limited to technical matters (facilitating the cancellation of contracts that are tacitly renewable and better controlled renewable credit).[40] Currently under study is the possibility of instituting a procedure for class action cases in France where they do not yet exist, taking inspiration from foreign experiences (in particular in Canada). While the United States reformed its own system in February 2005, France is searching for a new procedure for better protecting the consumer. Advocated by some political actors, such a project seems to provoke sharp reactions among industrialists.[41]

Distanced from both the forms of agitation and the nature of the great reform campaigns of the beginning of the twentieth century, the years from 1970 to 1980 were a decade in France of collective action on the theme of defending the consumer. These demands did not take the shape of an alternative economic model, as had been the case among co-operators in the 1920s, but were received by the state and political actors who, while occasionally instrumentalising them, responded by elaborating a complex legislative and institutional system. Setting aside the successive administrative and ministerial structures, the most important measures converged toward the creation of a consumption law that was rationalised in the Code published in 1993. Such an analysis fits well into the grid proposed by Gunnar Trumbull, who sees in the French experience the model of an approach centered on consumer protection.[42] France's difference from the other ideal-types that he offers, which are information (Germany, Great Britain) and collective negotiation (Sweden), no doubt derives from the very distinct roles played in France by entrepreneurs (more in retreat and bending only to strong constraint) and by the state (much more present through a legal-centric tradition and a specialised administration). This notion of 'consumer protection' does not summarise all of France's specific policies on consumption, to which must be added the important question, not treated here, of indebtedness and the equally major one of competition – not to mention standardisation, advertising, the role of the media and food safety, all of which are chapters in themselves.

Three major points seem to spring from this short overview. Consumerist mobilisation in France was characterised by a persistent fragmenting of associations, accentuated by French specificities (lasting throughout the twentieth century) such as divisions among trade unions and the existence of powerful family movements and many specialised associations. Far from suggesting a model hostile to associations that is quite illusory, French experience instead demonstrates the difficult coexistence of this diversity and the representativeness of each of these institutions, a permanently posed problem. The slow process that culminated in the Consumption Code is certainly original to France. This rationalisation of complex legislation going back two centuries, marked by a series of landmarks such as the 1905 law and the laws between 1972 and 1983, is an important element in the context of the judicialisation of a certain number of economic issues and social regulations. Finally, the scale of the European Union, henceforward determinant in these matters, obliges one to reopen the future prospects of a national path of defending the consumer. Faced with crises in food consumption that are by their very nature international, the question of the pertinent level for political intervention re-surfaces. Between the multiplication of legal arsenals and the creation of independent administrative authorities, it seems indeed that consumption policy looks much different today than it did in the 1970s heyday of consumerist demands in France.

Translated by Susan Emanuel

Notes

1 Jean Meynaud, *Les consommateurs et le pouvoir* (Lausanne, 1964).
2 Christiane Restier-Melleray, 'Experts et expertise scientifique: le cas de la France,' *Revue Française de science politique* 40:4 (1990): 546-85.
3 Alain Chatriot, *La démocratie sociale à la française: l'expérience du Conseil national économique 1924-1940* (Paris, 2002).
4 Pierre Rosanvallon, *Le Modèle politique français: la société civile contre le jacobinisme de 1789 à nos jours* (Paris, 2004).
5 Calliope Spanou, *Fonctionnaires et militants: étude des rapports entre l'administration et les nouveaux mouvements sociaux* (Paris, 1991).
6 Michel Wieviorka, *L'Etat, le patronat et les consommateurs: étude des mouvements de consommateurs* (Paris, 1977).
7 Alessandro Stanziani (ed.), *La Qualité des produits en France (XVIIIe-XXe siècles)* (Paris, 2003).
8 Nathalie Sauphanor, *L'Influence du droit de la consommation sur le système juridique* (Paris, 2000).
9 Maurice Deslandres, 'La Participation des consommateurs à la vie des corps publics', in *Le Rôle économique de l'Etat: semaines sociales de France, XVIe session, Strasbourg 1922* (Lyon, 1922), pp. 355-70.
10 These categories are taken from Marcel Garrigou, *L'Assaut des consommateurs: pour changer les rapports producteurs – vendeurs – consommateurs* (Paris, 1981), pp. 25-31. We also have detailed statements from consumers' associations, variously dated: *Les Organisations de consommateurs, Ministère de l'Economie et des Finances, Comité National de la Consommation* (Paris, 1975); Michel Bernard and Jacqueline Quentin, *L'Avant-garde des consommateurs: luttes et organisations en France et à l'étranger* (Paris, 1975), pp. 171-203; and *Guide des associations nationales de consommateurs, Les Groupes de travail de l'ILEC* (Paris, 2002).
11 The long-standing housing associations are the *Confédération Nationale du Logement* (National Housing Confederation, created in 1916) and the *Confédération Générale du Logement* (1954), and two others may be included in the housing category: the *Association Léo-Lagrange pour la Défense des Consommateurs* (1979) and the *Fédération Nationale des Usagers des Transports* (1978).
12 Alain Chatriot, 'Les coopérateurs' in Jean-Jacques Becker and Gilles Candar (eds), *Histoire des gauches en France vol. 2: à l'épreuve de l'histoire* (Paris, 2004), pp. 91-7.
13 Rémi Lenoir, *Généalogie de la morale familiale* (Paris, 2003). For the post-war years, we should mention the *Confédération nationale de la famille rurale* (created in 1944), the *Union nationale des associations familiales* (1945), the *Confédération syndicale des familles* (1946), the *Fédération des Familles de France* (1948) and the *Confédération*

nationale des associations populaires familiales (1952). In 2004, after complex recompositions, six different family associations were recognised as representative of consumers.

14 *50 Millions de consommateurs*, 41 (May 1974): 30-32.

15 Louis Pinto, *La constitution du 'consommateur' comme catégorie de l'espace public* (Paris, new ed., 1989) and 'Le Consommateur: agent économique et acteur politique', *Revue française de sociologie*, XXXI (1990): 179-98 and 'La Gestion d'un label politique: la consommation', *Actes de la recherche en sciences sociales*, 91-92 (March 1992): 3-19.

16 Alexandre Mallard, 'La presse de consommation et le marché: enquête sur le tiers consumériste', *Sociologie du travail*, 42 (2000): 391-409.

17 Pinto, 'La Gestion d'un label politique: la consommation', p. 16.

18 Called the Royer Law, after the name of its promoter, this law to defend small shopkeepers the creation of new hypermarkets in 1973 and gives the right to take legal action to consumers' associations.

19 Michèle Ruffat, 'L'Introduction des intérêts diffus dans le plan: le cas des consommateurs', in Henry Rousso (ed.), *La Planification en crises (1965-1985)*, (Paris, 1987), pp. 115-31.

20 Régis Boulat, 'Jean Fourastié et la naissance de la société de consommation en France', in Alain Chatriot, Marie-Emmanuelle Chessel and Matthew Hilton (eds), *Au nom du Consommateur: Consommation et politique en Europe et aux Etats-Unis au XXe siècle* (Paris, 2004), pp. 98-114.

21 Jeanne Picard, *L'Information du consommateur,* Study Presented by the Section on Modernisation of Distribution, 7 June 1960, Conseil Economique et Social, Archives du Conseil économique et social; *Les moyens d'information des consommateurs*, Conseil Economique et Social, Sessions of 2 and 3 July 1974, *Journal officiel de la République française*, 17 September 1974; *Bilan et perspectives de la politique française à l'égard des consommateurs*, Conseil Economique et Social, Sessions of 22 and 23 May 1984, *Journal officiel de la République française*, 20 July 1984. These three reports constitute essential sources for better understanding the situation of associations and institutions bearing upon consumption in France during this period.

22 Henri Estingoy, 'Fonctions de l'Institut National de la Consommation', *Concurrence*, 32 (1st trimester of 1970): 32-45.

23 *Le Figaro*, 15 January 1976; *Le Monde*, 20 January 1976; *L'Humanité*, 12 February 1976.

24 Report in the name of the Commission of Economic Affairs and the Plan on the draft law on the protection of and information to consumers by M. Jean Proriol, *Impressions du Sénat*, 2nd ordinary session, no. 376, appendix to proceedings of 16 June 1977, p. 3.

25 Law no. 78-22 and no. 78-23 of 10 January 1978, *Journal officiel de la République française*, 11 January 1978, 299-308.

26 Robert Boulin, 'Editorial', *Revue de la concurrence, des prix et de la consommation*, 1 (June 1977).

27 *Les Echos*, 10 April 1978.

28 'Cent dix propositions pour la France', *Regards sur l'actualité*, 74, (Sept/Oct. 1981).

29 Claude Romec, 'Consommation: un Ministère à part entière: interview de Catherine Lalumière, Ministre de la Consommation', *Coopération, distribution, consommation*, 3-4 (March-April 1982), 3-7, p. 4.

30 Law no. 83-660 of 21 July 1983 regarding consumer safety and modifying some clauses of the law of 1 August 1905, *Journal officiel de la République française*, 22 July 1983, pp. 2262-65.

31 Report made in the name of the Commission of Production and Exchanges on the Proposed Law relating to consumer security and modifying various clauses of the law of 1 August 1905, by Henry Delisle, *Impressions de l'Assemblée Nationale*, 2nd ordinary session, no. 1419, appendix to proceedings of the session of 12 April 1983, p. 7.

32 *Le Monde*, 31 August 1985.

33 Véronique Neiertz, 'Avant-propos', in Jean Calais-Auloy, *Propositions pour un code de la consommation, Rapport de la commission de codification du droit de la consommation* (Paris, 1990), p. 5.

34 Jean Calais-Auloy, 'La Protection légale et réglementaire du consommateur: lacunes, excès', in *Nouvelles données pour un droit de la consommation*, 2nd University-Business Meeting organised 17-18 November 1972 in Aix-en-Provence by the Institute of Business Law and the Centre for Improving Business Administration (Paris, 1974), p. 56.

35 Calais-Auloy, *Propositions pour un code de la consommation*, pp. 9, 10, 25.

36 Jean Calais-Auloy, 'La Communauté européenne et les consommateurs', in *Mélanges offerts à André Colomeri* (Paris, 1993), p. 127.

37 Marie-Christine Heloire, 'La Politique de la communauté européenne à l'égard des consommateurs', (Law Ph. D. thesis, Université Paris I, 1986); Philippe Gouband, 'La Protection des intérêts économiques des consommateurs en droit communautaire' (Law Ph. D. thesis, Université Paris II, 1996); and Béatrice Lamarthe, *La Défense du consommateur dans l'union européenne*, Paris, La Documentation Française, 2001.

38 Luc Chatel, *De la conso méfiance à la conso confiance*, Report to the Prime Minister of the Parliamentary Mission of the Secretary of State to small and medium enterprises, to business, to artisans, the liberal professions and consumption, on information, representation, and consumer protection, 9 July 2003.

39 In 2004, no less than 18 associations were recognised at the national level for defending consumers.

40 Law 2005-67 of 28 January 2005 tending to boost the confidence and protection of the consumer, *Journal officiel de la République francaise*, 1 February 2005, p. 1648.

41 *Le Monde*, 20 and 22 January 2005; *Libération*, 7 January and 15 February 2005.

42 Gunnar Trumbull, 'Strategies of Consumer-Group Mobilization: France and Germany in the 1970s', in Martin Daunton and Matthew Hilton (eds), *The Politics of Consumption. Material Culture and Citizenship in Europe and America* (Oxford, New York, 2001), pp. 261-82.

Chapter 8

Shopping for the 'People's Home': Consumer Planning in Norway and Sweden after the Second World War

Iselin Theien

Scandinavia represents a distinct approach to the organisation of the consumer interest after 1945, which cannot be understood without reference to the unique standing of the Labour parties in these countries. Rooted in a compromise between workers and farmers in the mid-1930s, strong and popular Labour governments steered Sweden, Norway and Denmark into the age of mass consumption from 1945 to the mid 1960s. The attitudes of these Social Democratic regimes to the market was deftly described by an American observer of 1950s Norway, who found that 'the liberal tenets of consumer sovereignty and free labour ... are accorded a prominent, but not entirely inviolate, place in the Norwegian socialist credo.[1] Indeed, the form of socialism espoused by the Scandinavian Labour parties paved the way for a comparatively strong state involvement in consumer affairs. The foundations of this Scandinavian model of consumer politics were laid down by the Swedish Social Democrats who, in the 1930s, suggested that regulation and economic planning could be something more than a transitory phase to socialism. What the Swedes envisioned as 'planned house-keeping' (*planhushållning*) also became the aim of Norwegian Labour, embracing this announced third way between state socialism and the free market as an independent, Social Democratic road to an egalitarian society after the period of reconstruction.[2]

To use another of the widely applied and ideologically charged metaphors of the Swedish Social Democrats, the vision of the state as the 'people's home' (*folkhemmet*) encouraged the view of consumption as a public matter in the Scandinavian countries. There were elements within this thinking that hinted at collectivist forms of consumption, most visibly in plans drafted in both Sweden and Norway for collective laundries, refrigerators and even common meals within housing estates in the 1950s, inspired by British 'community centre' ideas.[3] The promotion of universal welfare rights and public services in the broader fields of education, health and culture have also been regarded as forms of social consumption in the 'people's home'.[4] More commonly, though, the ideas of the

Social Democrats centred around erecting new public institutions to look after the consumer interest, maintaining a notion of individual consumer sovereignty but backed up by a state with regulatory powers which could be applied where necessary.

The distinction drawn by Gunnar Trumbull between the German consumer regime as essentially *means-based*, aimed at creating a fair market place, and the French as *ends-based*, aimed at creating legal protections for consumers, is useful for thinking about the Scandinavian model as well.[5] In contrast to France and to the Anglo-American liberal model, the Social Democratic regimes showed little interest in creating an ends-based, in the sense of legalistic, framework for consumer protection. This conforms neatly to a broader analysis of the regulatory approach adopted by the Social Democrats after 1945 as a marked departure from a liberal, rules-based order.[6] The difference between a liberal and the Social Democratic order has been described as one of a restraint on state powers (providing predictability for the individual) under the former, and a more flexible role for the state (with a greater degree on restraints on private interests) under the latter.[7] It was within this latter context that the Social Democratic model for consumer representation took shape, as a means-based but, in contrast to Germany, essentially state-oriented framework for constant negotiation of the consumer interest.

The regulatory framework for economic politics developed by the Social Democratic regimes encouraged the application of a wide network of experts and interest representation. In the growing field of issues that became subject to public scrutiny and planning in the post-1945 period, the Scandinavian states relied heavily on the creation of case-specific committees and expert opinions from interest organisations.[8] The two traditional partners for the state in these corporatist deliberations were, of course, the employers' associations and the trade unions. However, the Social Democratic states were remarkably quick at identifying the consumer as a separate entity for inclusion into the corporatist framework as an extension of their 'third way' orientation. For, in line with the progressive outlook of the Scandinavian Labour parties, which appeared far more ready to embrace the new fruits of affluence in the early 1950s than British Labour, the consumer soon emerged as an entity demanding political representation.[9] Moreover, as Matthew Hilton has suggested, the programme of nationalisation diverted the focus of the British Labour Party from establishing regulatory consumer bodies, whereas the ideological reorientation from socialisation to regulation among the Scandinavian Labour parties could be seen as a contributing factor to their interest in finding ways of representing the consumer interest.[10]

However, the question of where the true representatives of the consumer interest were to be found presented other problems. Identifying which people were to stand as 'consumer experts' was by no means as easy a task as that found within the labour market, where primary interests emerged with greater clarity in the organisation of employers versus employees. In corporatist literature, consumers have been regarded as an example of a disempowered group, due to their difficulties in enforcing 'closure around their interests'.[11] The commonly recognised heterogeneity of the consumer interest presented a particular challenge to the Social Democratic planners, as no single organisation could lay claim to representing the consumer interest for uncontested entry into the corporatist structure. Labour's recognition of the consumer interest in the post-war years did not, therefore, come with any ready solutions as to how this interest was to be mediated in the Scandinavian system of 'negotiated economies'.[12]

In her study of the Japanese consumer movement, and with reference also to the experiences of British and American consumerism, Patricia Mclachlan has suggested a typology of three consumer organisations; Consumer co-operatives, educational consumer organs, and consumer advocacy groups.[13] What is noteworthy in Scandinavia, is the absence of any organisation belonging to the third of these categories, corresponding to the US Consumers Union or the UK Consumers' Association. This may, of course, be understood in the context of the Social Democratic regimes having implemented their own model for consumer representation before the Consumers Union-type organisations had gained a foothold in Europe in the latter part of the 1950s. But the strong standing of the consumer co-operative movement has also been seen as a factor pre-empting the space for independent consumer advocacy groups modelled on the Consumers Union in Scandinavia.[14]

For the Social Democratic planners of the late 1940s and early 1950s, however, the absence of consumer advocacy groups meant that they could not base their consumerist institutions on any pre-existing acknowledged organisation of the 'pure' consumer interest. Whether such an ideal organisation for the consumer interest has ever existed is a matter for discussion. For instance, the standing of the Consumers' Association in Britain would seem to conform more closely to what Suzanne Berger has singled out as the Anglo-American pattern of autonomous interest representation, with groups reflecting 'essentially unmediated demands of socio-economic groups themselves', than any parallel Scandinavian organisation.[15] That is not to say that there were no organisations making claim to the consumer interest in Scandinavia. Both the consumer co-operative movement, a wide range of women's organisations and the trade unions formulated and sought recognition for consumerist agendas in the post-war years. In this article, these questions relating to how the consumer interest was sought and represented within the Scandinavian system will be addressed through a case study of Norway in the 1950s. Within the time-span of a few years, from about 1950 to 1954, a distinct Social Democratic model of consumerism was implemented in Norway, which set the course for how consumer expertise was to be understood up to the present day.

The issue of consumer representation was pushed onto the political agenda in 1950s Norway through two principal debates. Firstly, the heated discussions surrounding the introduction of a Price Control Act in the early 1950s, which gave the state a permanent right to intervene in the price-setting mechanisms of the domestic market, brought the issue of how the consumer interest was to be defined and represented to the core of the political debates of the era.[16] In this chapter, the debates over price regulation will be approached as a source for analysing the party-political attitudes to consumption, and, more specifically, to understanding how the Social Democratic notion of consumer interest representation was shaped. Secondly, there is the issue of how consumers situated themselves in relation to the increasingly complex framework of corporatist institutions underpinning the Social Democratic regime. The primary focus here will be on the creation of the state-sponsored Norwegian Consumer Council of 1953, which brought organised consumers into the corporatist framework of the Social Democratic regime.

Taking care of consumers: the 1954 Price Control Act

After five years of occupation, the language of reconstruction offered the Labour government a fresh opportunity to create 'a new work-day' for Norwegian society, with the aim of expanding the notion of democracy from the political to include also the economic sphere. In 1945, this notion referred to increasing both the influence and the responsibility of the 'democratic organisations' of different groups of producers and workers.[17] At the same time, the party called for the co-ordination of production with consumption, so that all production would be geared towards covering 'the real needs of the population'.[18]

In order to define what these real needs of the population amounted to, the government had a powerful instrument at its disposal in the temporary price control legislation which had been devised by the government-in-exile in May 1945, named the Lex Thagaard after the head of the Price Directorate, Wilhelm Thagaard. The state institution of the Price Directorate, originally a product of World War One, saw its powers greatly extended in the aftermath of World War Two. Under the Lex Thagaard, the Price Directorate was given the authority of controlling prices and expropriating profits from private businesses, as well as enforcing minimum output levels for producers, when it was deemed necessary for the functioning of the domestic market.[19]

In 1947, the Labour government invited representatives from the trade unions, the consumer co-operative movement and the principal producers' organisations to join a committee preparing a new and permanent price control mechanism. After prolonged internal debates, the majority of the committee agreed on a proposal for a new Price Control Act, which was eventually presented to the parliament in 1952. The representatives of the principal producers' organisations presented a dissenting proposition, calling for only temporary and much milder forms of price regulation.[20]

According to the dissenting voices of the producers, the proposed Price Control Act was trying to make permanent a crisis regulation associated with war-time remedies in order to construct a 'silent socialism'. As they saw it, the proposed Price Control Act was informed by a wish to redistribute wealth which was already sufficiently taken care of by the taxation of wages. By driving down the profit margins as a means to redistribute wealth, one would force producers to compromise on quality, or to channel production into more lucrative fields as the price controls were primarily intended to apply to basic goods. Moreover, the use of enabling laws designed to bring this form of redistribution into life would place the market permanently and firmly in the hands of government officials. In short, the trade and industry organisations warned that Norway would no longer belong to the realm of modern, Western democracies if the Price Control Act was implemented in its proposed form.[21]

The Labour Prime Minister Oscar Torp dismissed the accusation that the legislation was any means to introduce socialism on the grounds that it had nothing to do with the long-term aims of the Labour movement of changing the very modes of production.[22] The Price Control Act, then, was to be understood as a law essentially regulating the modes of consumption, through state controls of the price mechanism. Regardless of the prime minister's claim that this legislation had nothing to do with implementing socialism, it could be regarded as having rather a lot to do with implementing the programme of the Labour Party. In 1949, Labour had made some significant revisions of its party programme by redefining its scope from a working-class to a people's party, thus transforming it into one of the least dogmatic policy statements of the European social democratic parties.[23] This people's party defined socialism as a society where everybody would get access to increased living standards.[24] And, as the then Minister of Finance Erik Brofoss (who was otherwise regarded as something of an ascetic within the Labour movement) had defined increased living standards in 1947, this meant making more goods available for everybody.[25]

The Price Control Act proposition laid out a programme for the state to realise the vision of increasing the general living standard in terms of consumption. As the committee majority explained it, the post-war society differed from the interwar situation in the sense that whereas in the 1930s business had needed protection in a buyers' market, after the war it was the consumers who needed protection because it was now a sellers' market.[26] In order to secure a fair deal for consumers under these changed circumstances, the committee proposed that the state should be given a permanent right to intervene in the market, by setting maximum prices in areas where over-powerful producers attempted to take advantage of their position, and minimum prices in instances where the authorities suspected that producers were trying to squeeze out competition in order to establish a monopoly weakening the position of the consumers in the longer run.[27]

The reason why the Price Control Act committee thought it necessary to implement permanent legislation was that it believed the threat of depression to be constant, and not solely related to war-time shortages. Moreover, it pointed out that the patterns of consumption were undergoing substantial changes, in the sense that consumers now spent less on food and other necessities, and more on consumer durables such as fridges and radio sets, on fashionable goods and on leisure.[28] The committee regarded these new patterns of consumption as less stable than the demand for necessities. Moreover, in the open Norwegian economy a substantial proportion of the new consumer durables would have to be imported. According to the Ministry of Finance, 40 per cent of the goods consumed domestically had been imports in the period from 1949-51, and the Ministry believed that the desired further increases in living standards required continued high levels of imports.[29] Thus, the committee concluded, in order to make the regulation of the modern market efficient, the state would require a permanent right to control the price mechanism. A consequence of this expanded vision of the Social Democrats, which departed from their traditional focus on the sphere of production as the primary scene for the social redistribution of wealth, was that the category of consumers became increasingly visible.

An illustrative example of how consumers were pushed up the political agenda can be found in the comparison between two of the principal debates on price regulation in the post-war period. In 1947, when the Lex Thagaard was up for revision in the form of new, temporary price legislation, all of the party-political representatives in parliament were concentrating their arguments on how this legislation would influence producers. It was only in the afternoon of the second day of the debate that the Labour MP Rakel Seweriin reminded her colleagues that 'there has been much talk of the business interests in this debate, but there is also another party to the relationship that the legislation will regulate, and that is the consumers'.[30] She defended the price legislation by reference to the plights of housewives, to whom the state ought to guarantee continued access to necessities at fixed prices. According to Seweriin, the tacit agreement which had been reached on this point constituted the very essence of the social stability which had marked Norwegian society after the war.

When the discussion over the permanent price legislation reached its height in 1953, the consumer had assumed a more central role in political rhetoric. In the debate over the Price Control Act, Rakel Seweriin now had a very different concern on her mind. Again, she entered the parliamentary debate in the afternoon of its second day, but this time to remark that she found it quite astonishing that 'not a single member of parliament has openly defended the interests of producers and business in this matter ... It is equally remarkable that all of the political parties now appear to defend the interests of consumers.' She challenged the opposition's claim to represent the consumer interest, and stated that their 'free choice' arguments would be contradicted by 'every housewife and consumer knowing that they don't decide on what goods a shop manager puts on sale, or on what those goods cost'. Not only was business acting as a sovereign in these questions, she argued, but the producers also had strong organisations at their disposal, whereas the consumer had none. Seweriin thus thought it essential for the state to create permanent institutions to represent the interests of consumers in these matters.[31]

As both the proponents and the opponents of the Price Control Act claimed to speak on behalf of the consumer interest, the question of how the true consumer voice was to be heard remained a pertinent one. A former Labour cabinet minister, Reidar Carlsen, promoted a distinctly state-oriented view for regarding existing political institutions as the legitimate voice of the consumers: 'I perceive myself as a representative of the consumer. At least, I was under the impression that it was the consumer who elected me'.[32] Consequently, he stated that he could not envisage any more powerful channel for the consumer interest than parliament, and, correspondingly, that he regarded the general elections as the only way of empowering consumers. This faith in the expertise of parliament was also evident in the argumentation of the leading Labour politician of the post-war era, Einar Gerhardsen, who acted as Prime Minister for the larger parts of the period from 1945 to 1965. Gerhardsen used the example of the 'recent innovation of ballpoint pens' to argue that consumers lacked fundamental information. As the prices of these pens had fallen dramatically in the span of only a couple of years, Gerhardsen argued, how were consumers to know what the right price of the product actually was?[33]

The opponents of the Price Control Act in the Conservative and the Farmers' Party vigorously objected to the notion that the state was more equipped to look after the consumer interest than the actual shoppers themselves. In classic liberal vein, the leading Conservative politician, Sjur Lindebrække, argued that '[t]he aim of the economic policies must always be to give consumers the most plentiful, the best and the cheapest goods available according to how consumers themselves perceive their needs and wants.'[34] Accordingly, he called for a transfer of powers *out* of the government offices and back to the consumers. The Farmers' Party followed up on this lead, and added that the best form of price control consisted of informative product labelling, so that consumers themselves could compare price and quality.[35]

However, the Price Control Act committee and its defenders in parliament also suggested more direct ways for consumers to make their voices heard than through the elected politicians. The 1953 Minister of Finance, Trygve Bratteli, outlined this idea in his description of modern Norwegian society as one where organisation had eclipsed free competition. Within this system, he diagnosed 'housewives in their role as consumers' as the only principal economic group with no strong organisation at their disposal, which made free price-setting illusory since producers were efficiently organised.[36] This notion resonated with the main trade union AFL (*Arbeidernes Faglige Landsorganisasjon*), which supported the Price Control Act on the grounds that whereas labour and capital balanced each other through their organisations and thus did not require any state interference, there existed no corresponding balance of powers between the unorganised consumers and business.[37]

Outside of parliament, however, the consumer co-operative movement, with a membership of over 200,000 households, firmly protested against the notion that consumers were unorganised in Norway. Nevertheless, and in contrast to their traditional opposition to state regulation of the markets, the consumer co-operative union NKL (*Norges Kooperative Landsforening*) cautiously supported the Price Control Act.[38] One way of accounting for this change of direction would be to see it as an expression of a general rapprochement between the consumer co-operative and the Labour movements in the post-war years. But also, the NKL saw the Price Control Act as an opportunity to receive recognition for their position as 'the principal organisation for consumers in Norway.'[39] This was important, as it became increasingly evident that both social and political actors were looking for new ways of organising the consumer interest in the early 1950s. These attempts were eventually channelled into the creation of the 1953 Consumer Council.

Creating a new platform for consumers: the 1953 Consumer Council

The creation of the 1953 Norwegian Consumer Council was regarded at the time as something of an experiment.[40] This does not, however, imply that the Norwegian model was without precedents. In 1946, the Swedish parliament had established a commission on consumer education and product research, which led to the establishment of the state Institute for Informative Labelling in 1951. In addition to this recent Swedish innovation, the 1953 Norwegian parliamentary bill on the Consumer Council mentioned the Danish Housewives' Consumer Council as another source of inspiration. The *Danske Husmødres Forbrugerråd* had been established as an independent committee for a number of Danish housewives' organisations in 1947, with the aim of providing a platform for the representation of the consumer interest on the official price boards.[41]

While expressing their admiration for these two Scandinavian consumer bodies, the committee preparing the parliamentary bill on the Norwegian Consumer Council maintained that neither of them provided a complete model for a consumer organisation suited to the particular needs of Norway. Moreover, the committee dismissed the idea that any private consumer organisation, for instance along the lines of the US Consumers Union, represented a viable option for Norway. This was based on the perception that the consumer interests often appeared to be of a volatile, ad hoc nature, and thus were unlikely to produce the stability needed for forming a voluntary organisation. For instance, the committee remarked, a housewife would only be interested in the market for washing machines for a limited time, and once the item was bought, she would no longer have any interests in common with other washing-machine buyers. The consumer interest was simply regarded as too broad and diverse for any private organisation, and the committee thus believed that organising the consumer interest represented a legitimate task for the state.[42]

The notion that housewives as shoppers of washing machines and other modern goods were unable to organise independently was, however, somewhat problematic. Already in 1950, women's organisations of both Labour, Conservative and Co-operative origins had established a joint Committee for Consumer Education and Quality Control, which, as the name suggests, represented a clear-cut example of a privately organised educational consumer group, created to deal with consumer durables and other products associated with affluence.[43] This initiative originally met with support from the state, which, through the Ministry of Trade, promised 10,000 *Kroner* to the further work of the committee in 1951.[44]

However, this funding never materialised, and the Committee for Consumer Education and Quality Control dissolved shortly after its much publicised foundation meeting. Parallel to this consumerist initiative, however the state in the form of the Price Directorate had been drawing up plans of its own. The priorities of the Price Directorate differed from those of the women's organisations in the sense that the Price Directorate regarded quality considerations as secondary to price concerns for the consumer interest.[45] In particular, the Price Directorate was looking for ways of strengthening consumer representation on a number of trade-specific price boards, which had hitherto consisted of trade union representatives and selected housewives.[46] The Price Directorate was less than satisfied with these representatives, and was generally sceptical about having trade unions representing the consumer interest, as it believed that the priorities of the trade unions might 'differ from those of the general consumer, for example where price increases are deemed necessary to maintain production and thus employment levels.'[47]

Therefore, the Price Directorate suggested that a new consumer organisation be established as a permanent advisory body to the political authorities in matters regarding price regulation. Subsequently, and only a few months after the housewives had set up their Committee on Consumer Education and Quality Control, the Price Directorate invited the women's organisations alongside the Consumer Co-operative Union (NKL), the Trade Union (AFL) and the principal producers' organisations to discuss the creation of a 'Consumers' Council', the *Forbrukerrådet*.[48] In order to avoid any 'institutional overlapping', the Price Directorate made it clear to these organisations that the housewives' committee and the accompanying public funding would have to be channelled into the new, state body.[49] However, in what must be understood as a concession to the original women's organisations, the proposal drafted by the Consumer Council committee presented a body combining price regulation with consumer education and quality control.

It was the combination of these three fields within one, state-sponsored body that made the Norwegian Consumer Council, which was eventually passed through a bill in parliament in 1953, an experiment in Scandinavian consumer organisation.[50] Sweden, which in many other respects served as the leader in Scandinavian consumer politics, followed up on the Norwegian lead later in the 1950s, with the creation of the Swedish State Consumer Council, *Statens Konsumentråd*, in 1957. In the same process, the 1944 'Home Research Institute', *Hemmens Forskningsinstitut*, was transformed from a privately based centre for home economics, run by housewives' organisations (though partly supported by public means) to a fully-financed state institution.[51]

The creation of such state-centred consumerist institutions lends itself to conflicting interpretations of what constituted the driving force for the Social Democratic planners. To the opponents of the Norwegian Consumer Council in the principal trade and producers' organisations, this institution appeared as little more than an auxiliary power source for the Labour government. As the principal Conservative daily *Aftenposten* put it, the non-socialist sectors of Norwegian society feared that the consumer body would simply form 'another layer in the security wall around the Labour government'.[52] The trade and producers' organisations particularly reacted to the 'conspicuous timing' between the creation of the Consumer Council and the Price Control committees, and regarded the two as complementary schemes in Labour's efforts to place the market under political control.[53] A direct link between these two incentives had in fact been suggested by the Price Directorate, which had signalled that an eventual Consumer Council might play a role as an organ for the consumer interest under the proposed Price Control Act.[54]

However, the private roots of the state consumer institutions in the housewives' educational consumer groups may suggest a more dynamic perspective on this 1950s process. Both in Sweden and in Norway, the creation of the public consumer bodies were presented, and to a large extent perceived, as a particular concession to women.[55] The association of women, and, more precisely, housewives, with the consumer interest was partly a reflection of statistical observations showing that most purchases were made by women; a Swedish public trade commission estimated that female shoppers were responsible for two thirds of the purchases made nationwide.[56] In addition, it was sometimes suggested that women applied a somewhat different logic in their shopping decisions than men. For instance, the Swedish trade commission thought that whereas men were prone to spend 5 *kronor* on a product worth 2 *kronor* if they needed it, women were more inclined to spend 2 *kronor* on a product worth 5 *kronor* even if they did not need it.[57] More commonly, though, women were seen as more knowledgeable consumers than men, and the image of the consumer expert as a housewife was also heralded by state planners such as the Norwegian Price Directorate.[58]

The composition of the Norwegian Consumer Council may also be seen as reflecting the recognition of female expertise in consumption issues, as the housewives' organisations were given the majority of the seats on the council board, with additional representation granted to the Consumer Co-operative Union NKL and the Trade Union AFL.[59] From the perspective of the housewives' organisations, even the non-socialist National Council of Norwegian Women eyed the creation of a state consumer body as a golden opportunity to implement programmes to improve the standing of the consumer.[60] The establishment of the Consumer Council may thus be seen as a classical corporatist trade-off, by which various interest organisations, and most notably the housewife associations, gave up some of their independence in return for greater direct access to national policy formulation in the field of consumer affairs.

Conclusion: private consumption, public planning

By demonstrating that there existed strong consumer voices outside of parliament and the government offices, the women's organisations could be seen as tempering a more *dirigiste* approach to consumer protection in Norway. The notion that the state knew best how to look after the interests of the consumers in the market, which had been voiced most clearly by Labour in the debate over the Price Control Act, was challenged by such independent articulations of consumer demands. At the same time, both non-socialist women and consumer co-operators, traditionally sceptical of state regulation of the market, displayed a growing recognition of the political authorities as allies in their ambition to improve the standing of the consumer in the post-war years. The mutual recognition of the established consumer organisations and the political authorities in the field of consumer representation could be seen as an important factor in the creation of stable and relatively strong institutions for the consumer interest in the Scandinavian countries.

Beneath the institutional level lay the more fundamental question of whether the consumer was a public or a private actor. The Social Democratic notion of private consumption as largely a public matter was informed by several concerns. One was the general, productivist ambition of creating a national economy that literally delivered the goods to the 'people's home'.[61] The education of a nation of consumer experts was seen as an important element in this planning, as the Social Democrats believed that if consumers would make more enlightened choices, production would become more rational.[62] However, as has been discussed in this article with relation to the Norwegian Labour Party, the Social Democratic planners also increasingly focused on consumers as a social category worthy of attention and protection in its own right. From mildly paternalistic concerns over how gullible consumers were exposed to advertising and modern salesmanship in the market to more liberal concerns over consumer rights and representation, the Labour regimes saw a need to incorporate consumers into their planned housekeeping of the 1940s and 1950s.

As it emerged in relation to the establishment of the Norwegian Consumer Council, there was an apparent gender dimension to this growing recognition of the private consumer as public citizen. In Sweden, the inclusion of consumption among the new public tasks of the Social Democratic state was explicitly linked to feminist issues. The follow-up to the 1946 commission on product research and consumer education, the 1964 commission on 'More efficient consumer information', saw state consumerism in the context of deeper social changes. 'The relations between the private and the public have fundamentally changed', this commission argued, 'and at the core of these changes are the changes in family structures and the position of women'.[63] In explicit disagreement with what they regarded as the old liberal wish for keeping the private private, the Social Democratic planners argued that private housewifery should be viewed as a profession on a par with paid employment, and, correspondingly, that it was subject to public regulation like any other work-place.[64] State involvement in consumer affairs was thus presented as an aid to housewives, strengthening their position in society by moving their work out of the private and into the public sphere of the 'people's home'. The private had, in this respect, become political, and the public consumer bodies were seen as an important part of the arena for women's politics.

The gradual co-optation of private interests and voluntary organisations by state institutions in the field of consumer affairs would thus appear as one aspect of the reformist, regulatory socialism guiding the Social Democratic regimes. While many of the instruments applied to promote the consumer interest in Scandinavia, such as product research, quality labelling and information disseminated through comparative testing magazines resembling the British *Which?* or the French *Que Choisir?*, the logic of Social Democratic consumerism was comparatively unique. The corporatist structure developed for representing consumers and guiding consumption in Scandinavia expressed a blurring of the boundaries between the private and the public, in which neither producer nor consumer sovereignty was 'entirely inviolate'.[65]

Notes

1 Mark W. Leiserson, *Wages and Economic Control in Norway 1945-1957* (Cambridge, MA, 1959), p. 3.

2 On Sweden, see Leif Lewin, *Planhushållningsdebatten* (Uppsala, 1967). On Norway, see Rune Slagstad, *De nasjonale strateger* (Oslo, 2001), pp. 273 ff.

3 See the Swedish public report on collective town planning: *SOU 1956:32. Hemmen och samhällsplaneringen. Bostadskollektiva kommitténs slutbetänkande* (Stockholm, 1956).

4 Bengt-Olof Anderson, *Den svenska modellens tredje kompromiss. Efterkrigstidens välfärdspolitik med utgångspunkt från industrins kompetenssäkring och skolans reformering* (Göteborg, 2000), p. 27.

5 Gunnar Trumbull, 'Strategies of Consumer-Group Mobilization: France and Germany in the 1970s', in Martin Daunton and Matthew Hilton (eds), *The Politics of Consumption. Material Culture and Citizenship in Europe and America* (Oxford, 2001), p. 262.

6 See Trond Nordby, *Korporatisme på norsk, 1920-1990* (Oslo, 1994) and Francis Sejersted, *Demokratisk kapitalisme* (Oslo, 1993), Ch. 9.

7 Rune Slagstad, *Rettens ironi* (Oslo, 2001), p. 200.

8 See Leif Lewin, *Samhället och de organiserade interessena* (Stockholm, 1992).

9 See Lawrence Black, *The Political Culture of the Left in Affluent Britian, 1951-64: Old Labour, New Britain?* (Basingstoke, 2003).

10 Matthew Hilton, *Consumerism in Twentieth-Century Britain: The Search for a Historical Movement* (Cambridge, 2003), p. 146.

11 Alan Cawson, *Corporatism and Political Theory* (Oxford, 1986), p. 15.

12 Klaus Nilsen and Ove Pedersen (eds), *Forhandlingsøkonomi i Norden* (Norwegian edition, Oslo, 1989).

13 Patricia Maclachlan, *Consumer Politics in Post-war Japan: The Institutional Boundaries of Citizen Activism* (New York, 2002), p. 16.

14 See Tor Bjørklund, *Forbrukerinnflytelse på dagligvarehandelen*, (Oslo, 1984) and T. Janus Andersen, *Forbrugerpolitik og forbrukerorganisation i Skandinavien*, (Copenhagen, 1980).

15 Suzanne D. Berger, 'Introduction', in Suzanne D. Berger (ed.), *Organizing interests in Western Europe: pluralism, corporatism, and the transformation of politics* (Cambridge, 1981), p. 5.
16 A similar debate took place in Sweden: see *SOU 1955:45: Konkurrens och priser. Betänkande avgivet av 1954 års priskontrollutredning* (Stockholm, 1955).
17 Norwegian Labour Party programme, 'Arbeid til alle', 1945.
18 Labour Party election programme, 1945.
19 Trond Bergh, 'Plan, marked, fullmakter og demokrati' in Edvard Bull *et al.* (eds), *Arbeiderbevegelsens historie i Norge, Bind 5* (Oslo, 1987) pp. 224-49.
20 Norwegian parliamentary records: Ot.prop. 60, 1952.
21 Parliamentary records: Appendix 2 to Ot.prop. 60: Joint statement from the Organisation of Norwegian Industrialists, the Association of Private Retailers and the Craftsmen Guild, 1 July 1952, pp. 62-116.
22 Parliamentary records: St.forh. 1953 vol. 8, p. 437.
23 Even Lange, *Samling om felles mål, 1935-70. Bind 11 Aschehoughs Norgeshistorie* (Oslo, 1998), p. 132.
24 Trond Bergh, 'Norsk økonomisk politikk' in Trond Bergh and Helge Pharo (eds), *Vekst og velstand. Norsk politisk historie 1945-65* (Oslo, 1989), p. 47.
25 Parliamentary records: St.forh. 1947 vol 8, p. 480.
26 Parliamentary records: Ot.prop. 60, 1952, pp. 71-79.
27 *Ibid.*, p. 51.
28 *Ibid.*, p. 27.
29 Parliamentary records: Ot.prop. 60, 1952, p. 29.
30 Parliamentary records: St.forh. 1947 vol 8, p. 543.
31 Parliamentary records: St.forh. 1953 vol 8, p. 464.
32 *Ibid.*, p. 397.
33 *Ibid.*, p. 463.
34 *Ibid.*, p. 360.
35 *Ibid.*, p. 373
36 *Ibid.*, p. 388.
37 Parliamentary records: Appendix 2 to Ot.prop. 60: Statement from the AFL, 28 June 1952.
38 On the pre-war attitudes of the NKL, see Iselin Theien, 'Socialism, Liberalism or Political Neutrality? The Balancing Act of the Consumer Co-operatives in Inter-war Norway', *Journal of Co-operative Studies*, 106 (2002): 167-182.
39 Parliamentary records: Appendix 2 to Ot.prop. 60: Statement from the NKL, 25 June 1952, p. 30.
40 Norwegian Joint Committee on International Social Policy, *Social and Labour News from Norway* 4 (1953).
41 Parliamentary records: St.prp.1/11 1953, p. 18.
42 The Norwegian national library collection, NA/A k 7517: Instilling fra Forbrukerrådutvalget: I. Forbrukerrådet [Oslo, 1953], p. 24.
43 Utvalget for kvalitetskontroll og konsumentopplysning, UKK. See 'Samarbeid', *Mellom Oss. Meldingsblad til de kooperative kvinneforeninger*, 1 February 1951 and NKL archives, K4/5A/424: Copy of letter from the UKK to the Ministry of Trade, 23 June 1951.
44 Reference in parliamentary records: St.prp.1/11, 1953, p. 1.

45 The Norwegian national library collection, NA/A k 7517: Instilling fra Forbrukerrådutvalget: I. Forbrukerrådet [Oslo, 1953], pp. 3-4.
46 Price Board Regulations, §2, *Pristidende* 1/1948.
47 Parliamentary records: St.prp.1/11/11, 1953: Letter from the Price Directorate to the Ministry of Finance of 26 January 1952.
48 Norwegian National Archives: Nytt 1. sos.knt. A, 1263/11, D0607, FR/12.
49 Parliamentary records: St.prp.1/11/12, 1953.
50 Parliamentary records: St. tid. 1953, pp. 1998 ff.
51 Swedish public report *SOU 1964:4: Effektivare konsumentupplysning. Betänkande avgivet av konsumentupplysningsutredningen* (Stockholm, 1964), pp. 9-11.
52 'Forbrukerne og regjeringen', *Aftenposten*, 16 April 1953.
53 Parliamentary records: St. prp. 1/11/4,5,7, 1953.
54 NKL Archives, K4/5A/438: 'Orientering om innstilling fra Pris- og Rasjonaliseringskomiteen'.
55 See for instance editorial on 'Forbrukerrådet' in *Dagbladet*, 11 August 1952, and editorial on 'Forbrukerne og regjeringen' in *Aftenposten*, 16 April 1953.
56 Swedish public report on trade *SOU 1955:16: Pris och prestation i handeln. Varudistribusjonsutredningens betänkande* (Stockholm, 1955), p. 68.
57 *Ibid.*, p. 73. The example was attributed to the Norwegian economist Thomas Sinding.
58 See for instance reference in NKL Archives, K4/5A/416: Semmingsen PM, 17 November 1951.
59 Parliamentary records: St.prp 1/11, 1953. p. 28.
60 *Ibid.*, addition 2: Statement from the NKN, 23 March 1953.
61 See Even Lange, *Samling om felles mål, 1935-70. Bind 11 Aschehoughs Norgeshistorie* (Oslo, 1998), pp.154 ff.
62 Swedish public report on product labelling *SOU 1949:18: Kvalitetsforskning och konsumentupplysning. Betänkande avgivet av 1946 års utredning angående kvalitetsforskning och konsumentupplysning* (Stockholm, 1949), p. 15.
63 *SOU 1964:4: Effektivare konsumentupplysning. Betänkande avgivet av konsumentupplysningsutredningen* (Stockholm, 1964), p. 23.
64 Britta Lövgren, *Hemarbete som politik. Diskussioner om hemarbete, Sverige 1930-40-talen, och tilkomsten av Hemmens Forskningsinstitut* (Stockholm, 1993), pp. 32 ff. See also Gro Hagemann, 'Citizenship and Social Order: Gender politics in Twentieth-Century Norway and Sweden', *Women's History Review*, 3 (2002).
65 Mark W. Leiserson, *Wages and Economic Control in Norway 1945-1957* (Cambridge, Mass. 1959), p. 3.

Chapter 9

The Entrepreneurial Ethic and the Spirit of Consumerism:

Finances and Strategy in the US Consumer Movement

Robert N. Mayer

Who should speak for the consumer – experts who judge what is best for consumers or leaders of consumer-generated organizations who transmit member preferences? In many countries, consumer experts are officially designated and financially supported by the national government. In extreme cases, a single individual or organization is allocated the near-exclusive right to provide input on consumer policy questions and bring lawsuits on behalf of consumers. The assumption behind direct government-funding of consumer experts is that the consumer viewpoint is vital in public debate but vulnerable to under-representation by the 'free rider problem' so that consumer representation must be guaranteed by the state.[1]

The 'corporatist' approach to consumer representation in which government-sanctioned experts interpret the interests of consumers is best exemplified by the Nordic countries, but it applies to a lesser degree to most wealthy countries, especially the Netherlands, Germany, and Canada.[2] Even in the United Kingdom, where the privately-funded *Which?* (formerly the Consumers' Association) speaks effectively for consumers, government-supported consumer representation is accomplished as well by the National Consumer Council, whose mission is 'to safeguard the interests of consumers and to ensure that these interests are represented to, and are taken account of, by decision-makers.'[3] The potential drawback of government-provided consumer representatives is they may mute their voices when the interests of consumers conflict with the interests of the group in power.

In the United States, direct government support of private consumer organizations is forbidden, so a very different approach to consumer representation has evolved. As befits a country that raises the free market and democracy to near-divine status, consumer representation is expected to spring spontaneously from consumers themselves. If consumer organizations fail to coalesce to voice consumer concerns, this becomes evidence that consumer interests are weak and undeserving of consideration in public policy discussions. One risk of this approach is that, because consumer interests are diffuse and likely to be subordinate to other bases of political affiliation, effective consumer representation will not take place, even when most consumers feel strongly about a subject.[4] A second risk exists. When individuals or groups manage to voice a consumer perspective, their legitimacy can be undermined through charges of being 'self-appointed' or 'paternalistic.' An upside exists, however, under this arrangement for representing consumers. If the barriers to consumer mobilization can be overcome, representation by a varied set of well-funded, professionally-staffed, politically-independent consumer organizations is possible.

In essence, the US approach to consumer representation equates legitimacy with the ability to mobilize financial resources from the private sector. This forces the leaders of consumer organizations to act as political entrepreneurs who 'sell' goods and services to a variety of non-governmental entities.[5] This task of raising funds from consumers as well as philanthropists, businesses, and foundations is made more difficult by the fact that consumer organizations must compete with each other in obtaining money. A final challenge to representing consumers in a political environment that defines the legitimacy of a consumer organization by its ability to mobilize financial resources is the threat of 'corporate front groups,' that is, corporate-funded and corporate-directed organizations that pretend to speak for consumers but in reality pursue the interests of their corporate patrons.

There are several legal and tax policies in the US that aid private consumer organizations in mobilizing financial resources. Still, each organization must find its way to financial solvency and stability. After providing a few basics about the rules governing private consumer organizations in the US, this chapter examines the diverse ways in which four leading US consumer organizations have overcome the challenge of mobilizing resources on an ongoing basis. The organizations are the National Consumers League, Consumers Union, Consumer Federation of America, and Public Citizen. For each of these organizations, I highlight the unique features of its fund-raising strategy and consider the potential impact of the strategy on its political tactics. Next, I examine the phenomenon of corporate front groups and how they muddle public and policy maker perceptions of the consumer interest. Finally, I conclude with some final reflections on the exportability of a US-style system of consumer representation in which resources are conflated with legitimacy.

Some rules of the game

The most important distinction among consumer organizations is whether they qualify as a 501(c)(3) or 501(c)(4) entity under the US Internal Revenue Code. Both designations refer to non-profit organizations that are exempt from federal taxation, but only 501(c)(3) organizations are eligible for low-cost bulk mailing permits. Far more important, only donations to 501(c)(3)s are tax deductible for the donors. In essence, the federal government subsidizes donations to 501(c)(3) organizations and, hence, these organizations must be devoted to religious, charitable, scientific, public safety, literary, or educational purposes. This might seem to disqualify most consumer advocacy organizations; but as long as they refrain from endorsing particular political candidates and devote only an 'insubstantial' portion of their resources to lobbying for specific legislation, the organization can usually qualify. ('Insubstantial' is not specifically defined, but it is generally understood that spending somewhere between five to ten per cent of an organization's budget on legislative lobbying falls within the legal limits.) If an organization plans to devote a substantial portion of its resources to lobbying on specific pieces of legislation, it should incorporate as a 501(c)(4).

An organization established as a 501(c)(3) can exist side-by-side with one established as a 501(c)(4). The two organizations need to be incorporated separately and have different names, but the members of their governing boards can overlap. The staffs of the two organizations can also be shared. It is critical, though, that the two organizations keep separate financial records. For example, a person who works for both entities must keep time sheets that show work time allocated to each organization. Most importantly, funds given to the 501(c)(3) may not be used by or commingled with those of the 501(c)(4).

Although the incorporation of consumer groups and other activist organizations as a 501(c)(3) is common, it is controversial. Political conservatives and libertarians consider it unfair for activists to benefit from even indirect government support. Conservative think tanks such as the Cato Institute and Heritage Foundation have criticized activism by 501(c)(3) organisations, and members of Congress sometimes heed the call to reign in what they perceive as inappropriate subsidization of political advocacy.[6] Those who believe that 501(c)(3) organizations abuse their tax status say they are equally opposed to lobbying by left- and right-leaning groups. In practice, however, most of their targets are on the left, especially environmental, labour, and 'good government' groups.

Against the backdrop of the rules that govern non-profit organizations, how do consumer organizations solve the problem of resource mobilization? The next section of this chapter examines the efforts of four major consumer organizations in the US. They are arguably *the* four most important, but they also exemplify four different strategies for raising revenue without abandoning their core mission of faithfully representing consumers. The four organizations are treated in chronological order of their founding.

The National Consumers League

The National Consumers League (NCL) is not the largest or most powerful US consumer organization, but it is the oldest. It was founded in 1899 and has continuously pursued a worker- and consumer-focused agenda of social justice.[7] Having solved the resource mobilization problem for more than a century, NCL relies on its longevity as a primary source of its perceived legitimacy and expertise.

NCL's sources of funding have changed over time. Until fairly recently in its history, the League relied heavily on volunteer work and financial contributions from a small but deeply committed group of well educated and wealthy leaders. Most of these leaders had a strong sense of social responsibility toward workers; their desire to improve the condition of consumers was secondary.[8] It was not until the late 1930s, when the League was struggling in terms of leadership (NCL's guiding light Florence Kelley had died in 1932) and finances, that NCL placed greater emphasis on issues, such as monopolies and high prices, that might have appealed to consumers more directly. Again after World War II, the League continued championing genuinely consumer issues in addition to those reflecting the consumer's responsibility toward workers, but the League did not appeal to the general consuming public for financial support. As a result, the League continued to rely for human and financial resources on a small group of leaders, and it considered disbanding on several occasions. When NCL Chair Robert Nathan recruited Sandra Willett to become the organization's leader in 1976, he said to her, 'You are the League's last hope. If you don't succeed in raising money and developing programs, we will probably have to merge [with another consumer organization] or shut down.' The League had less than $7,000 in its bank account at the time.[9]

Fortunately, the organization stepped back from the brink. Beginning in the mid-1970s with the appointment of Willett as its executive director and continuing from 1984 to the present under the leadership of Linda Golodner, NCL has successfully met the challenge of raising enough money from new sources to become a professionally-staffed organization dedicated primarily to the consumer (although with a strong commitment to labour issues). With many other consumer organizations competing for funding and the consumer movement past its apex in the late 1970s, the League's leadership decided that it would have to rely on a broad range of funding sources, including individual businesses and trade associations.

The exact percentage of NCL's $2 million annual budget that currently comes from business sources is not a matter of public record, but it is safe to say that the proportion is at least half. (Key financial data for the four organizations examined in this chapter are found in Table 9.1, on p. 164.) Individual corporations and trade associations contribute to NCL in several ways. Some are unrestricted donations, but most contributions are designed to support specific projects, such as conferences, educational campaigns, the Lifesmarts consumer knowledge competition for high school students, a fraud reporting center, dinners at which awards are presented for service to consumers, and surveys of consumer opinion on important issues. Donors come from many industries, with telecommunications, financial services, health care, and pharmaceuticals being especially well represented among NCL's funders. In fairness to the League, it also receives financial support from a number of labour unions (often drawn from the same industries as its business donors) and procures ongoing funding from the US

Department of Justice in support of the League's National Fraud Information Center.

A final source of NCL funding is the receipt of *cy pres* awards.[10] These awards are made by courts in cases where consumers have been harmed but it is not feasible to compensate consumers directly. For example, in 2002, NCL was one of several non-profit organizations to receive a portion of a $1.9 million court settlement involving charges that Amazon.com's and Alexa Internet had illegally collected personal information. NCL's share was $150,000, to be used to educate consumers about their privacy rights.[11]

NCL's practice of accepting business funding has isolated the League somewhat from the remainder of the US and world consumer movements. Acceptance of business funding precludes the League from being a member of Consumers International, the umbrella group for the world's consumer organizations. Russell Mokhiber, author of several anti-corporate books and editor of the *Multinational Monitor*, described the League as having been 'taken over' by corporate America and turned into a 'corporate consumer group.'[12] NCL's executive director Linda Golodner is unapologetic about the League's fundraising methods, noting that NCL is open about its contributors and has stood up to corporate pressure when necessary. Moreover, Golodner believes that working in partnership with corporations provides an important 'reality check' to consumer organizations, helping them to pursue policy solutions that are feasible and therefore can be implemented quickly.[13] Most important, acceptance of business funds has allowed the League to amass a stable staff of full-time professionals who accumualte substantial expertise in areas of consumer policy. They are both invited to express the consumer point of view in government and business fora; these expert staffers also petition and submit comments to regulatory bodies on behalf of consumers.

Consumers Union

Consumers Union (CU) is the largest consumer organization in the world in terms of its annual budget. CU was founded in 1936 as a result of a strike by the workers of its predecessor, Consumers' Research.[14] For the past seven decades, CU has been at the heart of the US consumer movement and, in an important sense, the world consumer movement. CU's core enterprise is product testing, an activity that requires substantial scientific expertise. Among CU's 400 employees who earn more than $50,000 per year,[15] many are scientists and engineers. Others are professionals in various aspects of journalism and financial management. As a result, CU can lay claim to the largest amount of scientific expertise among the four organizations profiled in this chapter.

CU's legitimacy in speaking for the consumer has bases other than longevity and scientific expertise, however. For one thing, it has more than five million member-subscribers, far more than any other consumer organizations. CU also has an enormous budget by the standards of consumer organizations. Its annual revenues were over $164 million in the 2003 fiscal year, approximately twice that of its nearest global 'competitor,' the Consumers' Association in the United Kingdom.[16]

While the majority of Consumers Union's revenues come from the sale of its flagship magazine *Consumer Reports*, CU receives substantial amounts of funding from other sources, including foundation grants for special projects and bequests from its dedicated followers. An example of the former is CU's Consumer WebWatch program, which works to increase the credibility of consumer information found on the Internet. Consumer WebWatch was launched in 2000 with a $2.7 million grant from the Pew Charitable Trusts and a $2 million grant from the John S. and James L. Knight Foundation.[17] CU also aggressively encourages annual contributions from its loyal readers, some of whom donate as much as $10,000 to become 'patrons' of the organizations. Other members engage in 'planned giving' whereby members bequeath funds to CU to be available either after their death or before it in exchange for a lifetime annuity. A further source of revenue for CU is its annual raffle. Despite giving away more than $50,000 in cash prices to various winners, CU clears $4-5 million annually from its raffle.[18]

Among all of CU's sources of revenue, two are notable for their absence. One is revenue from advertisements placed in its published products. Under its 'No Commercial Use Policy,' CU does not accept any advertising. Nor does CU sell, rent, or trade its membership list. Both accepting advertising and selling the names of its members to marketers would generate significant revenue for CU in the short term, but these practices would likely undercut its long-term credibility.

The legitimacy and expertise of Consumers Union is enhanced not only by its longevity, scientific expertise, size, and scrupulousness in accepting money; CU's ability to speak for the consumer is also a function of how its spends its money. In addition to successfully running its own organization, Consumers Union has provided both initial and sustaining funding for a variety of consumer organizations, including the Consumer Federation of America, the American Council on Consumer Interests, and Consumers International. This financial support of other consumer organizations reflects CU's commitment to do more than help consumers choose among competing brands in the marketplace. CU is also dedicated to elevating the rules that govern the marketplace. Although CU is organized as a 501(c)(3), the massive size of its budget allows it to engage in a large amount of political activity, including those of its 'advocacy' offices in Washington, D.C., Texas, and California and its Consumer Policy Institute. Normally, consumer organizations need to be extremely circumspect about lobbying in support of specific legislation, but given the size of CU's annual revenues, it is allowed to spend $1 million annually on this form of lobbying. According to its tax filings, CU stays well under this limit, but it spends several million dollars per year on *general* advocacy with regard to consumer issues.

The Consumer Federation of America

The Consumer Federation of America (CFA) is the umbrella organization for the US consumer movement. CFA's 300 dues-paying members are organizations, not individual consumers, but these organizations have a combined membership of over 50 million individuals. As such, CFA does not speak *for* the consumer; it *is* the consumer. It was established in 1967 by 'reform-minded advocates during a period of change and social protest.'[19] These advocates included representatives of consumer organizations (like Consumers Union), labour unions (like the International Ladies Garment Workers Union), and consumer cooperatives (especially credit unions and rural electrical cooperatives); these constituencies continue to form the base of CFA. While annual dues payments range as high as $20,000, most organizations contribute between $75 and $1,000 annually. CFA's $3.5 million 2004 budget was spent on research, consumer education, services in support of its member organizations, and advocacy in all branches and levels of government.[20]

Like the National Consumers League and Consumers Union, CFA's core staff members are experts in various domains of consumer policy. Many of these experts, such as Marc Cooper (public utilities) and Barbara Roper (investor protection), have spent their entire careers within CFA. Recently, CFA has become a home base for political entrepreneurs who once ran their own consumer organizations. Examples of consumer experts who followed this career path are Carol Tucker Foreman and Arthur S. Jaeger (food policy) and Alan J. Fishbein (housing and credit).

Although CFA's largest member is Consumers Union, CFA's philosophy regarding sources of funding is closer to that of the National Consumers League than it is to that of CU. Unlike CU and like NCL, CFA is willing to accept funds from business and government sources *for specific projects*. For example, in 2000, CFA conducted a consumer survey and commissioned a research study with funding from the corporation Providian Financial. More typically, CFA accepts project funding from business-related foundations, such as the Bank of America Foundation, Ford Foundation, or Worldcom Foundation. Also like NCL, CFA relies on conferences and an awards dinner as important sources of revenue, both of which raise some funds from businesses or business-affiliated organizations.

Like NCL but unlike CU, CFA also accepts funds from the US government, and recently this practice turned into a headache for CFA. Until very recently, CFA was organized as a 501(c)(4), making it ineligible for federal government grants; but since 1972, CFA has operated a foundation organized as a 501(c)(3), which is eligible to carry out work for the government. Between 1996 and 2001, the CFA Foundation received almost $5 million dollars from the US Environmental Protection Agency (EPA) to educate consumers about the dangers of radon in their homes and methods of energy conservation. In the middle of 2003, about the same time that CFA itself converted to 501(c)(3), the EPA's Inspector General charged in an audit that the CFA Foundation was insufficiently separate from CFA in terms of personnel and facilities. The audit concluded that the CFA Foundation was therefore not eligible to do contract work for the government and that $4.7 million that had already been spent should be returned to the federal government.[21] The dispute is currently being litigated, and it is unlikely that CFA will have to return the entire amount of the funding, but the disagreement has cost CFA a considerable amount of money and staff time.

Like NCL, CFA's relationship with the business community has been attacked by more purist elements of the public interest community. For example, CFA was criticized for hiring Carol Tucker Foreman to head its Food Policy Institute in 1999. Ms. Foreman has a long and distinguished record in the consumer movement, but she also served as a lobbyist for Monsanto, a major agricultural firm, specializing in biotechnology, genomic, and breeding applications. Foreman's work for Monsanto was seen by some as badly compromising CFA's position on the issue of genetically-engineered food.[22] In response to critics of its relations with business organizations, CFA's executive director Stephen Brobeck admits, 'There is a gray area, and we do sell tables at events to corporations. We will accept payment on a project for research or education as long as we control the final product.' But, Brobeck insists, he uses a general litmus test in dealing with the perception of corporate influence: whether CFA would be embarrassed if the facts were printed on the front page of nation's leading newspapers, such the *Washington Post* or the *New York Times.*[23]

Despite sniping from critics within the consumer movement, CFA enjoys a high degree of legitimacy as a spokesperson for consumers. Its annual Consumer Assembly is essentially an annual convention of the US consumer movement. CFA's leaders and experts are sought by both members of the press and the US Congress for pragmatic articulation of a consumer position on pressing matters of consumer policy. When an organization was sought by the European Union and the US government in 1998 to launch the Trans Atlantic Consumer Dialogue among leading consumer organizations in the US and Europe, the job (and funding) was given to CFA.

Public Citizen

Public Citizen was founded in 1971 and serves as an umbrella for a variety of subunits organized along functional lines. These subunits include the Center for Auto Safety, Congress Watch, Global Trade Watch, the Health Research Group, the Litigation Group, and the Critical Mass Energy and Environment Program. From a legal point of view, Public Citizen is composed of two organizations— one a 501(c)(3) corporation, the other a 501(c)(4) foundation. Neither entity will accept direct business funding. The Public Citizen Foundation will accept project funding from foundations, even ones bearing the names of major industrialists like Rockefeller, Carnegie, and Ford, as long as these foundations have a long record of political independence.

Public Citizen Incorporated and the Public Citizen Foundation had a combined revenue of about $13.5 million in 2003, with almost $10 million flowing to the Foundation.[24] Of the total revenues, $7.5 comes from contributions and membership fees (there are 150,000 members), $2.5 million comes from grants (mostly from foundations and trusts), and $2.2 comes from the sale of publications. Other significant sources of revenue include rental property income, investment income, court awards, and commissions from selling oil through its Buyers Up energy cooperative program. Like Consumers Union, Public Citizen actively encourages financial contributions from individuals, including bequests (contributions specified to be paid upon a person's death) and annuities (receiving annual interest payments on the donated amount until the donor's death). Sixteen bequests were listed in Public Citizen's 2004 annual report, although the amounts are not specified.[25]

One surprising source of income for the Public Citizen Foundation is the sale of its mailing list, typically to other non-profit organizations. This practice is not unusual among advocacy organizations in the United States, even those organizations with a strong anti-business reputation. Within the consumer movement, the Center for Science in the Public Interest engages in this practice, earning over $345,000 from mail list rentals in 2002, down from a high point of $650,000 in 1999.[26] In the environmental movement, groups with anti-business reputations like Greenpeace, the Environmental Defense Fund, and Sierra Club make hundreds of thousands of dollars annually from mailing list rental fees.[27]

Although Public Citizen has been run by its president Joan Claybrook since 1982, it is still identified in the public mind with its founder, Ralph Nader. For most of its history, this relationship was both a financial asset for Public Citizen and a source of legitimacy as a consumer spokesman because Nader enjoyed the admiration of people on both the left and right of the political spectrum.[28] Public Citizen was able to brush off the occasional criticism that Nader and, by extension, Public Citizen is 'owned by' the trial lawyers.[29]

The advantage for Public Citizen of being associated with Nader may have turned into a liability after Nader's unsuccessful bid for the US presidency in 2000. Many people, including most members of the US consumer movement and other liberal organizations, attributed George W. Bush's extremely narrow victory over Albert Gore as the result of Nader's candidacy. As a result, Claybrook had to carefully separate Public Citizen from Nader's candidacy, both before and after the November 2000 election. Angry post-election letters to the editor appeared in Public Citizen's newsletter, but it is difficult to know the financial impact of Nader's candidacy on contributions to Public Citizen.

John Carlisle of the conservative National Legal and Policy Center argues that the partnership between Nader and the trial lawyers is 'too politically profitable for either to hold a grudge,'[30] but a few facts are clear from Public Citizen's tax filings. Between October, 1, 1999 and September 30, 2000, the Public Citizen Foundation received almost $8 million in contributions, gifts, and grants. From October 1, 2000 to September 30, 2001, the Foundation received only $5 million, and the amount declined to $4.4 the following year before climbing back to $5.5 million between October 1, 2002 and September 30, 2003 and to almost $7 million in the most recent tax year. Contributions to Public Citizen Inc. also dropped dramatically after the 2000 election. In Public Citizen's 1999 filing (October 1, 1999 - September, 2000), the organization received $4.6 million from contributions, gifts, and grants. In its 2000 filing, contributions, gifts, and grants dropped to a total $2.8 million.

It is impossible to know how much of the decline in public financial support for Public Citizen is attributable to Nader's presidential candidacy, but contributions to neither Public Citizen Incorporated nor Public Citizen Foundation have returned to their pre-election level. One can also observe that similar contributions to other major consumer organizations rose after the 2000 election. In any event, Nader's presidential bid serves as a cautionary tale for consumer organizations that hitch their wagon to a celebrity activist. The organization benefits when the activist's reputation is in its ascendency, but the organization may suffer when their leader (or perceived leader, as in this case) stumbles.

Front groups

The consumer organizations profiled above are only four of dozens of consumer groups in the United States. The Consumer Federation of America web site lists 110 state and local consumer organizations, and this number does not count consumer cooperatives or national consumer organizations (most of which are based in the District of Columbia).[31] The large number of consumer groups in the United States is a source of strength for the US consumer movement. A group of concerned citizens can easily form a consumer group as a vehicle for education, research, and/or lobbying. If the members of the organization can attract financial and human resources, the organization may achieve a reasonable degree of longevity. Expertise is not the basic criterion for political viability in representing consumers; the ability to attract financial resources is.

One problem, however, with a system with low 'barriers to entry' into the marketplace of consumer groups is that the corporate opponents of consumer organizations can easily set up competing consumer groups. These 'corporate front groups' may not have many real members, and they may take positions that are clearly harmful to the majority of consumers. Nevertheless, these front groups can blunt the efforts of legitimate consumer groups by affecting public opinion and the positions of government decision makers on issues of consumer policy.

The phenomenon of front groups is not new; nor is it confined to the domain of consumer politics. During the McCarthyism of the 1950s, many organizations were accused of being front groups for the Communist Party. During the last two decades, many groups operating in the area of environmental policy have been dubbed front groups by mainstream environmental groups.[32] In the 2004 US presidential election, an organization of veterans who disputed the Vietnam War record of candidate John Kerry was regarded by many people, especially

Democrats, as a front group for the Republican Party.[33] Indeed, alleged front groups have become so widespread that some observers view these groups as standard features of US politics.[34]

In the domain of consumer policy, charges of being a corporate front group have become common. The accusation of having set up and directed a front group has been leveled most frequently at tobacco companies, but telecommunications, health care, and pharmaceutical companies are often subject to the same criticism.[35] The problem with using a term like 'front group,' though, is that is presumes an objective standard for being a 'legitimate group.' Even the most artificial and cynically employed group can be said to have a few consumer members (other than public relations and lobbying professionals whose salaries are paid by a company or trade association) and can be viewed as representing the interests of at least some consumers (e.g., those who smoke cigarettes against those who would restrict smoking or those who drive large sports utility vehicles against those who would more heavily tax them). Conversely, some consumer groups, as we have seen, are not completely immune to working in partnership with business organizations. For these reasons, it is as easy to deny the charge of being a corporate front group as it is to level the charge in the first place.

It is best not to get too caught up in the problem of definitively distinguishing legitimate consumer organizations from front groups, for it is clear that several groups meet common sense definitions of a front group as 'an organization that purports to represent one agenda while in reality it serves some other party or interest whose sponsorship is hidden or rarely mentioned'[36] and 'enable corporations to take part in public debates and government hearings behind a cover of community concern.'[37] When a group presents itself as being composed of everyday consumers yet receives virtually all its funding from industry sources and is run by public relations professionals hired by those same industry sources, it seems reasonable to use the term front group.

During the 1990s, the tobacco industry hired public relations firms like Burson-Marsteller and Bonner & Associates to establish groups like the National Smoker's Alliance, the American Smokers Alliance, and Consumers for Responsible Solutions.[38] While there is no question that some smokers supported the activities of these organizations, little if anything was asked of those people who signed up as 'members.' The public relations firms did all the work when it came time to lobbying against a proposed law or ballot initiative that would have restricted smoking.[39] At the federal level, groups like Citizens for Better Medicare, United Seniors of America, Voices for Choices, and Connect USA spent tens of millions of industry dollars on advertising in support of industry positions on drug and telecommunications legislation.[40] Even when front groups are unsuccessful in achieving their political ends, legitimate consumer organizations must spend their very limited resources to counter them; in this sense, front groups are always at least partially successful.

The larger point illustrated by the existence of front groups is that a political system that encourages the formation of multiple, privately-funded consumer organizations leaves the door open to the formation of corporate front groups. It is impossible to have one without the other, for every act of public policy that facilitates the formation of legitimate consumer groups also makes it easier to establish front groups. Given the complexity of most consumer issues and honest differences of opinion among consumers, front groups can often make a plausible – and well-financed – case that they are pursuing the 'true' consumer interest. And given the fallibility of legitimate consumer groups, front groups may even turn out to be right about what is best for consumers. Nevertheless, front groups point out the dual task facing consumer organizations in a pluralistic system of consumer representation: protecting legitimacy as well as mobilizing resources.

Conclusion

US consumer organizations must be admired for their entrepreneurial ethic in mobilizing financial resources without direct government help. Not only have these organizations managed to balance their revenues and expenses on an annual basis, but several have even managed to accumulate assets that yield investment income year after year. Each of the four major consumer organizations examined in this chapter has tapped several sources of income without unduly competing with each other for funding. More important, each of the organizations discussed here has accomplished the task of resource mobilization without losing its political integrity, although some have been accused of being too dependent on business funding and thereby violating the spirit of consumerism. Mainstream consumer organizations have not only overcome the substantial barriers to resource mobilization; they have done so in an environment in which corporate front groups are free to challenge their specific policy positions and their broader legitimacy as spokesmen for consumers.

The American model of pluralistic consumer representation has a number of advantages. Any single organization, lacking the responsibility of covering the entire consumer policy waterfront, is free to specialize in those domains of consumer policy that best suit its personnel, geographic, and tactical assets. Unlike the vulnerability of an agricultural monoculture to a particular pest or climactic threat, a national consumer movement based on a single all-encompassing organization may be more vulnerable to political threats than a diverse, decentralized movement. Even in the absence of external threats, a pluralistic system of consumer representation may be better suited to meet the challenge of leadership turnover. The US consumer movement has already weaned itself from the leadership once provided by Ralph Nader. And, for example, if Steve Brobeck were to retire after a quarter century at the helm of the Consumer Federation of America, the US consumer movement would still enjoy the overall leadership provided by Consumers Union's president, James Guest, as well as the heads of many other consumer groups.

Perhaps the greatest advantage of a diverse consumer movement with multiple organizations that can speak with expertise and legitimacy on behalf of consumers is the ability for some organizations to take 'extreme' and 'unrealistic' positions on consumer policy issues without precluding other organizations to be more accommodating to other groups and points of views. Indeed, the extreme positions taken by consumer organizations that are largely outside negotiations among interest groups may strengthen the hand of more moderate consumer representatives who are invited inside the process of political compromise. Through this 'outside-inside' strategy,[41] defeat for one consumer organization may be instrumental in victory for another.

One could no doubt point out advantages to a less pluralistic, more centralized system of consumer representation. Even if one believed that, on balance, a pluralistic approach is preferable to a centralized one, a US-style system might be easily exported to other nations. The US approach depends on a specific set of circumstances, including tax policies favoring private, non-profit consumer organizations and wealthy foundations with liberal sympathies. Ironically, it is not the United Kingdom or Australia, with political cultures and institutions similar to those of the US, that most closely resembles the US system of consumer representation. Rather, the diversity and pluralism of the US is better approximated in India, a country with more than a dozen member organizations in Consumers International. India is a huge country with democratic traditions, but its experience suggests that a system of consumer representation based on political entrepreneurship is not unique to the United States. Although an entrepreneurial system of multiple consumer representatives may leave some organizations by the wayside, one can hope that the survivors of a competitive system emerge stronger for the experience.

Table 9.1 Key Financial Features of Four Leading US Consumer Organizations

CONSUMER ORGANIZATION	Founding Date	Tax Status	2003 Revenues*	Net Assets
National Consumers League	1898	501(c)(3)	$2.8 m	$.8 m
Consumers Union	1936	501(c)(3)	$164 m	$54 m
Consumer Federation of America	1967	501(c)(3) and 501(c)(4) until 2003; now 501(c)(3) only	$3.5 m	$1.6 m
Public Citizen	1971	501(c)(3) and 501(c)(4)	$13.5 m	$13 m

* Revenues exceeded expenses for all four organizations in 2003.

Tax Status Definitions:
501(c)(3) : A non-profit organization operated primarily to promote charitable, religious, educational, scientific, literary, or public safety goals.
501(c)(4): A non-profit organization operated exclusively to promote social welfare, that is, primarily to further the common good and general welfare of the people of a community (such as by bringing about civic betterment and social improvements).

Source: 'Tax Return of Organization Exempt from Income Tax: Form 990 for 2003' available at www.guidestar.org

Notes

1 Mancur Olson, Jr., *The Logic of Collective Action* (Cambridge, MA, 1965).
2 Benedicte Federspiel, 'The Role of Consumer Organizations', in Hans Jeleby (ed.), *Facts and Views on Nordic Consumer Policy* (Nordic Council of Ministers, 1995), pp. 17-25; Lawrence E. Rose, 'The Role of Interest Groups in Collective Interest Policy-Making: Consumer Protection in Norway and the United States', *European Journal of Political Research*, 9 (1981): 17-45.
3 National Consumer Council, 'About Us,' National Consumer Council Web Site: http://www.ncc.org.uk/.
4 Mark V. Nadel, *The Politics of Consumer Protection* (Indianapolis, 1971), pp. 235-8.
5 Paul N. Bloom and Stephen A. Greyser, 'The Maturing of Consumerism', *Harvard*

Business Review, 59 (1981): 130-39; John D. McCarthy and Mayer N. Zald, 'Resource Mobilization and Social Movements: A Partial Theory', *American Journal of Sociology*, 82 (1978): 1212-41.

6 James T. Bennett and Thomas J. DiLorenzo, *Destroying Democracy: How Government Funds Partisan Politics* (Washington, D.C., 1985); John Samples, Christopher Yablonski and Ivan G. Osorio, *More Government for All: How Taxpayers Subsidize Anti-Tax Cut Advocacy-Policy Analysis #407* (Washington, DC, 2001), p.10; Marshall Wittmann and Charles P. Griffin, *Restoring Integrity To Government: Ending Taxpayer-Subsidized Lobbying Activities-Backgrounder #1040* (Washington, DC, 1995); Jon Kyl, 'Should the EPA Award Grants to Politically Active Environmental Organizations?' *US Senate Republican Policy Committee* (Washington, DC, 2005), pp. 1-8, (http://rpc.senate.gov/_files/Apr0705EPAGrantsPG.pdf).

7 Erma Angevine, *History of the National Consumers League, 1899-1979* (Washington, DC, 1979).

8 Maud Nathan, *The Story of an Epoch-Making Movement* (Garden City, NY, 1926).

9 Sandra Willett, *telephone interview with the author* (May 8, 2001).

10 Robert E. Draba, 'Motorsports Merchandise: A Cy Pres Distribution Not Quite "As Near As Possible"', *Loyola Consumer Law Review*, 16 (2004): 121-57.

11 Linda F. Golodner, *email correspondence with the author* (May 2, 2005).

12 Russell Mokhiber, 'Corporate Consumer Group', *Multinational Monitor*, 19 (1998): 6.

13 George Idelson, 'Golodner Adresses Critics of NCL Partnering Policy', *The Consumer Affairs Letter*, 19 (1998): 6-9.

14 Norman I. Silber, *Test and Protest: The Influence of Consumers Union* (New York, 1983), pp. 17-38.

15 Consumers Union, *Tax Return of Organization Exempt from Income Tax: Form 990 for 2003* (Yonkers, NY, 2004).

16 Consumers' Association, *Which? Annual Report for 2003/4*. (London, 2004).

17 'About Us' on Consumers Union WebWatch Project Web Site. Available at: http://www.consumerwebwatch.org/about-consumer-reports-webwatch.cfm, 2005.

18 Consumers Union, 'Raffle Winners Announced', *Test, Inform, Protect Newsletter* (June, 2003).

19 Stephen Brobeck, 'Consumer Federation of America', in Stephen Brobeck (ed.), *Encyclopedia of the Consumer Movement* (ABC-CLIO, 1997), pp.146-51.

20 Consumer Federation of America, *2004 Annual Report* (Washington, DC, 2005).

21 US Environmental Protection Agency, Office of Inspector General, *Audit Report: Consumer Federation of America Foundation–Costs Claimed Under EPA Cooperative Agreements, Report No. 2004-4-00014* (Washington, DC, 2004).

22 Russell Mokhiber and Robert Weissman, 'Which Way CFA?' Distributed via lists.essetial.org listserve, June 8, 2000.

23 *Ibid.*

24 Public Citizen Foundation, *Tax Return of Organization Exempt from Income Tax: Form 990 for 2003* (Washington, DC, 2004); Public Citizen Incorporated, *Tax Return of Organization Exempt from Income Tax: Form 990 for 2003* (Washington, DC, 2004).

25 Public Citizen, *2004 Annual Report* (Washington, DC, 2005).

26 Center for Science in the Public Interest, *Tax Return of Organization Exempt from Income Tax: Form 990 for 2003* (Washington, DC, 2004).

27 Ronald Shaiko, *Voices and Echoes for the Environment: Public Interest Representation*

in the 1990s and Beyond (New York, 1999): 93-100.
28 Robert N. Mayer, 'Gone Yesterday, Here Today: Consumer Issues in the Agenda-Setting Process', *Journal of Social Issues*, 47 (1991): 21-40.
29 Peter Brimelow, Peter and Leslie Spencer, 'Ralph Nader, Inc.', *Forbes*, 146 (September 17, 1990): 117-22; Neil Hrab, 'Association of Trial Lawyers of America: How It Works with Ralph Nader Against Tort Reform', *Foundation Watch* (January, 2003): 1-7.
30 John Carlisle, 'Public Citizen Thwarts Consumer Access to Promising New Drugs', *Organization Trends*, (May 2003): 1-7.
31 Consumer Federation of America, 'State and Local Members.' CFA web site http://www.consumerfed.org/backpage/statelocal_main.cfm, 2005
32 Carl Deal, *The Greenpeace Guide to Anti-Environmental Organizations* (Berkeley, CA, 1991); Thomas P. Lyon and John W. Maxwell, *Corporate Environmentalism and Public Policy* (Cambridge, UK, 2004); Mark Megalli and Andy Friedman, 'Fronting for Business', *Multinational Monitor*, 14 (1992): 20-24; Sheldon Rampton and John Stauber, *Trust Us, We're Experts* (New York, 2001).
33 Maria Newman, 'Bush Urges End to Attack Ads by Outside Groups on All Sides', *New York Times* (August 23, 2004): 1; Lois Romano and Jim VandeHei, 'Kerry Says Group Is a Front For Bush', *Washington Post* (August 20, 2004): A1.
34 Arianna Huffington, *Pigs at the Trough: How Corporate Greed and Political Corruption Are Undermining America* (New York, 2003), pp. 100-103; Samuel Loewenberg, 'Business Meets Its Match', *The American Prospect*, 14 (2003): 55-58.
35 Consumers Union, 'Public Interest Pretenders', *Consumer Reports*, 59 (1994): 316-20; Bill Hogan, 'Pulling Strings From Afar,' *AARP Bulletin* (February, 2003): 3-5; John Stauber and Sheldon Rampton, *Toxic Sludge Is Good for You!* (Monroe, ME, 1995), pp. 25-96; United States House of Representatives, Prescription Drug Task Force, *Seniors Beware: The Need for Medicare Prescription Drug Coverage, How Drug Pricing Has Harmed Seniors, and Debunking the Myths of Drug Makers* (Washington, DC, 1999). http://www.house.gov/stark/Presdrugtask/pharmfacts.html
36 'Front Groups' in SourceWatch, a project of the Center for Media and Democracy. Available at: http://www.sourcewatch.org/wiki.phtml?title=Front_groups, 2005.
37 Sharon Beder, 'Public Relations' Role in Manufacturing Artificial Grass Roots Coalitions', *Public Relations Quarterly*, 43 (1998): 21-23.
38 *Ibid*; Ken Silverstein, *Washington on $10 Million A Day: How Lobbyists Plunder the Nation* (Monroe, ME, 1998), pp. 88-133; John Stauber and Sheldon Rampton, *op. cit.*
39 Theodore Tsoukalas and Stanton A. Glantz, 'The Duluth Clean Indoor Air Ordinance: Problems and Success in Fighting the Tobacco Industry at the Local Level in the 21st Century', *American Journal of Public Health*, 93 (2003): 1214-21.
40 Andrew Benore, Alex Knott, and Emily Quesada, *United Seniors Association: Hired Guns for PhRMA and Other Corporation Interests* (Washington, DC, 2002); John McCoy, *Citizens for Better Medicare: The Truth Behind the Drug Industry's Deception of America's Seniors* (Washington, DC, 2000); Alan C. Miller and T. Christian Miller, 'Election Was Decisive in Arena of Spending: Ever-Higher Sums', *Los Angeles Times* (December 8, 2000), 1-2.
41 Michael Pertschuk, *Smoke in Their Eyes: Lessons in Movement Leadership from the Tobacco Wars* (Nashville, TN, 2001).

Chapter 10

Living in the City Differently: The Birth of New Expertise in France in the 1960s and 1970s

Odile Join-Lambert and Yves Lochard

'We are an association of residents. We do not consider ourselves *users*. The 'user' is like a passive consumer. We are more conscious users, meaning we know how to use things – first or all, you have to share them. Somehow we are also actors in the organization of using things.'[1] This statement from the former president of a residents' association of a Paris *arrondissement*, the *Association pour le Développement et l'Aménagement du XIIIe Arrondissement* (ADA 13, Association for the Development and Renovation of the 13th Arrondissement), mentions three groups of actors in a city: the resident, the consumer, and the user of public services (such as transportation).

At the moment ADA 13 was formally created in 1964, consumers' associations already existed that took into account the consumption of services and *usagers*[2]; in particular, there were school-parents' associations and family associations – all part of the same vague nexus but issuing from different spheres of influence: the family movement, the trade union movement, and certain professional and political influences. The most active generalist organisations, like the *Confédération Syndicale du Cadre de Vie* or the *Confédération Syndicale des Familles*, were the heirs of a family movement that began at the end of the 1930s, when activists within the Catholic Church created associations centred on working-class families, focusing on the domain of social services through direct engagement in producing them (e.g. assistance to the unemployed, home help, leisure activities). The *Mouvement Populaire des Familles* (1946), the *Fédération Française des Familles* (1948), the *Confédération Nationale des Familles Rurales*, and the *Union Féminine Civique et Sociale*, which in the 1950s all promoted the theme of the '*bonne acheteuse*' (wise shopper) were getting involved in domains connected to consumption and the living environment, by defending the buying power of working-class families. At that time, the theme of the wise usage of public services appeared to be an aspect of protecting consumers. More generally, the consumer movement was reconsidering administrative issues at the end of the 1960s and beginning of the 1970s. Between 1969 and 1973, the first press articles appeared dealing with 'consumer' opinion about public services. The magazines of the *Union Fédérale des Consommateurs*, *Que Choisir?* and *Que Choisir Budget?*, whose take-off began in the 1950s, and that of the *Institut National de la Consommation* (INC), created in 1966, launched the first investigations into (and rebukes of) the conduct of government bodies and elected officials. Alongside consumers' associations, some users' associations reconfigured themselves or created new offshoots, like the *Association Française des Utilisateurs du Téléphone* (AFUT, French Association of Telephone Users), founded in February 1969.

Residents' associations aimed at securing collective facilities, such as ADA 13, were set up in opposition to the *user* and *consumer* duality, in order to create a specific new space and expertise. These were associations of residents interested in the use of collective facilities, not limited to the problems of housing or some particular service like transport, but belonging to a wider vision of the development of a *quartier* or an *arrondissement*. They dealt with interlocutors who were indeed different from those of consumers' associations (not business companies but the state and elected officials), and this determined the way they saw themselves. Their objective was partly different, too: whereas consumers organised to request that the state rectify inequalities between producers and consumers, the *usagers* took an almost diametrically opposite approach, united by a critique of the state as a furnisher of services. But it was especially out of the 1960s context that residents' associations construed themselves in opposition to both the consumer and the user. The reluctance to call themselves 'users' sprang from a more general distrust of consumption itself that we find at the heart of the Christian movement[3] from which most of these associations had issued. They thought it desirable to promote forms of collective consumption (cooperatives, bulk buying groups) as most able to 'promote people'. Collective consumption in effect implied 'participation', the 'keyword of any people promotion', whose best tool was 'democratic planning'.

In this context, ADA 13 and groups like it belonged to a movement to pluralize expertise: they contributed to constructing specialised know-how on the city and to spreading it horizontally, all the more understandable because governing the city gives rise to a great diversity of types of knowledge; one cannot pretend to influence a city's evolution without being armed with this kind of knowledge. However, far from considering or designating themselves as 'experts', members of ADA 13 instead conceived of themselves as intermediaries between the population and the managers, between the aspirations of residents and the state's technocratic management. Nevertheless, the construction of a particular competence was on its way to becoming one of the major resources in the quest for recognition that was animating associations with respect to the state and elected officials. Was this movement the counterpart of economic, technical or political disinvestment by the state in this sector? Or was it a matter of 'conquests' that would result from the mere mobilisation of associations and their involvement in urban development policies? This research thus belongs to the social history of urban experts in a larger sense, that is to say, those who intervene in debates over controlling the evolution of urban forms. For those who participated in the debates and campaigns over urbanism in the years from 1960 to 1970, city planning was, as it had been at the beginning of the twentieth century, an enterprise that was as much social as physical, designed to modify the forms of society as well as the shape of the city.[4]

This chapter will show first how the sites of specialised knowledge of the city multiplied in the 1960s and 1970s, in both the state and diverse associations. It will then examine whether the composition of generalist residents' associations, in particular ADA 13, corresponded to the advent of new socio-professional categories addressing the problem of collective facilities, and hence to a social diffusion of expertise. Finally, through the evolution of forms of mobilisation and kinds of campaigns mounted by ADA 13, we will see how achievements and expertise about the city were diffused and how such learning was transferred outside the association to other spheres and to other actors.

The state and the town environment: new sites of knowledge about city planning

Between 1959 and the start of the 1970s, France underwent a period of strong economic growth. The policy of economic modernisation was reinforced by a vigorous program of improving public facilities (infrastructure and urban amenities). Within the state there was a de-concentration of power with respect to city studies, extension plans, and urban rehabilitation. A new Ministry for Facilities (*Equipement*) was created in 1966, and the reorganisation of ministerial departments dealing with housing construction and the elaboration of urban development plans meant a fragmentation of functions and expertise regarding the city. The formula of '*Schémas Directeurs d'Aménagement et d'Urbanisme*' (SDAU, Master Plans for Urban Development) was inaugurated by such a plan for the Paris region that was adopted in 1965. The SDAU defined the general orientations of city planning and projected those infrastructure extensions that were considered desirable.

In this context, the new economic and social stakes linked to the evolution of housing were especially noticeable. The period between 1945 and 1953 was marked by renovation and the primacy of housing problems, as well as by the central role played by the state as both decision-maker and financial investor.[5] From 1953 to 1963, a fundamental reorientation of housing took place: the insufficiency of financing was remedied by appealing simultaneously to diverse resources (for example, contributions from businesses obliged to devote 1 per cent of their payroll to the financing of housing for their workers, appeals to savings banks, etc.). During this decade, for the first time in France, housing with full amenities was built on a large scale. But 1963 marked a new break: a new urban policy aimed at a balance among jobs, housing and facilities, by focusing on the notion of 'poles of development' (or urban centres) alongside circulation;

moreover the role of the state as banker was superseded by private capital in the construction sector. The state chose to reserve its aid strictly for those who had a real need for housing subsidies, thereby releasing funds for other tasks like land redevelopment. It was then up to the state to set the conditions conducive to developing the real estate market, and at the same time to strengthen its intervention of a welfare kind so as to limit the effects of such an orientation.[6]

This policy encountered three principal challenges. The first was born of a revolt by *usagers* and residents. The state's financial disengagement from the housing construction sector, the search for savings and speed in building projects, and the logistics of using concrete as a principal material all induced a concept of 'mass provision' which resulted in standardized and repetitive apartment tower blocks that were calibrated to the domestic requirements of a nuclear family of medium size.[7] Since they did not receive from public bodies the necessary directives about the qualitative characteristics of housing, the builders stuck to habitual distribution schema. The technocratic character of the decisions taken in this domain was aggravated by the paucity of architectural research, the lack of preparation for new building programmes and the volume of demand. The low interior quality of the housing was compounded by the poverty of accompanying facilities, by limited green space and by poor collective services.

Thus the 1960s was a period of both the development of the service sector and the take-off of the associative sector, whose size was approaching the level of other countries while keeping the structure and resources specific to France.[8] In parallel with an increase in the number of associations created each year, a certain number of common traits were emerging. There was a noticeable link between membership in the salaried middle classes and investment in associations.[9] The city was a privileged theatre for this associative flowering. Compared to previously existing associations linked to the city, the years 1964 to 1974 saw the creation of urban associations related to the new urbanism and to local democracy, which laid claim to citizen initiative and acted in favour of decentralization. Consequently, most operations decreed by public authorities to reorganise the city of Paris, even if they were already underway, were one by one halted. The demands of associations of residents and neighbourhood groups reached the political arena in 1974 during the Presidential campaign run by Valéry Giscard d'Estaing.[10] Here we should mention the specific status of Paris: it was not a *commune* with its own political life and in the 1960s was still ruled by a Prefect, hence the particular need of Parisian inhabitants for political representation. Whatever the case, these associations formed sites in which specialised points of view about aspects of the city were formed. They constituted a new source of knowledge about urban realities.

The new revolt by residents and the creation of new associations were part of the 1960s logic of renovation and provision of amenities for towns. In the course of the 1970s, protests were directed less at the insufficiency of facilities or their falling behind schedule than they expressed urbanistic biases – increasingly, a rejection of concrete and a demand for protection of the environment. One event epitomises the revolt by *usagers*: the adoption of a charter by the *Groupes d'Action*

Municipale (GAM, Municipal Action Groups) in 1971. Demonstrations by these groups took place in several cities during the municipal elections in 1971 and one of their leaders, Hubert Dubedout, even became mayor of Grenoble. In 1972, the first *Plan d'Architecture Nouvelle* (PAN, New Architecture Plan) concentrated on housing design and led to the production of housing that was less fixed in its definitions; programmes integrating critiques by *usagers* and from social science researchers superseded the knee-jerk functionalism of the preceding generation. The idea of 'mass provision' was also challenged and a stop was put to huge blocks of 500 units. This movement enjoyed much media and public attention with the success of Christian de Portzamparc at PAN in 1975, when he completed 209 homes organised along a real street of the 13th *arrondissement*, the part of Paris most disfigured by rehabilitation.[11] Another challenge was born from the very consequences of privatisation and the economic crisis: on the one hand, real estate investment was becoming less profitable, while on the other, the crisis diminished the number of credit-worthy buyers and it had a dissuasive effect on potential first-time home owners. Ultimately, the law of 31 December 1976 decided to involve organisations of *usagers* in the urban planning process.

Of course, not all this was a result of the urban activist associations. Up to that point, the state as planner held a quasi-monopoly of expertise in these matters and it was not overly concerned with consultation, if we may believe Paul Delouvrier, a delegate-at-large to the District of the Region of Paris. Asked about the lack of consultation over the siting of 'new towns' created around Paris at that time, Delouvrier replied: 'The State, and thus the government, had the power to decide: my role was only to develop a scheme and submit it to consultation … The elaboration of any project demands time to mature, if not in silence then at least in relative solitude. To sum it up, let us say that we were autocratic in our preparation because General De Gaulle was like that in decisions of this kind, and democratic in the game of persuasion.'[12] But the state contributed rather directly to the emergence of other forums on the city that gradually gained legitimacy on urban issues. The public services had all created autonomous bodies for making reports and set up networks of internal research in administrations that were more or less decentralised (*Groupes d'étude et de programmation* and *Centres techniques spécialisés* were established in Paris, such as the *Centre d'études des transports urbains* and the *Laboratoire central des Ponts et Chaussées*). More generally, the General Council on Bridges, for example, had a deliberate policy to have representation from associations. The state could not take care of everything, so it supported an association like ADELS (*Association pour la Démocratie et l'Education Locale et Sociale*), founded in 1959 at the national level. Inside the institutions of the state clear attention was paid by the planners to scholarly institutes and there was an emerging explicit interest in the social sciences for the support they might lend to the conceptualisation and conduct of urbanisation. Public authorities slowly withdrew from granting the steering of projects exclusively to senior civil servants who relied on technocrats – particularly planning economists. More generally, 'participation' as a democratic method enjoyed success after the movement of May 1968, when it meant neither power sharing nor a means of employing the new capacities of citizens who were increasingly well educated, but rather participation as a means of educating and transmitting expertise to those who were being administered. Starting in 1971, the commission of cultural affairs of the *Commissariat Général du Plan* stressed: 'All the current demands concerning regional or municipal freedom, like all the spontaneous initiatives to create local committees or councils, for the neighbourhood or even the building, express the desire for autonomy and the unification of living at the level where that can be really appreciated.'[13] And by the middle of the 1970s, public authorities expressed their desire that the users of public services organise themselves and constitute a lever for reform of government. At least that was the wish of the *usager* commission within the *Commissariat Général du Plan* a little later, in 1975: 'A great difficulty arises when the users are not organised as such ... Nothing decisive will be done in all these domains without the intervention of users acting as a pressure group.'[14]

In this evolution, the social sciences played the role of intermediary between the state and the associations, between scholarly and grassroots activist spheres.[15] At the end of the 1960s, Jacques Delors was at the *Commissariat Général du Plan*, before becoming an advisor to the Prime Minister in 1969. At the Plan, he took an interest in urban questions and had a project for a national institute for urban research, one that would have scientific competence and be a site for meeting and interaction among actors, with mutual education: national planning would make global efforts encounter local actors and give voice to needs, with negotiation between the two sides enabling rationalization. In the 1960s, people expected the social sciences to be 'sciences auxiliary to action, practical disciplines aiding decision-making'[16] and to allow people to appreciate the wider degree of acceptance by a population subject to changes conducted in a voluntarist manner. Those responsible for urban research at the Ministry of Equipment (Loïk Le Floch-Prigent and Michel Conan) approached the universities in search of teams able to undertake such studies. Qualitative research 'took over from quantitative, and to a certain extent, sociology took over from economics'.[17] Urban studies gradually disengaged from the notion of *milieu* so dear to the disciplines like geography that had been traditionally chosen for the role of princely advisors in matters of land development. The concept of 'living environment' posed the urban issue as a social issue and invited a wider contribution from sociology and the social sciences.

The new favour accorded to sociology even pushed certain sociologists to claim supremacy for specialists in the social sciences over the city planners. For Paul-Henry Chombart de Lauwe, this was a veritable *leitmotiv* of the mid-1960s. In a memorandum entitled 'Dialogue with the Municipalities: Development of Cities of a Million Inhabitants in 1964',[18] he wondered if it 'might be up to sociologists or any representative of the social sciences to define city plans ... It is impossible for the city planners to elaborate plans without relying on social science studies. Teams ought to be set up to allow more effective collaboration.' In 1965, he was pleased at 'efforts made in France at the *Commissariat Général du Plan* in liaison with sociologists, demographers and economists' for urban planning nourished by this co-operation. Later, he would say that he intended in this booklet to take a position 'vigorously against the weaknesses in housing policy, against urban speculation, tower blocks and more widely, against any city planning that refused to take into consideration the problems of underlying social structures.'[19] While he did not, on his own, represent the whole field of urban sociology, Paul-Henry Chombart de Lauwe (along with Henri Coing) was a significant element in it.

Thus it was in a context of diversification of the expertise convoked to guide public policies of urban development that we must appreciate the new credit granted to residents' associations as a source of knowledge about the social world. In 1968, 'the previous idea of a global system of expertise allowing the gradual and overall mastery of the evolution of diverse elements in the economic and social structure begins to lose its credibility within the government... What then is expected of the social sciences? Reality frustrates analysis… on the internal plane... it is social movements, and no longer experts in Administration, that make meaning.'[20] If this formula might appear a little excessive, it stresses a turning point in the relative position of the associative world in society and in its capacity to make its voice heard on urban issues, in particular, and to propose alternative solutions. The 'urban movements' and the associations that animated from them appeared as new actors in policies for managing urban life, distinguishing themselves from associations of consumers or users, as we shall see through the case of ADA 13.

Composition of a residents' association: autonomous expertise?

ADA 13 is particularly interesting for the way in which it contributed in the 1960s and 1970s to raising the question of expertise and competences regarding the city and of the sharing of roles between the state and inhabitants. It seemed to succeed at what public bodies did not manage to achieve: dialogue between specialists and non-specialists, diffusion of knowledge and information from inhabitants to elected officials, managers and administrators – and vice versa. Between 1964, the date of its creation, and 1977, the year its idea of creating new urban bodies of reduced dimensions was generalised to all the Paris *arrondissements*, an original construction of knowledge about the city was developed and disseminated. The creation of ADA 13 belongs to the tradition of participation sought by the administration of the *Commissariat Général du Plan*. It also appealed to those civil servants (within the Plan especially) who believed in social experience at the local level. Would ADA help introduce real elements from the outside world into future administrative organizations? And was it really independent of the 'expertise' produced by state services? To answer these questions, we must first look at its composition. Was there actually an increase in the number of households with information about the city? Since many members of these associations were in fact government or municipal employees, we may wonder if true decentralisation was happening.

Urban life and its management call for a great diversity of expert knowledge, mobilizing skills both technical (from architects and planners) but also sociological and demographic, neither of which can be dissociated from political choices or styles of governance. This helps explain the social composition specific to this type of association. While the propensity to join and become involved in any association (especially consumer ones) is higher among middle and high social strata than among the working class, this is particularly the case for associations linked to the living environment. Here the middle classes occupy a dominant place, sometimes out of proportion to the socio-professional composition of the neighbourhood. Marxist sociologists at the time suspected the dominant classes of over-valuing land management and urban planning in order to mask the struggles over demands for housing and transport. But the generalist associations concerned with collective amenities in fact privileged tentative steps, showing that other paths were possible and that technical diagnoses did not merit the adherence that politicians sometimes so easily gave them. This will to measure up to the administration and its technicians on the terrain of information and skills is therefore inseparable from the socio-professional composition of these associations and explains their dissimilarity from tenants' associations and transport user groups. Furthermore, among such associations we can detect a specific orientation to particular forms of knowledge: 'information, truth in information, seriousness about it, realism that takes account of the possible, education of the citizen, the search for possible technical solutions for each particular sector, socialism succeeding thanks to the accumulation of realizable reforms within the framework of the French Republic, with a style one could call technocratic but balanced by a real concern for dialogue and participation and by the vigilance of certain inspirational people worried about the apparent demotion of purposes, values and doctrinal preoccupations'.[21]

More precisely, the case of ADA 13 belongs to the social evolutions of the 13th *arrondissement* of Paris in the 1960s. This association was created in a Parisian *arrondissement* then being transformed by the departure of industry and the construction of housing projects.[22] Onto this area traditionally occupied by workers (and which was regarded as a place of innovative social experience), the developers projected their hygienic, social and financial ambitions. But in this *quartier* favourable to militancy, the inhabitants organized against the developers, at first in the tradition of working-class Catholicism which was attentive to an alliance with the French Communist Party. Other militants and residents quickly mobilised.[23] In the periphery of Paris, the late departure of industry had led to a drop in the working population of the 13th *arrondissement*, with a decline of 27 per cent in industrial jobs and a growth of 38 per cent in the tertiary sector.[24] The number of artisans and small shopkeepers dropped significantly between 1954 and 1968 (down 36 per cent) and the number of workers went down 31 per cent between the same dates. Moreover, there were few schools, means of transport or shops. The transformation of this *arrondissement* thus offered a space of possible action to young householders concerned with their living environment. In 1960, the first residents of the new apartment buildings constructed in the 13th *arrondissement* demanded the building of a school nearby, the establishment of a market and the renovation of Rungis Square. They ran up against bureaucratic compartmentalisation because each service was preoccupied with its own user. These first residents would be the first members of the association.[25]

The composition of the association is interesting because it changed as a function of the *arrondissement*'s social evolution and new definitions of its modes of action. When it was created, the association shared three characteristics with consumers' movements: the influence of Catholicism; of women and young couples; and, finally, of university people. But its composition would evolve. ADA 13 was born from the encounter between a humanitarian aid network and people with wider aims, united by a common struggle against the war in Algeria. Faced with the first demolitions of dilapidated buildings, a 'committee of the badly housed' was set up to agitate in favour of the expropriated and the tenants of small furnished hotels. Alongside but distinct from this committee was a group of Catholic activists who represented the original ADA 13 network: gathered around Saint-Hippolyte Church, their social origins were modest.[26] In the years that followed the Liberation, this church had been taken over by priests of the *Mission de France* who tried to give life to the surrounding community. Jean-Charles Guilloteau, a lawyer by profession, became in 1964 the first president of ADA 13. Sociologist Paul-Henry Chombart de Lauwe was on the parish committee with him. His political engagement and academic practice were closely intertwined: 'Our research was at the time closely tied to daily working-class life, either in the neighbourhoods or in the unions.'[27] Close to this founding kernel but distinct from it were members of a religious community produced by popular Scouting, the *Amitiés Scoutes,* and the *Vie Nouvelle.* A third informal group of Christian activists worked in liaison with the Communist Party, strongly implanted in this formerly working-class *quartier*: in total there were 30 to 40 men and women, whose point in common was their political commitment against the war in Algeria. There were also journalists involved, including *Le Monde*'s Gilbert Mathieu, deputy head of the economics section as well as being active in the *Parti Socialiste Unifié* (PSU) and with his wife, a member of *La Vie Nouvelle.* Gilbert Mathieu had been covering housing issues and was very active in the founding of the association.[28]

The creation of ADA 13 belongs in part, then, to a change in Catholic activism in the 1960s. Post-war economic growth had transformed ways of living and cultures and had posed a challenge to the Church's organisation into movements specialised according to social milieux, as it had been before the war. In brief, the working class confronted the middle class, as the latter was becoming the central group in French society. ADA 13's creation belongs to a modernising Catholicism attached to expertise and technical competence, anxious for social transformation that included social justice.[29]

The second characteristic in the social composition of ADA 13 was shared with many consumers' associations: the crucial role played by women and young couples. It was a woman, Agnès Planchais, who pursued the contacts necessary for the creation of what she called the 'Development and Population Committee', before it named itself ADA 13. She did so independently of any political affiliation, although the ties with the PSU, to which some founding members belonged, were close. Born in 1924, Agnès Planchais was secretary to the *Jeunesse Etudiante Chrétienne Féminine* (JECF) in 1944, then secretary general in 1949. She created one of the first international school exchanges after the war. The year she helped found ADA 13, she was also a member of the national city planning team of the *Union Féminine Civique et Sociale* (UFCS) for women's continuing education and for female consumers. Thus within the administrative council of the new organisation were women and young couples from the new middle classes. Agnès Planchais was not the only one to make the link with the consumer movement as a whole: Maïté Mathieu, the wife of journalist Gilbert Mathieu, was in contact with the National Confederation of Popular Family Associations (which became the *Confédération Syndicale du Cadre de Vie* in 1975/76); other women on the council were also members of the *Mouvement Populaire des Familles* (MPF).

However, soon after the formal creation of the association, between 1966/67 and 1970, a second generation of activists born in the second half of the 1930s (i.e., a decade after the founding members) entered the ADA council and modified its social composition. The third characteristic was thus linked to the sociological evolution of the *arrondissement* and the very nature of the association: the use of surveys became more systematic and attempts to master and spread information were at the core of the campaigns undertaken. In this second generation one finds white collar employees in both the private and public sector, individuals such as Jacques Remond (a white collar worker who joined the association in 1967 and became its president in 1970), Jean-Marc Favret (an administrator in the Ministry of Education), and somewhat later, Robert Lion (senior civil servant, director of construction and then secretary general of the HLM subsidised housing office). This general evolution was sometimes contested: during a general assembly in 1966, for example, ADA 13 was reproached for devoting too much effort to studies to the detriment of its role as basic educator.

This orientation, however, allowed ADA 13 to meet a goal it had chosen, to confront a problem others had diagnosed: to gather information (at the time non-existent) on redevelopment projects, either underway or being planned, that would be understood and discussed by residents, and not a mere alibi produced by the renovators. The issue was all the more crucial because a gigantic project had been planned for the 13th *arrondissement*: the construction of 80 hectares in the form of towers named 'Operation Italy'. With the constructors running the risk of seeing their project fail due to the 'bad will of certain property owners', the city envisaged new legal entities, *Associations Foncières Urbaines* (AFU, Urban Landowners Associations) 'to allow participation and to facilitate agreements with owners who did not want to be associated with it'.[30] These associations of owners could be substituted for the renovation bodies. 'Consultation' was thus limited to owners and promoters, and the public enquiry was really to protect owners.

At the same time, in the 14th *arrondissement* of Paris, the association VDL XIV was formed largely by students, professors, those in the liberal professions and those knowledgeable about habitats. The most active people were even recruited outside the *quartier*. Olivier Mongin, future director of *Esprit*, the journal of personalist Christianity, was an organiser. The journal played a part in the urban movement and devoted a special issue to the topic in March 1979 titled '*Habiter la Ville*'. Jacques Charoux, a member of Paul-Henry Chombart de Lauwe's team, wrote the introduction. In Roubaix, while the association's composition more reflected that of the *quartier*, the *Atelier Populaire d'Urbanisme* (APU) worked closely with scholars and various city-planning professionals to find solutions to local problems.

This gave these associations a particular contour: they were mostly marked by an over-representation of middle and upper classes, especially members belonging to the university, press, government and business milieux who were endowed with specific competences that they placed at the service of the movement – as was the case with many consumers' associations in Great Britain, for example.[31]

Construction of collective expertise and transfers

The case of ADA 13 shows us not only how during this particular period in France a form of collective expertise was created among residents, leaders of associations, practitioners in the mental health centre of the 13th *arrondissement*, sociologists and specialists in various city planning domains, but also how such knowledge, initially generated within the association, was simultaneously disseminated and transferred to other spheres. Consequently, the story of ADA 13 is also the history of increased recognition of the association itself. Of course, it was limited to a single Parisian *arrondissement* and the number of its members never exceeded a hundred – a figure which was tiny compared to national associations such as ADELS. But its capacity to negotiate and its contemporary legitimacy in relation to the political parties and union organisations was very important. It had gradually acquired status as interlocutor of both public bodies and elected officials. Its audience was linked to the political context at the end of the 1950s and to the arrival of Gaullism, to the search for a less stifled political life and to the failings of the traditional political parties over the war in Algeria. It built a reputation for seriousness, especially during the fundamental experience of 'Operation Italy'. In the second half of the 1970s, its representativeness was now measured by its capacity to negotiate with public authorities: it was henceforth represented on an *arrondissement* commission alongside elected officials and public bodies.

The achievement of this legitimacy cannot be separated from the gradual construction of a collective competence. Over the years, the association became a collective expert. It gained the co-operation of various specialists and advisors (city planners, civil servants, journalists) who were brought to its councils: Robert Lion, for example, brought directors of the HLM office before members of the association to get information about the specific problems in this sector. The part played by another striking figure in sociology who was living in the 13th and was a member of the association, Renaud Sainsaulieu, is also important in terms of methodical survey and target analysis. The association was, however, more than a compendium of specialised knowledge. Its bulletins demonstrated a generalist discourse that borrowed from various competences but resulted in overall position-takings which imagined the *arrondissement* an 'entity to inhabit'.

The association preferred to define itself as an association of residents rather than users. The latter were suspected of passivity – content to use goods and services – and even, in the Marxist tradition, of being invented for the sole purpose of breaking working-class solidarity in the event of a strike. So while the term *usager* was sometimes employed in the beginning, after 1971 it was no longer current except for users of public transportation.[32] Nor did ADA 13 place itself under the consumer banner, partly because its interlocutor was the state and the Plan rather than private enterprise, but also because the nature of its engagement was political participation and not acting as a pressure group. For the Christian movement, in fact, the structure of consumption and its purpose were clearly revealed in the Plans, and at this level discussion and participation might have been fruitful. However, in 1975, in the Plan's working group ADA 13 found itself labelled '*Usager*' and placed among residents', users' and consumers' associations (specifically, ADA 13, the Civic & Social Feminine Union, the Family Welfare Fund, the National Consumption Institute, the Federation of Social and Socio-Cultural Centres, the National Confederation of Working-Class Families, the National Federation of Consumer Cooperatives).[33] But ADA 13 had built up its own expertise, like other residents' associations, by differentiating itself from users and consumers.

If ADA 13 was in a position to produce something more than technical counter-expertise, it was because its efforts were enveloped in a value system that gave it identity. It implemented its explicit desire to exchange knowledge, to share it among association members and beyond them to ordinary inhabitants, so that it did not remain the prerogative of licensed specialists. The signs of this choice are many. Conceiving of itself as a movement for popular education, it took a significant part, either directly or through the leanings of its most active members, in the experiment of the Popular University of the 13th. Moreover, from the start the association organised training sessions; its publications repeatedly highlighted workshops for continuing education organised by ideologically related groups. Most especially, its regular recourse to the practice of surveys implemented this desire to produce knowledge constructed collectively, associating specialists and laypeople in offshoots of 'Economy and Humanism', a Christian movement that went back to 1942 and which had been active in thinking about land development and urban issues. For it, scientific knowledge should not belong to an inner circle but to everybody. The 'participatory survey' aimed to allow people to enquire about themselves and prepare them for assuming responsibility.

Thus expertise was constructed by sociologists and professionals in urban planning in dialogue with local activists and was put in touch with the skills of practitioners on the ground, sometimes combined with those of specialised civil servants. We will give three examples of such dissemination of information by ADA 13: to administrators by means of answers to public surveys, to the politicians who took up its ideas about consultation, and the sharing of what was learned with other associations.

The 1960s saw the re-organisation of urban operations: public authorities regularly practiced a form of delegation of power to public/private hybrid companies, mostly based in Paris, and then to a second wave of private companies, as was the case with Operation Italy and with Belleville. This was city planning through delegation of power for the realisation of 'mass plan' projects, including their conception and budget forecasting. The problems of controlling development bodies were considerable. In response to a public enquiry about Operation Italy, ADA 13 elaborated a collective response that was discussed with other local associations, then sent out as a press release and co-signed by a dozen associations, and finally sent to the investigating commissioner and to elected officials. In order to obtain information directly from residents, a method was tested on a selected sample of a hundred families on the perimeter of Operation Italy.[34] ADA 13 requested that a permanent information centre for residents be installed on site. It also created billboards that showed, for example, a diagram of the decision-making process for building a primary school, in this case demonstrating the effective status of the mayor as a civil servant and the difficulty for residents of making themselves heard.[35]

The reactions to this operation raised the problem of local institutions in Paris: the special status of the capital was depriving its *arrondissements* of autonomous public life and of the possibility of knowing public opinion among the citizens concerned. The association analysed this and by 1968, at the time of the reform of local collectivities and regionalisation, it was developing ideas about a new status for the capital. In December 1970, the association proposed reforming Paris by creating new urban units of smaller size that would allow inhabitants to be situated in relation to the city as a whole and to intervene in its functioning and transformations. This reform involved a new division of Paris into twenty-five units, each grouping together three or four *quartiers* of 40,000 to 50,000 inhabitants, rather than the current 20 *arrondissements*. Each unit would have an elected council and the mayor would be elected from the members of this council.[36] This project culminated at the Parisian level in 1977 with the new status of the capital's elected officials. The ideas ADA had tried out passed into the political and administrative sphere.

Movements like ADA 13 privileged the circulation of their experiences because they drew upon a logic of *doing*. Developing counter-data – or at least data from its own surveys – and counter-projects (Alma-Gare inventing solutions that public authorities had not imagined; ADA 13 creating a popular university) made them different from associations of public service users or consumers, which drew on a logic of *demanding*. The 'new urban movements' wanted to try out experiments themselves. The case of the *Atelier Populaire d'Urbanisme* (APU) is significant in this respect. It was created by the residents of the Roubaix (Alma-Gare) *quartier*, confronted with the renovation of their degraded habitat, who decided to stay put and supervise this renovation. 'APU does not want to be just a defence committee for residents but also to have the means to analyse renovation projects that concern them and respond to them. Even more, it wants to develop counter-projects.'[37] APU organised residents and regularly gathered them to imagine solutions to concrete problems posed by the renovation (putting fencing around work sites so they did not turn into rubbish tips, preventing pillaging, rent freezes, etc.).

In the dissemination of Parisian experiences, the exchange among associations played an important role in this period, especially in Paris, which had no municipal politics before 1977. This was the sense of the lessons drawn by ADA 13 from the experience of the Italy sector renovation: 'When they manage to obtain indispensable information, combined with the technical skills necessary to analyse it, associations may discern risks in the choices made by those in authority, point them out and offer alternatives. Strong local power and a clear method of consultation are indispensable. The creation of the Paris mayor's office in 1977 and its consultation commission should avoid decisions being taken by irresponsible and totally impenetrable authorities. In cases of this importance, associations ought to work in close coordination and from the initial stages.'[38] Beyond the exchange of competences internally, there were also forms of reciprocal learning with movements collaborating on similar initiatives, with groups nourished by the same inspiration. These interventions were accentuated by the fact that most activists belonged to many groups, with a 'tendency of associative accumulation of advantages'.[39]

The journal of ADELS, *Correspondance Municipale*, gives a good account of the exchange of experiences made in various *arrondissements*, which must be contextualised. In 1975, the President of the Republic had asked the Prime Minister to allow groups of users and associations for the safeguarding and promoting of the living environment to participate in activities assisting public collectivities, especially local ones. This period was one of the rare moments in the history of city politics when real participative techniques were thought through, as shown by Table 10.1 below that summarises the experiences of various associations, including ADA 13.

Table 10.1 The Constraints of Evaluation

Stage of the process	Constraints	Activities
	Financial; Non-accessibility; Non-organisation of information	Budget for information activities Foresee access to organised info
1. Information	Lack of comprehension on the part of those who should receive it	Set up mechanisms for sensitising, pedagogic presentation of info, Set up mechanism for objective supervision & dissem. of info, Clarify the issue
2. Identification of the problem to resolve	Legal difficulties Politics Standard, norms	Plan if necessary for loosening of constraints, Make sure legal mechanisms understood by all, Define the responsibilities of each body, Indicate mode of conflict resolution
3. Propose different choices	Lack of technical studies Feasibility study & anticipation of consequences of each choice, Insufficient info from the public	Plan complementary budget, Relaunch info campaign and call for participation before any decision taken
4. Synthesis & Evaluation of decisions	Quantitative & qualitative criteria insufficiently precise, Lack of coordination with the decisions of other structures, Legal difficulties	Refine economic & social criteria Re-do some studies on these bases Enlarge consultation Define legal responsibilities of each authority, Appeal to other authorities
5. Execution	Financial difficulty Lack of technical skill	Designate those responsible for follow-up, Set up evaluation mechanism, Plan budgets
6. Evaluation Revision	Lack of follow-up	Put in place procedures for revision

Source: *Correspondance Municipale, No. 182-183* (November-December 1977)

The term 'evaluation' is not used here in the abstract sense that it would later acquire in 'evaluation of public policies': in 1977 it was used to specify the constraints of thinking and analysis in the domains of city planning and communal facilities. It was a pedagogic effort on the part of associations of residents who wanted to participate in collective life, to facilitate collective debate, and to identify possibilities for campaigns to be undertaken and hence for participation. It testifies to the experience of activists issuing from trade unionism with respect to the living environment (*Syndicat du Cadre de Vie*), from Catholic social action or from the ADELS, trying to analyse and publicise what they had done within various associations.

Conclusion

The example of associations of city-dwellers in the years 1960 to 1970 thus shows the emergence of a desire by activists to take part in debates from which they had been excluded and so to influence the evolution of the city. Several of these associations emanated from trade unionism and from working class Catholic groups, which had tried local involvement while waiting for the hoped-for possibilities of political engagement on the national level: on the left, the political parties had failed over the war in Algeria and political life was stifled by Gaullism. This militancy was linked to the wish for a more lively political life than there had been at the start of the 1960s.

An association like ADA 13 constituted both a centre of expertise (through the knowledge capital it accumulated) and a generator of proposals (especially for apparatuses and procedures enabling local democracy to thrive). Its trajectory during the period under consideration suggests that urban movements should not be considered to achieve things solely through a struggle for new rights, nor judged under the opposite hypothesis that the state favoured a surge in themes like unity in the living environment, links between habitats and working environments, with the intention of distracting popular movements from real stakes like housing or transport. Rather, a study of this association illuminates a complex skein of factors: the initiatives of local activists from Catholic social action groups, from the *Syndicat du Cadre de Vie* and the *Mouvement de Libération des Familles*, matched with the desires of a generation of middle-class professionals, especially within the *Commissariat Général du Plan*, who were anxious to see *usagers* organise as a pressure group – all in a political conjuncture where 'participation' was gradually acquiring acceptance.

The association's path illustrates the progressive construction of types of knowledge that can procure influence on the evolution of city development and more widely on the forms of local democracy. Whereas under the Fourth Republic, the urban development process had been divided among three figures – the city architect, the technical administrator of construction (serving the state) and the politician (working at the municipal or national level and facing re-election votes and the obligation to obtain results), starting with the Fifth Republic and throughout the 1960s, it was more and more difficult to define the task and place of developers and creators of cities, whose roles were fragmented.[40] This was one of the reasons for the aspirations of such associations as ADA 13: both to referee the state, which it could not pretend to replace in defining priorities, and to represent the aspirations of residents; the latter did not have the same sense of time as politicians, decision-makers, developers, or even architects. Thus, the process of city planning ought not to be understood simply as a conflict between the local and the national, or as the articulation of local interests in opposition to some more general national public interest.

Associative expertise is not limited to the types of technical knowledge that would have led it to rival the professionals or the municipality, as the ADA experience shows. It nourished its own expertise from many sources: first and foremost, the experience of residents and of practitioners at the local level, then the social sciences, approaching the variegated uses of the city according to social groups. Then there was socio-political reflection about governance of the city and about the most appropriate procedures to enable local democracy. Thus, associative expertise is itself composite and fed by different fields of knowledge. The influence of its expertise contributes, too, to convictions about good rules for living together and to a vision of city life. One finds the same practical project among researchers and activists: 'to realise, thanks to a revived local community, the social integration of populations into a democratic order. We expect from urban change (and the science that guides it) some progress in the political order'.[41] Finally, the temporal sense of ADA 13 was that of long-term militancy, and for this reason no doubt it was rather distanced from forms of engagement that are more localised or more scholarly, as we have today. The militant-resident of the 1960s did not rival the technician but reminded both technicians and politicians that they alone could not decide on the common good. In this sense, the experience of these associations prefigured contemporary debates about the abrogation of decision-making by experts to the detriment of elected representatives. Various current mechanisms (citizen forums, consensual conferences, etc.) that have been envisioned to contain expert discourse and to circumscribe experts within the procedures of both representative democracy and participative democracy, are in fact the heirs of those invented in France in the 1960s and 1970s.

Translated by Susan Emanuel

Notes

1 Interview by the authors with Marc Ambroise-Rendu, 18 February 2004.

2 In France, one differentiates between the 'client' of a commercial entreprise, the 'user' of collective services furnished by the state (like education) or under state control (like public transportation), the 'person subject' to taxes, the 'patient' in a hospital, and

finally the 'insured' of Social Security. These designations have changed over time. So for example, the term 'client', often linked to the privatisation of a public service – or to the commercialisation of one – has been introduced since the mid-1970s in the administration of public entreprises.

3 Jacques Chaumeny, 'Personne et consommation socialisée', *Economie et Humanisme*, 141 (Annual Supplement 1962): 93.
4 Pierre-Yves Saunier, 'Où l'auteur propose un plan de travail pour une histoire dite sociale de l'aménagement urbain', *Recherches contemporaines*, 3 (1995-1996): 33-46.
5 Antoine Prost, 'La périodisation des politiques urbaines françaises depuis 1945: le point de vue d'un historien', *Cahiers de l'IHTP*, 17 (December 1990); Annie Fourcaut (ed.), *Banlieue rouge: 1920-1960* (Paris, 1992).
6 René Ballain, Francine Benguigui, *Loger les personnes défavorisées* (Paris, 1995); Annie Fourcaut, *La Banlieue en morceaux: la crise des logements défectueux en France dans l'entre-deux-guerres* (Grâne, 2000).
7 Jean-Paul Flammand, *Loger le peuple: essai sur l'histoire du logement social en France* (Paris, 1989); Hélène Frouard, *Les Politiques patronales de logement en France (1894-1944): de l'initiative privée au devoir national* (Ph. D. thesis, University of Paris I, 2003); Sabine Effosse, *L'Invention du logement aidé en France: l'immobilier au temps des Trente Glorieuses* (Paris, 2003).
8 Martine Barthélémy, 'Les Associations et la démocratie: la singularité française', in Yves Michaud, *Qu'est-ce que la société?* (Paris, 2000), p. 418.
9 See a comparison done by Johns Hopkins University on the non-profit sector, and Edith Archambault, *Le Secteur sans but lucratif* (Paris, 1999).
10 Mathieu Flonneau, 'Parisiens, citadins, citoyens et automobilisme: du rôle de quelques associations dans la ville', in Claire Andrieu, Gilles Le Béguec, Danièle Tartakowsky (eds), *Associations et champ politique: la loi de 1901 à l'épreuve du siècle* (Paris, 2001), pp. 611-23.
11 Jean-Paul Flammand, *Loger le peuple*, pp. 303-4.
12 Roselyne Chenu, *Paul Delouvrier ou la passion d'agir* (Paris, 1994), p. 259.
13 Archives Nationales [AN], Commissariat Général au Plan, CAC 890617/51, Préparation du VIe Plan, Rapport de la Commission des Affaires Culturelles, 'L'Action Culturelle', 1971.
14 AN, Commissariat Général au Plan, CAC 890617/51, Commission de l'aménagement du territoire et du cadre de vie, Preliminary Report by the '*Usager*' Working Group, February 1975.
15 Cf. Bernard Lepetit, Christian Topalov (eds), *La Ville des sciences sociales* (Paris, 2001).
16 Alain Drouard (ed.), *Le Développement des sciences sociales en France*, Paris, 1983, p. 138.
17 Robert Fraisse, quoted in Michel Amiot, *Contre l'Etat, les sociologues* (Paris, 1986), p. 93.
18 Paul-Henry Chombart de Lauwe, *Des Hommes et des villes* (Paris, 1965), p. 239.
19 Paul-Henry Chombart de Lauwe, *Un Anthropologue dans le siècle: entretiens avec Thierry Paquot* (Paris, 1996), p. 163.
20 Robert Fraisse, quoted in Amiot, *Contre l'Etat, les sociologues*, p. 93.
21 Jeanine Mossuz, *Les Clubs et la politique en France* (Paris, 1970).

22 AN/Institut Française d'architecture, fonds ADA13, 176 IFA, carton 1. We thank Agnès Planchais for authorisation to access the association archives. See also Henri Coing, *Rénovation urbaine et changement social. L'îlot no 4* (Paris, 1966).
23 Jacqueline Gauthier, 'L'espace social et la vie quotidienne dans un secteur prolétarien', in Paul-Henry Chombart de Lauwe *et. al.*, *Paris et l'agglomération parisienne,* vol. 1 (Paris, 1972), first published in Mario Robirosa and Elia Perroy, *Notes sur l'évolution d'un arrondissement de Paris* (Paris, 1962).
24 Figures from the Atelier Parisien d'Urbanisme, quoted in *Correspondance municipale, Revue mensuelle de l'ADELS*, 123 (September 1979): 9.
25 Agnès Planchais, 'Histoire de l'association', p. 12.
26 Interview by the authors with Jean-Charles Guilloteau, 24 March 2004.
27 Paul-Henry Chombart de Lauwe, *Un Anthropologue dans le siècle*, p. 157.
28 On Gilbert Mathieu, see Patrick Eveno, *Le Monde: histoire d'une entreprise de presse, 1944-1995* (Paris, 1996).
29 Denis Pelletier, *La Crise catholique: religion, société, politique en France, 1965-1978*, (Paris, 2002).
30 Atelier Parisien d'Urbanisme (APUR), Centre de documentation, 101BioPA24, Préfecture de la Seine, direction de l'urbanisme, Aménagement et rénovation du secteur Italie, mémoire au conseil municipal, 13 November 1965.
31 Matthew Hilton, *Consumerism in Twentieth-Century Britain: The Search for a Historical Movement* (Cambridge, 2003).
32 *Correspondance municipale,* 'Le rôle des habitants dans leur quartier: l'exemple du XIIIe arrondissement à Paris,' no 123 (September 1971).
33 AN, CAC 19890617, art. 51, CGP, Commission aménagement du territoire et du cadre de vie, Preliminary report of the working group '*usagers*', February 1975.
34 Cf. AN/IFA, fonds ADA 13, 176 IFA, carton 4, manuscript note by Agnès Planchais, 1966.
35 University of Paris VII, Sciences of the City, 'Le XIIIe à faire: comment? avec qui?', 1968.
36 AN/IFA, fonds ADA 13, 176 IFA, carton 2, *Bulletin de l'ADA 13*, 1, December 1970.
37 Gaëtane Lamarche-Vadel, Ariane Cotlenko, 'Alma-Gare: le singulier et le politique', in Eddy Cherki and Dominique Mehl, *Contre-pouvoirs dans la ville: enjeux politiques des luttes urbaines* (Paris, 1993).
38 Jacques Remond, *ABC 13, Special Issue*, 'Les mémoires de l'ADA 13', September 1997, p. 18.
39 Martine Barthélémy, 'Itinéraires militants et univers symboliques dans les associations de filiation catholique et laïque', in Dan Ferrand-Bechmann (ed.), *Les Bénévoles et leurs associations* (Paris, 2004), p. 114.
40 Danièle Voldman, 'Aménager la région parisienne: Février 1950-Août 1970', *Les Cahiers de l'IHTP*, 17 (December 1990).
41 Christian Topalov, 'Marché, solidarité, équité', *Courrier du CNRS*, 81 (1994).

Chapter 11

The Organised Consumer Movement since 1945

Matthew Hilton

This book has shown that there are several different moments in the history of the 'expert consumer' and that many have sought to position themselves as the authoritative voice of the consumer. The first section of the book dealt with those organisations which mobilised consumers as expert market agents who could act in support of others, be they slaves or maltreated workers, while the second pointed to the growing professionalisation of consumer expertise after the First World War. Of the final period, that covering the society of mass consumption, the attention has been on the different regimes of consumer protection and the different types of consumer expertise being articulated. What this final chapter seeks to provide is a more general overview of the modern consumer movement, that is those organisations in which shoppers professed their own expertise and sought to speak against those businesses, professions and public officials who had often spoken in their name.

It will firstly outline the growth of comparative testing organisations and magazines such as *Which?*, *Que Choisir?* and *Consumer Reports* which have formed something of a social movement, before comparing different consumer protection systems operating in the affluent West. However, what this chapter will also do is point to the global nature of modern consumerism, no more seen than in growth of the International Organisation of Consumers Unions (IOCU, subsequently CI, or Consumers International) which became one of the most prominent international non-governmental organisations (NGOs) of the late twentieth century. This is an aspect of the expert consumer which has often been overlooked, yet today consumer organising takes place in just about every country in the world and, as the case study of Malaysia will demonstrate, has produced remarkable instances of consumer activism which call into question existing academic understandings of consumer politics. As developing-world consumer advocates have articulated a notion of consumer rights based more on the access to basic needs than the choice between branded commodities, they have found themselves at times in confrontation with the interests of western consumers. But, it has also led to the expansion of the consumer interest and the idea of consumer expertise such that the modern consumer movement has contributed profoundly to the workings of contemporary consumer society. However, choice – and its satisfaction – has become the property not only of the consumer movement: the last two or three decades have witnessed a renewal in the number of organisations seeking to provide the expert consumer voice. As such, the modern consumer movement, spearheaded internationally by IOCU, may well have had its moment as new consumer voices emerge. Whether this is the case or otherwise – and this paper offers no predictions on the future of expert consumerism – the contest of speaking for the consumer remains as ever relevant as all the other chapters in this volume have demonstrated for the previous one hundred years.

The growth of the modern consumer movement

The modern, comparative-testing form of consumer expertise began in the United States. In 1927, a civil servant for the Labor Bureau, Stuart Chase, and an engineer, F. J. Schlink, published *Your Money's Worth*, a critique of the exploitation of the consumer in the modern marketplace.[1] Drawing on Veblen-esque attacks on consumption as well as anti-trust traditions within American politics, the book epitomised a desire to empower the consumer that was one of the founding principles of Consumers' Research, which began publishing its *Bulletin* in 1929. The organisation embodied a new spirit of what Charles McGovern has called 'consumer republicanism' or consumer citizenship: 'a form of ideal Jeffersonian independence not only in the marketplace but also in society at large.'[2] Consumers' Research sought to overcome the ignorance of the consumer and make him or her adept at assessing the quality of goods while at the same time maintaining a healthy distance from modern commercial values. It rode the wave of a developing consumer consciousness in 1930s America which saw the establishment of a consumer infrastructure within the New Deal bodies and the flourishing of several other consumer organisations.[3] However, in 1936, a strike broke out among Consumers' Research staff and in the ensuing split, Arthur Kallet, a former collaborator of Schlink, went on to form the longer lasting, and ultimately more successful, Consumers Union. Schlink had attempted to focus consumerism on product testing rather than broader social and economic issues and he would, in fact, later denounce his former radical colleagues – now connected to Consumers Union – as Marxists, especially since the new organisation did make efforts to link its model of consumerism with the social and economic concerns of the labour movement. However, by the end of the 1950s, when it had asserted its non-political role to the House Un-American Activities Committee, CU had been steered by its President, Colston Warne, and the socially conservative tendencies of the readers of *Consumer Reports*, towards a focus on value-for-money testing. This is not to say that CU has not gone on to fund a number of social and economic issues, but its primary focus on testing has proved extremely popular with American shoppers. It has remained a financially successful publishing organisation and it has had an uneasy relationship with some of the more aggressive voices in post-war American consumerism, most notably that of Ralph Nader.[4]

Nevertheless, the focus on the testing of goods and services was clearly an inspiration to European shoppers. In the 1950s, a number of consumer testing organisations began to emerge. In France, in 1951, the *Union Fédérale des Consommateurs* (UFC) was formed and began publishing its testing magazine, *Que Choisir?*, in December 1961. This form of organising built on strong consumer traditions which stretched back to the co-operative movement and the theory of consumer politics articulated by Charles Gide.[5] Thus, the UFC soon found itself joined by family and rural groups which had formed previously in the 1940s as well as co-operative groups (*Fédération Nationale des Coopératives de Consommation*) and trade unionists through bodies such as the *Organisation Générale des Consommateurs* (ORGECO, 1959), set up specifically to represent consumers who were also union members. In response, the state initially created the National Consumer Council (*Conseil National de la Consommation*) in 1960 to act as a forum for consumers to interact with government, though this has been followed with more comprehensives measures, most notably the National Consumption Institute (*Institut National de la Consommation*) in 1968, which published *50 millions de consommateurs* from 1970, and the creation in 1976 of a Secretariat of State for Consumption, converted into a full ministry by Mitterand in 1981.[6]

Most importantly, organised consumerism in France has taken the form of something of a social movement. By 1978, while only 3 per cent of the adult French population identified themselves as members of a consumer organisation, 27 per cent claimed to be willing to join one. Furthermore, in 1976, around 800 *clubs de consommateurs* around the country were affiliated to the *Associations populaires familiales*, inspired and motivated by such campaigns as the 3-6-9 boycott which urged protesting consumers to stop buying meat for three days, fruit for six, and mineral water for nine.[7] While no other European country witnessed such high levels of grassroots mobilisation, it is clear that French consumers were responding in part to a set of general issues facing a rising generation of affluent shoppers. That is, as western economies moved into an increasingly technological and complex age, where the traditional skills attributed to the housewife-shopper were no longer useful in the assessment of products, both male and female consumers sought institutional support to guide and protect them through the marketplace. Thus, it was not only the UFC which mirrored the activities of the American Consumers Union. In the Netherlands, *Consumentenbond* was formed in 1953, joining other rural, family and women's bodies, particularly the Netherlands' Union of Housewives, the Netherlands' Family Council and the Foundation for Household Information in Rural Areas, which had increasingly turned their attention to consumer affairs in the period of economic growth. *Consumentenbond* has, however, remained the pre-eminent consumer organisation, its 650,000 members or subscribers to its testing magazine in the late 1990s representing the highest market penetration rate of any consumer publication in the world, reaching one out of every nine Dutch families.[8] Similarly, in Belgium, the *Association des Consommateurs* was formed in 1957 as a private organisation of individual shoppers keen to imitate the success of *Consumer Reports*. In 1993, it had 325,000 member-subscribers and has played a leading role internationally in promoting consumer organising. At home, while it has always been the most prominent consumer organisation, it has also worked alongside a wider network, spearheaded by the women's, co-operative and labour movement which came together to form, in 1959, the *Union Féminine pour l'Information et la Défense des Consommateurs*, although this ended in 1984 when the socialist authorities withdrew their financial support.[9]

In financial terms at least, though, the most successful imitator of the American product-testing model has been the United Kingdom's Consumers' Association (CA). Formed in 1956 by a group of professionals broadly, if not entirely, associated with the centre-left traditions of the British Labour Party, CA first began publishing *Which?* in 1957. Its success was immediate and membership peaked in 1987 when subscriptions to *Which?* reached one million. While its core work has remained servicing its members with better information about the quality of branded products, the income generated from the sale of its magazine has enabled CA to play a leading role internationally and to become a prominent advocate at the national level. Although it is a purely private organisation, it has maintained a close relationship with the state and its staff and ideas have heavily influenced such government initiatives as the Consumer Council in the 1960s, the Office of Fair Trading from 1973 and the National Consumer Council from 1975. Furthermore, it also gave rise to something of a social movement. In the 1960s it encouraged the establishment of local consumer groups around the country. For the moderately-minded professionals associated with post-war planning and economic regeneration – lawyers, engineers, managers and accountants – the groups offered the opportunity for a new type of citizen to play a role in local and national civic life. Although Britain never witnessed the same degree of grassroots consumer mobilisation as in France, by March 1963 there were 50 consumer groups in existence with a total of 5,000 members. They had all come together under the National Federation of Consumer Groups (NFCG) and, in 1967, the movement peaked with the existence of 100 groups and a total membership of 18,000 consumers.[10]

While the growth of the western European consumer movement attests to the importance of explaining its rise through variables such as affluence, an increasingly technical marketplace and the growth of advertising and sales techniques which confused individual shoppers, the experience of other countries should not blind us to the fact that much consumer motivation emerges from adversity and detriment rather than the perplexities of expanding choice. Private testing organisations may have emerged in the 1950s, but they often found themselves working alongside pre-existing consumer groups, most notably co-operatives and women's organisations, the former of which had been recognised as the principal consumer experts in periods of necessity, and the latter of which had risen to prominence as expert consumers in the Second World War. In Japan, the main organisations which have become the dominant spokesbodies for consumers in an age of affluence all emerged in the period of shortages, rationing and controls associated with the Allied occupation in the late 1940s and early 1950s. Women especially protested against the restrictions of a recovering marketplace, the protests over rationing in Osako in October 1945 and the 'give-us-rice movement' leading eventually to the establishment of the *Kansai* Federation of Housewives' Associations in 1949. Similarly, a protest over the sale of defective matches – a particular problem for a country experiencing structural difficulties in the supply of electricity – led to the creation of the Japanese Federation of Housewives' Associations (*Shufuren*) in 1948. Within a year *Shufuren* had 500,000 members in the Tokyo region alone and by the early 1990s it consisted of around 400 local affiliates from all around the country. Other, more conservative, women's organisations have further bolstered the movement and, even as the Japanese began to enjoy unprecedented levels of economic prosperity, local co-operative clubs have flourished, a movement which, if highly diverse, nevertheless boasts 44 million members, as housewives in particular have sought to maintain a greater degree of control over an increasingly anonymous and alien marketplace.[11]

What the Japanese situation highlights is the specificities of different national consumption regimes. The factors which gave rise to consumer organising across the industrialised world may have been remarkably similar but how this consumer consciousness manifested itself as a consumer politics varied from one state to the next. Again, in Japan, the collective responsibilities of consumers have been just as relevant as their individual rights and this has meant consumer organisations have recognised the importance of protecting fledgling Japanese industries. This has led many commentators on Japan to conclude that its consumer movement has been especially pro-business.[12] Recently, this view has been questioned by Maclachlan's in-depth study of consumer politics which stresses the oppositional voice of Japanese consumer groups. Nevertheless, business and commercial interests have clearly eclipsed consumer voices within national public and private institutions and thus a large grass-roots consumer movement has had very little impact on economic and social policy when compared to, for instance, the United States. There, a more plural central bureaucracy has created a diverse number of opportunities – and, consequently, strategies – for consumer activists to pursue and, prior to an anti-consumer backlash beginning in the late 1970s, a more aggressive form of consumer politics was able to emerge in the US which achieved notable victories both in the courts (through class action suits) and in the legislature.

Different institutional contexts also provide part of the explanation as to why consumer movements have not taken off to the same extent at the grassroots level in other countries. In northern Europe, for instance, stronger state involvement in consumer protection measures has meant consumers have not had to flock to independent, and specifically consumer-based, organisations to realise their interests. In Germany, organisations of consumers emerged as elsewhere in the post-Second World War period, and the *Arbeitsgemeinschaft der Verbraucherbände* (AgV, Alliance of Consumer Associations), which was established as early as 1953, has subsequently gone on to co-ordinate different groups' activities, engage in consumer education and provide information to support its role as an advocacy organisation. However, it has not sought to become a mass movement, preferring instead to use its technical expertise to become an equal partner in the development of products and services. It has sought a negotiated role with government and, although business interests have predominated, the German consumer movement has developed a strong representative function. To some extent, this has meant the government has taken the initiative on many consumer activities. Several attempts had been made to start comparative testing magazines, but no lasting publication appeared until *Test* in 1966. German businesses had previously blocked the testing and reporting activities of AgV in the early 1960s, but with the support of the Social Democrats, a government-funded testing body, *Stiftung Warentest*, was established to publish *Test*. By the 1990s, sales had reached one million, and *Stiftung Warentest* was no longer reliant on government subsidies. As the pre-eminent national consumer publication, *Test* differs from other European publications, since the constitution of *Stiftung Warentest* allows for the input of business at all levels of the product examinations. This, in essence, reflects the German consumer protection regime more generally. German consumers have an impressive representative and negotiating role at the federal level (a situation replicated at the state level thanks to the creation of state-based *Verbraucherbände*), though this is strongest only in technical areas. What the absence of a strong, independent consumer movement has meant is that German consumer groups have not enjoyed the same freedom of action or ability to set their own agendas as, for instance, in the French case.[13]

In Scandinavia, limited populations have been held to prevent the economies of scale enjoyed by testing magazines with a mass circulation and thus, no such organisation as the Consumers' Association or Consumers Union has been able to emerge. Beyond this, however, strong co-operative, trade union and social democratic traditions have ensured the state has often initiated a range of consumer interest activities that have elsewhere emerged from 'below'. In Sweden, for instance, involvement in consumer affairs in the 1940s and 1950s by trade unions, co-operatives, voluntary and women's organisations was later taken up by the state (i.e., the *Statens Konsumentråd*). Later still, Sweden established the world's first consumer ombudsman as well as a Market Court in 1971 and, in 1973, the state-sponsored National Board for Consumer Policies (*Konsumentverket*, merging with the ombudsman in 1976). With such top-down consumer protection, no national federation of independent consumer groups was thought necessary until the Co-operative Union established a Consumer Policy Council to serve as a forum for the co-operative, labour and consumer movements (becoming the Consumer Council from 1992). In Sweden, then, the role of the state has been particularly strong and it has offered a specifically Scandinavian model of consumer protection which has been an inspiration for consumer movements elsewhere campaigning for greater state intervention. However, it has also ensured that consumer consciousness has been directed away from those organisations usually held to be more typical of a social movement.[14]

The global consumer movement

No matter how consumer politics have become institutionalised in different national contexts – be it according to models of information provision, corporatist negotiation or social democracy – it is clear that in the 1950s rising concerns about an increasingly complicated marketplace had given rise to a consumerist 'identity' among the populations of the richer countries of the world. It is no surprise, then, to learn that several of these national consumer movements believed progress could further be achieved through co-operation at the international level.

In 1958, Elizabeth Schadee of the Dutch *Consumentenbond* and Caspar Brook of the UK Consumers' Association discussed opportunities for international collaboration. They approached Colston Warne of the US Consumers' Union who enthusiastically embraced the project and who was able to devote $10,000 of his organisation's money to setting up an international body. In the spring of 1960 the First International Conference on Consumer Testing was held to discuss opportunities for future collaborative efforts. A Technical Exchange Committee was established and a range of goods identified where the pooling of testing facilities would be beneficial to all concerned. More significant still was the creation of the International Organisation of Consumers Unions (IOCU) on 1 April 1960. On its Council sat the representatives of the four comparative testing organisations from France, Belgium, the Netherlands and the UK that had been largely founded on the American model, as well as Colston Warne of the US Consumers' Union. The original aims of the new body were simply to extend the comparative testing type of consumerism: 'It was to act as a clearing house for information on test programmes, methods and results; to regulate the use of ratings and reprints of materials of member organisations; and to organise international meetings to promote consumer testing.'[15]

IOCU's growth was impressive. Although in 1970 the Council still consisted of the core of the five founding members, five further organisations had become co-opted members (*Forbrukerrådet* of Norway, *Forbrugerrådet* of Denmark, *Statens Konsumentråd* of Sweden, the Consumer Council of the UK and *Stiftung Warentest* of West Germany) and another four were elected members (*Verein für Konsumenteninformation* of Austria, the Consumers Institute of New Zealand, the Israeli Consumers' Association and the Consumers' Association of Canada). A further 16 Associate members and 23 Corresponding members ensured that organised consumerism now reached into Asia, Africa and Latin America, if only into the richest nations of these areas.[16] By 1990, however, IOCU had extended well beyond the affluent West. The Council now consisted of representatives of most western European states, but also of consumer organisations in Argentina, Hong Kong, India, Indonesia, Jamaica, Japan, Mauritius, Mexico, Poland and South Korea. An Executive had been formed which showed the domination of the founding members (excluding Belgium) though even here South Korea and Mauritius were represented and the Presidency was held by Erna Witoelar of the *Yayasan Lembaga Konsumen*, Indonesia.[17] Today, IOCU is called Consumers International, and in November of 2003 it held its Seventeenth World Congress in Lisbon, Portugal. Its headquarters are in London, but there are thriving regional offices in Africa, Asia and Latin America. At the turn of the millennium, it had 253 members from 115 different countries which ranged from all the states of the western world to post-communist Eastern Europe and a whole collection of developing states (China, Chad, Guatemala, El Salvador, Gabon, Nigeria, Malawi and Burkina Faso) which, on first instinct, one might suppose had other interests that needed defending than those of consumers.[18]

The significance of the consumer movement as an international phenomenon has been generally overlooked by contemporary historians who have preferred instead to observe the campaigns, tactics and agendas of more headline-grabbing social movements concerned with human rights and environmentalism. Certainly, the consumer movement holds less of the excitement connected to the radicalism of other social movements and, indeed, many of the affluent and socially (if not politically) conservative subscribers to the comparative-testing magazines would hardly have regarded themselves as at the forefront of a new transformative, non-government organisation-focused (NGO) politics. Yet, it is the very respectability of the consumer movement which held the key to its influence, together with its expansion into the global South at a rate more development-based NGOs could only dream of. Within just a few years, then, IOCU had become much more than just a facilitator of collaborative testing mechanisms.

Almost from the very beginning of its existence, IOCU decided to structure its activities in a manner in line with the American government's espousal of a rights-based liberalism. In March 1962, President Kennedy made a significant speech in the history of consumer protection. In it, he outlined four basic consumer rights that were to act as the guiding principles for legislative and voluntary action: the right to safety; the right to be informed; the right to choose; and the right to be heard. IOCU immediately incorporated these four rights as its own *raison d'être*, binding its member organisations to the pursuit of consumer protection ideals articulated and advanced from within a changing US context. Such a rights-based model was also at the heart of liberal politics internationally and IOCU was able to use its respectable bases in western Europe and the US to obtain a foothold within the institutions of the United Nations. Along with women's organisations and the labour movement, the consumer movement was one of the earlier sections of civil society to be invited to participate within the UN. It quickly had an influence with the UN Economic and Social Council and it went on to have a voice in other bodies such as the World Health Organisation and the Food and Agriculture Office. It has been granted Category I status within the General Assembly, enabling it to sit at the table and speak like a national delegation (although it cannot vote on issues). Just as the respectable professionals who made up the national consumer movements were often able to find a representative role within different states in the 1960s and 1970s, so too were they able to secure a role within the institutions of global governance. Due to IOCU lobbying, in 1982 the UN General Assembly voted to establish a Consolidated List of of Products Whose Consumption and/or Sale Have Been Banned, Withdrawn, Severely Restricted or Not Approved by Governments. IOCU has been particularly concerned with food standards and has worked hard to influence the highly technical guidelines of Codex Alimentarius (the Commission for which exists within the WHO). In 1985, IOCU lobbying also led to the establishment of the UN Guidelines on Consumer Protection which have essentially acted as a model law for the implementation of consumer protection regimes around the world. In the mid-1990s, these were subsequently extended by the UN Commission on Sustainable Development and the UN Economic and Social Council to include the promotion of sustainable consumption. Less successfully, but more indicative of the role IOCU was playing in global civil society, was the campaign it spearheaded to obtain a Code of Conduct for Multinational Corporations. This ultimately failed due to US opposition and the weakening of the social and economic role of the UN with the creation of the World Trade Organisation and the post-Uruguay Round global trading system. Nevertheless, by the 1980s, IOCU had become a leading NGO as civil society organisations increasingly looked to the UN to implement more socially-minded forms of global justice.[19]

Part of the explanation for IOCU's prominence at this time lies in the absence of other NGOs, compared to the explosion of civil society organisations in the 1990s, and partly because it developed new forms of campaign tactics which gave it a greater legitimacy as the spokesbody for civil society. As IOCU expanded into the developing world in the 1970s, it encountered new sets of consumer problems not experienced by affluent westerners. Firstly, it had to deal with the problem of baby food formulas which were marketed to developing-world consumers as nutritious substitutes to breast milk. For poor consumers, such an expense was an unnecessary outlay, yet infant formula companies promoted their products as medical advances, even though evidence mounted that poor water supplies meant that babies were being fed disease-ridden foodstuffs.[20] Secondly, while the environmental movement and Rachel Carson's pioneering *Silent Spring* had raised the consciousness of American consumers to the dangers of pesticides, the problem seemed all the more acute for developing-world consumers who were often exposed to the harmful chemicals in their roles as agricultural labourers as well.[21] Thirdly (although many other examples might also be cited), developing-world consumer organisations were increasingly concerned about the high prices of western drugs and the inappropriate marketing of patent medicines which were either ineffective or were dangerous, the international pharmaceutical companies taking advantage of weak consumer protection legislation to dump products which had been banned in western markets.[22]

All three of these issues were subjects which fell within the remit of a variety of developmental NGOs concerned with economic and social justice. Not all of these organisations had such a prominent voice as IOCU, however, particularly at the UN, while IOCU, for its part, was too diverse an organisation to be able to collect the primary evidence needed to mount campaigns against the alleged market abuses. The solution pioneered by IOCU was to create networks of pre-existing organisations prepared to work together on a specific issue. Although campaigning networks had clearly existed at the national level for some time, and more general networks – or federations – existed within the labour and women's movements, the creation of single-issue, international campaign networks in the late 1970s was an important precedent which in many ways still has a fundamental influence on the nature of global civil society today. In response to the three issues cited above, IOCU initiated the International Baby Food Action Network (IBFAN) in 1979, Health Action International (HAI) in 1981 and the Pesticide Action Network (PAN) in 1982. Led and administered by IOCU, the networks brought together a variety of NGOs and enabled many smaller and – perhaps in the eyes of those who determined who could obtain a formal voice at the UN – less reputable groups to have a say in which issues should be brought to the attention of the UN. Not only did IBFAN, PAN and HAI, as well as other networks and campaigns at this time, provide a new direction for global activists, they focussed attention on the international marketplace and created further impetus for the campaign, for instance, to obtain a code of conduct on the activities of multinational corporations in the 1980s.[23]

Such campaigns also led to the incremental expansion of the consumer rights at the heart of IOCU's operating philosophy. Over the years, IOCU has added four more rights to those set out by Kennedy in 1962. They now include the right to redress; the right to consumer education; the right to a healthy environment; and the right to basic needs. These latter two rights in particular reflect the influence of the global South on the international consumer movement. The rights to a healthy environment and to basic needs are not so much rights but duties, since they invoke the responsibility of consumers to ensure that all other consumers can enjoy goods and services in an equally inhabitable environment, or else they call upon the duties of affluent western consumers to campaign to ensure that poor consumers around the world can also participate at the most basic level in the consumer society. As developing world consumer activists are keen to point out, if the right to basic needs is not met, then all other consumer rights effectively become meaningless. IOCU expanded in the 1960s and 1970s with a missionary fervour that thought better informed consumers could empower themselves to provide the correctives to imbalances of power within the marketplace. But as the focus of consumer concern in these new countries shifted from cars to rice and refrigeration to water supply, it soon became obvious that the majority of the world's consumers were facing a very different set of questions. As IOCU set up regional offices, first for the Asia Pacific in 1973 and then for Latin America in the late-1980s and for Africa in the 1990s, it took on board new agendas such that the 'expert consumer' has more often been concerned with meeting the demands of necessity rather than the desire for luxury.

Consumerism in the developing world: the case of Malaysia

How a new type of expert consumer emerged in the 1970s and 1980s is best understood with reference to a single country. Malaysia in particular has been instrumental in promoting an alternative type of consumer activism and pushing for the inclusion of basic needs as a fundamental consumer right. From the 1960s, Malaysian consumer activists have been some of the most prominent in the global South and many of its leaders have gone on to play key roles in IOCU, not least because IOCU's first regional office was based in Penang. However, although there is much that is specific about Malaysian consumer history its attention to questions of poverty make it also representative of policy shifts inspired by consumer movements across Asia, especially India, Indonesia and the Philippines and, subsequent to that, to developments in Latin America and Africa. As with so many post-colonial societies, consumerism as an organised movement first took off in Malaysia among the small groups of professional urban middle classes who, in 1965, came together in protest over the price of newspapers in the capital, Kuala Lumpur, and formed the Selangor Consumers' Association.[24]

Yet more significant, though, was the Consumers' Association of Penang (CAP), an organisation set up immediately after the ethnic-based riots of the 1969 general election. CAP consisted of the same small but expanding number of urban professionals who had joined together in Selangor, though they also sought a deliberately non-racial organisation which could find a new space to articulate social and economic issues in a political system dominated by ethnicity (Malaysia's population is currently around 55 per cent Malay, 30 per cent Chinese and 10 per cent Indian). CAP soon turned its attention to basic consumer goods and to the issues of adulteration, fraudulent sales, pesticide use and inappropriate marketing, all of which were rife in a country missing the same consumer protection mechanisms enjoyed by western consumers. But as a civil society organisation tolerated by an at times oppressive regime for its supposedly non-radical nature, it soon found itself entering upon questions of social and economic injustice as few other NGOs were in existence to tackle them. Thus by the end of the 1970s, CAP had extended its definition of consumerism to include women's rights, the plight of fishing and farming communities threatened by development projects, the land rights of the Orang Asli (indigenous) community, environmental destruction (CAP has gone on to set up Friends of the Earth Malaysia), and the appropriate direction to take for an expanding economy which at times has seemed more concerned with prestige projects than promoting the standard of living of the majority poor.[25]

By the mid-1980s, CAP had developed a consumerism which posited consumers as the expert commentators on the whole nature of economic development, not only fighting for the rights of individuals shoppers, but as the agents of a society being built in their name and who could therefore speak as to the nature of that society. CAP has gone on to outline a general critique of global economic policy which champions the rights of developing nations to enjoy the profits of their own resources.[26] Indeed, to this end, CAP has established Third World Network, now a leading player in global civil society and whose economist, Martin Khor, still an officer with CAP, has achieved a prominence at events organised by the European and World Social Forums.[27] At the heart of this politics is an assumption that development projects should be focussed on providing the majority of the population with access to a basic standard of living, rather than assuming a trickle-down effect from the high profits granted to a few well-positioned rent-seekers. Here then lies a wider critique of economic globalisation which offers the chance for the expert consumer to fight for the right to basic needs as the main platform of a human rights manifesto which places as much importance on economic and social rights as political and civil rights.[28] Indeed, this is precisely what has occurred, especially through individuals such as Anwar Fazal, one of the founders of CAP, who went on to become the regional director for IOCU from 1974 to 1990 and who, from 1978 to 1984, also served as the international movement's President. During this time, when he served as both figurehead and employee, IOCU's centre of gravity shifted firmly from its supposed headquarters in The Hague to the regional office in Penang, and IOCU came to be articulating an agenda more in line with other development agencies than with the concerns of affluent shoppers who purchased the testing magazines of *Que Choisir?*, *Which?*, *Test* and *Consumer Reports*.

If the 1960s and 1970s had been the age of the affluent western consumer, spearheaded by such prominent activists as Ralph Nader in the US, then by the 1980s, the consumer movement had become increasingly concerned with the needs of the world's poor. Having taken on board these agendas, the consumer movement then came to play a prominent role in global civil society, especially in the negotiations with the UN and in its promotion of networking as an international campaign tactic. In the 1990s, IOCU has retreated to some extent from this apparent radicalism, seeking to work with rather than protest against the new institutions of global trade, especially since the purchasers of testing magazines have increasingly questioned the use of their subscriptions to promote an international agenda irrelevant to their immediate, value-for-money, interests (indeed, this raises one of the key sources of potential conflict within a consumer movement which attempts to serve the both of both the North and the South, the affluent and the poor). Global civil society has also expanded exponentially over the last ten years, such that the consumer movement now finds itself eclipsed by a range of other organisations dealing with questions of basic needs.[29] Yet, developing world consumer organisations are still promoting a model of the expert consumer concerned more with the fight for a basic standard of living than the testing of branded commodities. Associations in Latin America and Africa have been forced to address the issues arising from deregulation and the conditions of structural adjustment programmes, while countries such as India have implemented consumer protection legislation (in 1986) which has encouraged the NGO community to expand enormously as institutions are empowered to take class actions on behalf of everyday consumers. Here is a new form of expert consumer, making a claim for a stake in the economic development process, though it is a form of modern citizenship which still has to compete with other experts speaking in the name of the consumer.

Conclusion

Since the 1990s national and international consumer movements have had to face a number of challenges which suggest that this form of consumer expertise may well be specific to the post-Second World War period. In many ways, the raft of consumer protection measures that were implemented in their various forms across western Europe and North America in the 1960s and 1970s actually met the demands of the consumer activists. Furthermore, improvements in standards, marketing and product development, together with a growing consumer awareness among competitive industries, ensured that products were less likely to be either faulty or even dangerous. In this regard, the comparative testing consumer movement has achieved many of its goals and removed the primary rationale for its existence. The same too might be argued for the rise of the expert consumer in the developing world, though this is not to suggest that questions of poverty have been eradicated. Firstly, the relevance of consumer groups has to be called into question. A problem faced by organisations such as Malaysia's CAP is that their demands for a more regulated, just and even moral marketplace are not shared by a new generation of an expanding middle class that has appeared in Latin American and South East Asia over the last two decades. It is clear that many consumers have been prepared to trade off civil and political liberties for economic advantages and, for those consumers who desire a share in the fruits of affluence, the nostalgic glorification of an indigenous pre-market culture comes across as an anti-modern, un-progressive and out-of-tune political discourse which pays little heed to the aspirations of developing nations which find themselves moving toward 'first world' status. This, of course, does not deny the continued relevance of campaigns to ensure all consumers enjoy access to the basic needs of life – water, fuel, shelter – but a second problem emerges here as well. With the explosion of NGO activity over the last ten to twenty years, the consumer movement has seen many of its topics dealt with more ably by more focussed single-issue organisations. Thus, in Africa, new groups have emerged to deal with questions of water and electricity supply, while the right to food is now being addressed by a whole spectrum of organisations loosely banded together as the 'anti-globalisation' movement. To return to Malaysia, the lead CAP and the consumer movement enjoyed in the 1970s and 1980s has now been taken away with the rise to prominence of human rights groups, women's groups, economic development agencies and even the formerly hostile Prime Minister, Mahathir Mohammad, who has been keen to appropriate the developmental arguments of NGOs to fit in with his broader vision of a developing world alliance against the institutions of global governance.[30] For the affluent of the developing world, the consumer movement may no longer meet their needs, while for the poor, the consumer movement is less well placed to deal with their problems than a plethora of new organisations.

A final issue emerges in the whole nature of consumer expertise. As the market and consumerism (in its acquisitive individualist sense) come to be regarded as the benchmarks of global economic policy and as choice becomes the watchword of politicians, so many different groups, institutions and political parties seek to position themselves as the expert consumer. Consumers now find themselves at the heart of the modern world and, as such, the consumer interest is held to be as diverse as that world itself. In an earlier intervention into the academic debate about the nature of consumer society, Gabriel and Lang in 1995 identified several different types of consumer. The consumer as 'chooser' was the idealised shopper who sees satisfaction in the endless choice between various branded commodities, never realising that choice itself can take place at other places than the supermarket shelf. Gabriel and Lang take on board the cultural critique of consumer society favoured by post-modernists which has argued that consumers are not manipulated by the forces of advertising (the consumer as 'victim'). Instead, the consumer can be a 'communicator' and an 'identity-seeker' in the meanings they wish to present about themselves through the goods they consume. The consumer can be an 'explorer', endlessly searching for new experiences and appropriating the meanings presented by manufacturers and their agents. Consumers are also the creators of their own meanings and can be 'hedonists' but also 'artists'. But the consumer can also be a 'rebel', boycotting goods to support alternatives ways of life, and he or she can be an 'activist', organising through co-operatives, consumer association and ethical, green and fair trade movements. Finally, the consumer can be a 'citizen', positioning consumption as the means through which contemporary citizenship can be exercised and suggesting that consumers ought not to be restricted to commenting on the goods and services the market offers, but engaging with the whole nature of modern society so that they have a say in the creation, shape and structure of that market in the first place.[31]

All these manifestations of the consumer are currently in existence. Some are the work of individual consumers, others are the work of consumers acting collectively and through institutions. But some too are the products of other interests in society, actively seeking to create a consumer that fits in with agendas appropriate to those other than consumers. In this sense, the consumer remains a contested entity and as business and political rhetoric continues to speak for the consumer it also means that the expert consumer is now more diffuse and varied than it has ever been in the past. This suggests that the modern consumer movement is unlikely to maintain its dominant position as the expert consumer in the future, if indeed it can lay claim to still being the authoritative expert on consumer affairs today. The modern consumer movement has excellent resources at its disposal and a global reach which will continue to make it a sought after voice. However, it will do so while competing with other expert consumers and constantly trying to maintain that its take on the consumer interest is the most valid, regardless of the arguments of environmentalists, ethical consumers, corporate front groups and co-opting populist politicians who will always appeal to matters of consumption as the lowest common denominator in electorate mobilisation. Yet, in terms of this book, it makes it clear that power relations, interests and institutional politics will remain as relevant as they ever have been over the last century in the jostling to become the expert consumer.

Notes

1 Stuart Chase and F. J. Schlink, *Your Money's Worth: A Study in the Waste of the Consumer's Dollar* (New York, 1927).

2 Charles McGovern, 'Consumption and Citizenship in the United States, 1900-1940', in Susan Strasser, Charles McGovern and Matthias Judt (eds), *Getting and Spending: European and American Consumer Societies in the Twentieth Century* (Cambridge, 1998), p. 51.

3 Lizabeth Cohen, *A Consumers' Republic: The Politics of Mass Consumption in Postwar America* (New York, 2003); Meg Jacobs, *Pocketbook Politics: Economic Citizenship in Twentieth-Century America* (Princeton, NJ, 2005); Gary Cross, *An All-Consuming Century: Why Commercialism Won in Modern America* (New York, 2000); Kathleen G. Donohue, *Freedom from Want: American Liberalism and the Idea of the Consumer* (Baltimore, 2003).

4 Lawrence B. Glickman, 'The Strike in the Temple of Consumption: Consumer Activism and Twentieth-Century American Political Culture', *Journal of American History*, 88:1, (2001): 99-128; Robert N. Mayer, *The Consumer Movement: Guardians of the Marketplace* (Boston, MA, 1989); Norman Isaac Silber, *Test and Protest: The Influence of Consumers Union* (New York, 1983); Michael Pertschuk, *Revolt Against Regulation: The Rise and Pause of the Consumer Movement* (Berkeley, CA, 1982).

5 Charles Gide, *Consumers' Co-operative Societies* (Manchester, 1921); Rosalind Williams, *Dreamworlds: Mass Consumption in Late Nineteenth Century France* (Berkeley, CA, 1982); Ellen Furlough, *Consumer Co-operation in Modern France: The Politics of Consumption* (Ithaca, 1991).

6 Chatriot in this volume; Gunnar Trumbull, *The Contested Consumer: The Politics of Product Market Regulation in France and Germany* (forthcoming); Luc Bihl, *Consommateur: défends-toi!* (Paris, 1976); Gunnar Trumbull, 'Strategies of Consumer Group Mobilisation: France and Germany in the 1970s', in Martin Daunton and Matthew Hilton (eds), *The Politics of Consumption: Material Culture and Citizenship in Europe and America* (Oxford, 2001), pp. 261-82; A. Morin, 'French Consumer Movement', in Brobeck *et al.*, *Encyclopaedia*, pp. 279-83.

7 Trumbull, *Contested Consumer.*

8 Joop Koopman, 'Dutch Consumer Movement', in Brobeck *et al.*, *Encyclopaedia*, pp. 227-32; Consumers International, *Balancing the Scales, Part 2: Consumer Protection in the Netherlands and Germany* (London, 1995).
9 T. Bourgoignie and A-C. Lacoste, 'Belgian Consumer Movement', in Brobeck *et al.*, *Encyclopaedia*, pp. 61-4.
10 G. Smith, *The Consumer Interest* (London, 1982); Matthew Hilton, 'The Polyester-Flannelled Philanthropists: The Birmingham Consumers' Group and Affluent Britain', in Lawrence Black and Hugh Pemberton (eds), *An Affluent Society? Britain's Post-War "Golden Age" Revisited* (Aldershot, 2004), pp. 149-65; Matthew Hilton, *Consumerism in Twentieth-Century Britain: The Search for a Historical Movement* (Cambridge, 2003); Lawrence Black, '*Which?*craft in Post-War Britain: the Consumers' Association and the Politics of Affluence', *Albion*, 36:1 (2004): 52-82.
11 Patricia L. Maclachlan, *Consumer Politics in Postwar Japan: The Institutional Boundaries of Citizen Activism* (New York, 2002); David Vogel, 'Consumer Protection and Protectionism in Japan', *Journal of Japanese Studies*, 18:1 (1992): 119-54; M. Imai, 'Japanese Consumer Movement', in Brobeck *et al.*, *Encyclopedia*, pp. 341-2.
12 K. van Wolferen, *The Enigma of Japanese Power* (New York, 1990); G. Fields, *Gucci on the Ginza* (Tokyo, 1989).
13 Trumbull, *Contested Consumer*; Consumers International, *Balancing the Scales, Part 2*; E. Kuhlmann, 'German Consumer Movement', in Brobeck *et al.*, *Encyclopaedia*, pp. 289-93.
14 K. Blomqvist, 'Swedish Consumer Movement', in Brobeck *et al.*, *Encyclopaedia*, pp. 544-547; Consumers International, *Balancing the Scales, Part 1: Consumer Protection in Sweden and the United Kingdom* (London, 1995).
15 Foo Gaik Sim, *IOCU on Record: A Documentary History of the International Organisation of Consumers Unions, 1960-1990* (New York, 1991), p. 27.
16 IOCU, *Knowledge is Power: Consumer Goals in the 1970s. Proceedings of the 6th Biennial World Conference of the International Organisation of Consumers Unions* (London, 1970), pp. 115-17.
17 IOCU, *Consumer Power in the Nineties: Proceedings of the Thirteenth IOCU World Congress* (London, 1991), p. 113.
18 Consumers International, *Annual Report, 1999* (London, 1999), pp. 37-41.
19 Esther Peterson and Jean M. Halloran, 'United Nations Consumer Protection', in Brobeck *et al., Encyclopaedia*, pp. 581-583; David Harland, 'The United Nations Guidelines for Consumer Protection', *Journal of Consumer Policy*, 10, 1987, pp. 245-66.
20 C. Williams, *Milk and Murder: Address to the Rotary Club of Singapore in 1939* (Penang, 1986); IBFAN, *Babies, Breastfeeding and the Code: Report of the IBFAN ASIA Conference, Sam Phran, Thailand, 5-12 October 1986* (Penang, 1987).
21 IOCU, *The Pesticide Handbook: Profiles for Action* (Penang, 1984); Foo Gaik Sim, *The Pesticide Poisoning Report: A Survey of Some Asian Countries* (Penang, 1985).
22 Charles Medawar, *Drugs and World Health: An International Consumer Perspective* (London, 1984); IOCU, *Forty-Four Problem Drugs: A Consumer Action and Resource Kit on Pharmaceuticals* (Penang, 1981).
23 G. Goldenman and S. Rengam, *Problem Pesticides, Pesticide Problems: A Citizens' Action Guide to the International Code of Conduct on the Distribution and Use of Pesticides* (Penang, 1988); K. Balasubramaniam, *Health and Pharmaceuticals in Developing Countries: Towards Social Justice and Equity* (Penang, 1996); IOCU and

IBFAN, *Protecting Infant Health: A Health Wokers' Guide to the International Code of Marketing of Breastmilk Substitutes* (Penang, 1985); IBFAN, *Breaking the Rules 1991: A Worldwide Report on Violations of the WHO/UNICEF International Code of Marketing of Breastmilk Substitutes* (Penang, 1991).

24 Matthew Hilton, *Choice and Justice: Forty Years of the Malaysian Consumer Movement* (forthcoming); Mohd Hamdan Adnan, *Understanding Consumerism* (Petaling Jaya, 2000).

25 Hilton, *Choice and Justice*; D. and T. Tiranti, *People with a Purpose: The Consumers' Association of Penang* (Penang, 1985).

26 S. M. Mohamed Idris, *For a Sane, Green Future* (Penang, 1990); S. M. Mohamed Idris, *Reflections on Malaysian Society: Where Do We Go From Here?* (Penang, 2003); S. M. Mohamed Idris, *Malaysian Consumers and Development* (Penang, 1986).

27 Martin Khor, *Globalisation and the South: Some Critical Issues* (Penang, 2001).

28 Education Research Association for Consumers (ERA), *Understanding Economic, Social and Cultural Rights* (Kuala Lumpur, 2001).

29 John Clark (ed.), *Globalising Civic Engagement: Civil Society and Transnational Action* (London, 2003); John Keane, *Global Civil Society?* (Cambridge, 2003).

30 Lim Teck Ghee, 'Nongovernmental Organisations in Malaysia and Regional Networking', in Tadashi Yamamoto (ed.), *Emerging Civil Society in the Asia Pacific Community: Nongovernmental Underpinnings of the Emerging Asia Pacific Regional Community* (Singapore, 1996), pp. 165-82; Vidhu Verma, *Malaysia: State and Civil Society in Transition* (Petaling Jaya, 2004), p. 54; E. T. Gomez and K. S. Jomo, *Malaysia's Political Economy: Politics, Patronage and Profits* (Cambridge, 1997); M. L. Weiss and S. Hassan (eds), *Social Movements in Malaysia: From Moral Communities to NGOs* (London, 2003)

31 Y. Gabriel and T. Lang, *The Unmanageable Consumer: Contemporary Consumption and its Fragmentation* (London, 1995).

Index

For Product Safety Concerns and Information please contact our EU representative GPSR@taylorandfrancis.com Taylor & Francis Verlag GmbH, Kaufingerstraße 24, 80331 München, Germany